Islam in Uganda

RELIGION IN TRANSFORMING AFRICA

ISSN 2398-8673

Series Editors
Barbara Bompani, Joseph Hellweg, Ousmane Kane and **Emma Wild-Wood**

Editorial Reading Panel
Robert Baum (Dartmouth College)
Dianna Bell (University of Cape Town)
Ezra Chitando (University of Zimbabwe)
Martha Frederiks (Utrecht University)
Paul Gifford (SOAS)
David M. Gordon (Bowdoin College)
Jörg Haustein (University of Cambridge)
Paul Lubeck (Johns Hopkins University-SAIS)
Philomena Mwaura (Kenyatta University, Nairobi)
Hassan Ndzovu (Moi University)
Ebenezer Obadare (University of Kansas)
Abdulkader I. Tayob (University of Cape Town)
M. Sani Umar (Northwestern University)
Stephen Wooten (University of Oregon)

Series description
The series is open to submissions that examine local or regional realities on the
complexities of religion and spirituality in Africa. Religion in Transforming Africa will
showcase cutting-edge research into continent-wide issues on Christianity, Islam and
other religions of Africa; Traditional beliefs and witchcraft; Religion, culture and society;
History of religion, politics and power; Global networks and new missions; Religion
in conflict and peace-building processes; Religion and development; Religious rituals
and texts and their role in shaping religious ideologies and theologies. Innovative, and
challenging current perspectives, the series provides an indispensable resource on this
key area of African Studies for academics, students, international policy-makers and
development practitioners.

Please contact the Series Editors with an outline or download the proposal form at www.
jamescurrey.com.

Dr Barbara Bompani, Reader in Africa and International Development, University of
     Edinburgh: b.bompani@ed.ac.uk
Dr Joseph Hellweg, Associate Professor of Religion, Department of Religion, Florida
     State University: jhellweg@fsu.edu
Professor Ousmane Kane, Prince Alwaleed Bin Talal Professor of Contemporary Islamic
     Religion & Society, Harvard Divinity School: okane@hds.harvard.edu
Dr Emma Wild-Wood, Senior Lecturer, African Christianity and African Indigenous
     Religions, University of Edinburgh: emma.wildwood@ed.ac.uk

Previously published titles in the series are listed at the back of this volume.

Islam in Uganda

The Muslim Minority, Nationalism & Political Power

Joseph Kasule

James Currey
is an imprint of
Boydell & Brewer Ltd
PO Box 9, Woodbridge
Suffolk IP12 3DF (GB)
www.jamescurrey.com
and of
Boydell & Brewer Inc.
668 Mt Hope Avenue
Rochester, NY 14620–2731 (US)
www.boydellandbrewer.com

© Joseph Kasule 2022
First published 2022

The right of Joseph Kasule
to be identified as the author of this work has been asserted in accordance with
sections 77 and 78 of the Copyright, Designs and Patents Act 1988

All Rights Reserved. Except as permitted under current legislation
no part of this work may be photocopied, stored in a retrieval system,
published, performed in public, adapted, broadcast, transmitted,
recorded or reproduced in any form or by any means, without the
prior permission of the copyright owner

The publisher has no responsibility for the continued existence or accuracy of URLs for
external or third-party internet websites referred to in this book, and does not guarantee
that any content on such websites is, or will remain, accurate or appropriate

British Library Cataloguing in Publication Data
A catalogue record for this book is available from the British Library

ISBN 978-1-84701-243-2 (James Currey hardback)

This publication is printed on acid-free paper

For my family, near and distant,
and to the victims of bad governance

In memory of Abdul Karim

Contents

Acknowledgements		ix
Note on Language and Transliteration		xi
Chronology		xiii
Glossary		xix
List of Abbreviations		xxi
1	Introduction	1
2	Islam in Pre-Colonial Buganda	31
3	Muslim Communities in the Colonial Era	67
4	Milton Obote Founds his Muslim Alliance	111
5	Idi Amin Attempts to Islamize the State	132
6	Islamic Reform and Intra-Muslim Violence	151
7	NRM Statecraft and Muslim Subjects	185
8	Conclusion	214
Bibliography		221
Index		235

Acknowledgements

This book is the outcome of a very challenging research process that included new encounters with various individuals, groups and communities. While I have turned these researches into the present book, I could not have done this without the support of many people. First, I acknowledge the financial support of the Carnegie Corporation of New York for the research grant to the Makerere Institute of Social Research (MISR) that enabled me to undertake this research. I have also benefited from a postdoctoral fellowship at MISR, which enabled me to access relevant resources and to converse with various experts. I owe thanks to Hayde Bangerezako, Yahya Sseremba and Mahmood Mamdani at the Institute.

I am also deeply grateful to the many people who took risks (including possible incarceration) to provide me with details of sensitive information regarding particular Muslim personalities in Uganda, and the designs of the state on Muslim subjects. I acknowledge the tremendous support accorded to me by specific people in Iganga, Jinja, Mbale, Soroti, Mbarara, Bushenyi, Kabale, Ntungamo, Mukono, Wakiso, Gulu and Kampala, who gave me much of their time and offered me kind hospitality beyond my expectations. I would also like to thank colleagues and friends in intellectual networks in Uganda and beyond who have made extensive comments on various drafts of this book. Lastly, I appreciate the support of Thurayya Islamic Media who gave me access to their audio and visual database.

Note on Language and Transliteration

All direct quotations translated into English are my own translations, unless otherwise indicated. For quoted translations that are not my own, I have kept to the spelling and orthography of the translator. Arabic words that commonly occur in English such as 'Imam' 'jihad' 'Salat', 'Hadith', 'Maulid', remain in their English approximations. All other Arabic terms not in common use, including the titles of Arabic manuscripts, are transcribed following the *International Journal of Middle East Studies (IJMES)* transcription system and appear in italics followed by an English translation in brackets on first occurrence, if appropriate.

Chronology

c. 500 CE	Bantu people begin to inhabit present-day Uganda.
c. 900–1400	Buganda kingdom is founded.
c. 1700	Bunyoro kingdom begins to disintegrate.
1840s	Zanzibar Arab traders introduce Islam to the palace of Kabaka Ssuuna II of Buganda.
1850s	Kabaka Muteesa I allows Islam to be taught in Buganda.
1862	Explorer John H. Speke becomes first European to visit Buganda.
1867	Islamic fasting is observed in Buganda.
1871	Muteesa I makes Islam state religion.
1875	Muteesa I requests Christian missionaries from Queen Victoria.
1876	Muteesa I murders his Muslim pages.
1877	CMS missionaries arrive in Buganda from England.
1879	Roman Catholic White Fathers arrive from France.
1884	Death of Muteesa I. Kabaka Mwanga I ascends the throne.
1885	British missionary Hannington of the CMS is murdered in Eastern Uganda; persecution of Christians begins.
1886–87	Kabaka Mwanga I murders his Christian pages.
1888	Three kings govern Buganda in one year: Kabaka Mwanga, Kiwewa and Kalema. Muslims depose Kiwewa for refusing circumcision and instead enthrone Kalema.
1889	Christian factions fight to reinstate Mwanga as Kabaka.
1890	Britain and Germany sign Heligoland-Zanzibar Treaty, giving control of Germany's claims to the Zanzibar Protectorate to Britain, and ceding Heligoland to Germany. This treaty paves way for British territorial claims inside the Eastern African mainland. Captain F.D. Lugard arrives in Buganda.

1890	Apollo Kaggwa becomes Katikkiro (Prime Minister) of Buganda.
1892	Catholics and Protestants battle at Mengo. Lugard intervenes to ensure a Protestant victory.
1893	Gerald Portal arrives in Buganda representing the Imperial British East Africa Company (IBEAC).
1894	A British Protectorate is declared over Buganda.
1895	Mill Hill Fathers Mission arrives in Buganda.
1896	British rule extends to Tooro, Ankole and Bunyoro; Uganda Protectorate is born.
1897	Kabaka Mwanga II revolts against British rule. August: Sudanese soldiers mutiny and kill English officers.
1898	British rule is extended to Bunyoro; Omukama Kabarega begins guerrilla warfare.
1900	Buganda Agreement is written and Buganda becomes a constitutional monarchy.
1906	Elite Christian schools founded at Buddo, Gayaza and Kisubi.
1919	Uganda Native Ordinance promulgated to govern native chiefs and their courts.
1920	Legislative Council established (no Ugandans).
1921	Muslim Prince Nuhu Kyabasinga Mbogo dies.
1929	Muslim Chief Twaibu Magatto dies.
1936	Uganda Muslim Education Association (UMEA) is founded.
1942	Walugembe Muteesa II becomes Kabaka of Buganda.
1945	First native representative to the Legislative Council is appointed.
1952	Ignatius K. Musaazi founds Uganda National Congress, precussor to Uganda People's Congress (UPC).
1953	Kabaka crisis begins as Governor Cohen deports Kabaka Muteesa II to England.
1955	Kabaka Muteesa II returns to Uganda.
1956	First direct elections to the Legislative Council.
1960	Colonial Secretary announces general elections for internal self-government to be held in March 1961; Buganda government boycotts the elections.

1961	Benedicto Kiwanuka's Democratic Party (DP) wins parliamentary majority and Kiwanuka becomes Prime Minister of Uganda. Kabaka's government and UPC (both Protestant) detest Catholic-based DP government and ally to challenge DP. Kabaka Yekka (King Alone, KY) party is formed by Buganda loyalists to secure its interests in an independent Uganda.
1962	Apollo Milton Obote becomes Prime Minister of Uganda due to a KY and UPC alliance. Uganda becomes independent.
1966	Apollo Milton Obote amends constitution; a state of emergency is declared over Buganda as it declines to recognize the constitutional amendments. The Kabaka crisis ensues as Obote orders the army to invade the Lubiri.
1967	Milton Obote abolishes all kingdoms.
1968	Obote becomes first republican president as a republican constitution is promulgated.
1969	Obote formally adopts the Common Man's Charter and the Move to the Left. November: Kabaka Walugembe Muteesa II dies while exiled in London. December: Obote survives an assassination attempt, declares a state of emergency throughout Uganda, bans non-UPC political parties and makes Uganda a one-party state.
1970	Obote promotes officers in the Uganda Armed Forces. Idi Amin becomes Chief of Joint Staffs and Commander of the Uganda Armed Forces.
1971	In a coup d'état, Idi Amin becomes President of Uganda and Commander-in-Chief of the Armed Forces.
	April: The remains of Kabaka Walugembe Muteesa II are returned from England for burial in Kasubi tombs.
	October: A national census targeting all Asians is ordered.
	December: Many Asians' applications for citizenship are denied.
1972	Amin tells Asians that Uganda is not an Indian country.
	May: Uganda Muslim Supreme Council (UMSC) is founded. Sheikh Abdul Razzaq Matovu becomes first Mufti of Uganda.
	August: Idi Amin proclaims a 90-day deadline to non-Ugandan Asians of British nationality to leave. Later, the expulsion is extended to Asians with Indian, Bangladeshi and Pakistani nationalities.

1973	Yoweri Kaguta Museveni founds Front for National Salvation (FRONASA) and begins his guerrilla activities against Idi Amin.
1979	January: Idi Amin regime ends and Yusuf Kironde Lule becomes President.
	June: Godfrey Lukongwa Binaisa becomes President after Lule is deposed.
1980	May: Paulo Muwanga becomes Chair of Military Commission after Binaisa is deposed.
	Apollo Milton Obote wins a second presidency after a disputed general election. Yoweri Museveni of the Uganda Patriotic Movement (UPM) joins other aggrieved groups to begin guerrilla struggle against Obote.
1985	A military coup makes Tito Okello Lutwa President. Apollo Milton Obote flees Uganda.
1986	Yoweri Kaguta Museveni becomes President after his guerrilla National Resistance Movement/Army (NRM/A) captures Kampala.
1989	General election conducted to choose representatives to the National Resistance Council.
1994	Elections to Constituent Assembly.
1995	A new constitution is enacted and promulgated.
1996	First general and presidential elections since 1980 are conducted. Yoweri Kaguta Museveni begins first term as elected president.
2001	Yoweri Kaguta Museveni wins second term of office as elected President following a general election.
2002	Uganda and Sudan agree to operate against Lord's Resistance Army (LRA) rebels acting within the vicinity of their common boundaries.
	December: Uganda government signs agreement with rebels of the Uganda National Rescue Front (UNRF).
2003	Last contingent of Ugandan troops leaves the Democratic Republic of the Congo (DRC) escorted by many Congolese civilians seeking asylum in Uganda.
2004	LRA rebels attack an internally displaced persons (IDP) camp in Barlonyo, Lira and murder more than 300.

2005	Referendum conducted to return Uganda to multi-party political dispensation; the NRM officially becomes a political party.
2006	Yoweri Kaguta Museveni begins his third term as elected President after a general election.
2007	Ugandan troops deploy to Somalia under the African Union Mission in Somalia (AMISOM) peacekeeping contingent.
2011	Yoweri Kaguta Museveni wins fourth term as elected President.
2012	Violence engulfs the Muslim community as some clerics and important personalities are murdered while others die under mysterious circumstances.
2016	February: Incumbent Yoweri Kaguta Museveni begins fifth term as elected President.
2017	Parliament votes to remove age limit for presidential candidates, to enable Museveni to contest for another term beyond the age of 75 years.
2018	Protests rock Kampala as lawmakers and civilians contest the removal of age limit for presidential candidates. Leading opposition figures are arrested.
2020	March: Uganda declares a state of emergency and a lockdown due to outbreak of the coronavirus (Covid-19).
2021	January: Yoweri Kaguta Museveni wins a sixth elected term to remain President after 35 years in power.

Glossary

Bataka	Custodians of lands held by the clan systems in Buganda.
Buganda	One of the largest of the historical Bantu kingdoms of present-day Uganda. Located in central Uganda, its people are Baganda and their language is Luganda.
Darasa	Islamic lecture(s).
Dawah	Islamic propagation.
Fatwa	Islamic religious ruling.
Jamat	Islamic congregation.
Jihad	Holy struggle. Mostly used herein to indicate armed violence.
Kabaka	Small representative (historically). After late eighteenth century, meaning changed to 'king'.
Kabaka	Yekka (King Only) political party.
Kasubi	Offical burial tombs for the Kabakas of Buganda.
Khutba	Islamic sermon(s).
Kintu	Considered to be the founder of the Buganda kingdom.
Lord's Resistance Army	Rebel movement based in Northern Uganda from the mid-1980s.
Lubiri	Kabaka's palace.
Lukiiko	Buganda's representative assembly.
Maulid	Celebration to mark Prophet Muhammad's birthday (PBUH).
Misr	Egypt (Arabic).

Mengo	Official capital of Buganda kingdom, located near Kampala.
Salaf Salih	Pious predecessors, used to refer to the first, second and third gerations of Muslims after the death of Prophet Muhammad (PBUH).
Salafism/Tabligh	Interpretation of Islamic sources close/similar to the Salaf Salih.
Ssaza	Unit of territory composed of more than one district; county.
Tabligh	Call to propagate Islam. Also the name of an Islamic *dawah* movement formed around the 1950s in northern India.
Tabliq	Ugandan sect of Sunni Islam that identifies with Salafism.
Takfir	Islamic apostasy.

Abbreviations

ADF	Allied Democratic Forces
CMI	Chieftaincy of Military Intelligence
CMS	Church Missionary Society
DP	Democratic Party
DRC	Democratic Republic of the Congo
FGD	Focus Group discussion
FEDEMU	Federal Democratic Movement
FRONASA	Front for National Salvation
IBEAC	Imperial British East Africa Company, also 'the Company'
IGP	Inspector General of Police
KY	Kabaka Yekka
LRA	Lord's Resistance Army
MISR	Makerere Institute of Social Research
NAAM	National Association for the Advancement of Muslims
NRA	National Resistance Army
NRM	National Resistance Movement
OIC	Organisation of Islamic Cooperation
PBUH	'Peace be upon him', recited by Muslims with every mention of the Prophet Muhammad
RC	Resistance Council
SPLM/A	Sudanese People's Liberation Movement/Army
UMC	Uganda Muslim Community
UMSC	Uganda Muslim Supreme Council
UNFM/A	Uganda National Freedom Movement/Army
UPC	Uganda People's Congress
UPDF	Uganda People's Defence Forces

CHAPTER 1

Introduction

Between 2012 and 2016, Uganda experienced a wave of violence targeting Muslim clerics and important personalities. Acts of murder, death under mysterious circumstances, verbal death threats, assassination attempts, physical acts of torture and general acrimony were widespread. The violence acquired a specific pattern that reflected its organized character. As the murders continued, leaders in the Muslim community called on the Uganda government to investigate not only the cause of this violence but to also take responsibility for the fear and insecurity which gripped the general public, Muslim or not. The public outcry from both Muslim and non-Muslim leaders influenced the government to institute a commission of inquiry to investigate the matter and publicize its findings. Before the investigations could proceed to furnish a thorough report, different government officials were on numerous occasions heard making statements that alluded to knowledge of who was killing the Muslim clerics, but were silent about the cause.

It should be noted from the outset that the Muslim community in Uganda has experienced internal leadership wrangles spanning a period of over twenty years, involving the opposing camps of Kibuli and Old Kampala (named after locations of their headquarters). These also receive allegiance from the leadership of other Muslim sub-groups throughout Uganda, especially in the urban areas. In the quest to take over the management and leadership of Muslim offices and endowments, the allies of these camps have on several occasions participated in episodes of violent brawls. The scale of planning, precision in execution and persistence of the 2012–16 violence revealed a complex dynamic hitherto unseen in Muslim leadership wrangles in Uganda. As multiple actors struggled to explain this wave of violence, competing explanations emerged.

Leading officials in the government of Uganda said on numerous occasions that the wave of murders targeting Muslim clerics and important personalities was orchestrated by a rebel movement called the Allied

ISLAM IN UGANDA

Democratic Forces (ADF). The President of Uganda[1] and the then Inspector General of Police (IGP)[2] purveyed[3] this explanation. From the outset, the response from government leaders seemed to provide an answer to the public's thirst for information regarding the source of the murders and the cause. A closer examination reveals that the government's response concealed more than it disclosed. Since the rebel movement spoken of (ADF) was allegedly founded and led by a Muslim who had a history of identifying with Salafism/Tabligh (interpretation of Islamic sources similar to that of the Salaf Salih – 'pious predecssors'), which the Uganda government had since the early 1990s defined as practising a 'radical' version of Islam, the government's response insinuated that a Muslim-led group was murdering fellow Muslims. The hidden implication was that members of the general public concerned about the murders in the Muslim community should blame Muslims identified with 'radicalism'. The government's response caused a ripple effect and intra-Muslim finger pointing began. We should remember that once the wave of violence of 2012–16 had begun, the pattern of killings, death threats and assassination attempts targeted Muslim clerics and important personalities allied to just one Muslim camp, that of Kibuli. The Muslim groups allied to them therefore began asking why the ADF had chosen to direct acts of violence at only the Kibuli. Muslim groups allied to Old Kampala denied that ADF was the instigator and argued instead that the murder of Muslim clerics was not in fact limited to Uganda but was more common, even being seen in neighbouring Kenya. The explanations and counter-explanations put forward by the various actors in the attempt to understand the wave of violence that gripped the Muslim community are analysed in this book, but I argue that it is in a broader historical 'Muslim question', which I seek to address, that the explanation for the murders lies.

The broader historical Muslim question that this book examines concerns the status of Islam as ideology and the relationship of individual Muslims and masses – in their quest for autonomy – to existing configurations of power. I wrote this book for a number of reasons. First, to investigate how Muslims have articulated Islam in Uganda under changing political regimes in Uganda's political history, and specifically how individual Muslims have understood and practised different forms of Islam

---

[1]   'Museveni blames Sheikhs' killing on ADF', *Daily Monitor*, 1 July 2016.
[2]   'Police link killing of Muslim leaders to ADF rebel group', *Daily Monitor*, 31 December 2014.
[3]   On three separate funeral ceremonies for the murdered Muslim clerics in Uganda, the IGP emphasized this narrative.

leading to multiple and contradictory practices. Second, to establish how the various political authorities have responded to Muslim articulations of Islam. This springs from the constitution of the various forms of political authorities across history, that is, in pre-colonial Buganda, the colonial state and post-colonial governments. Third, to highlight the seminal role of British colonial rule in laying the structure of inter-religious relations and how these were, in turn, reproduced in various ways by post-colonial governments in Uganda to govern Islam and Muslims. The book interrogates the way in which when British colonial authorities took state control, they formulated religion for their own ends, making interventions that took advantage of the splits within and between Muslim communities, including passing new laws and creating and supporting elite factions. These laws were not only designed to confine religious practice to the private sphere, but to keep them away from the political forum and any impact on governance. Fourth, to investigate the nature and character of the relationship between and among Muslim groups and the Muslim community on the one hand and how this relationship, in turn, induces state intervention. The overriding reason is to provide a historical anchor for the conditions that framed the Muslim subjects as a political minority and the social-cultural-economic consequences that such a minority status engenders.

The book is arranged in chapters that correspond with a political period, intended to show how techniques of Muslim subjectivity either continued or discontinued under different political regimes and how those in power cultivated a role for Islam and Muslims within the state.

Chapter 2 focuses on the pre-colonial political community in Buganda. I show how Islam was the first among the foreign religions to enter Buganda and how the reigning Kabaka Muteesa I (1854–84) attempted to Islamize society and the state. Muteesa I's reign begins the seminal moment of the Muslim puzzle, which posed questions unique to that epoch, such as how Islam as an ideology intersected with the Ganda social-political structure of the time and how Muteesa I would deploy Islam to become the fulcrum of social-political and economic organization. I reveal in this chapter how Muteesa's Islamization of Buganda allowed a particular state project to emerge, one that deployed Islam as an ideology to achieve specific interests without totally rupturing the existing social-cultural ethos existing in Buganda. The period also witnessed episodes of violence committed against Muslim and non-Muslim subjects of Muteesa I, and my analysis sets this in a wider context and unpacks the events and reasons leading to their occurrence. With the death of Muteesa I and the entry of Christianity, Islam shifted from a superior to a defensive position, especially with the onset of the colonial administration. British colonial officials imagined a state project different from the pre-colonial community in Buganda, one in which the public role of Islam and Muslims would be distant.

In Chapter 3, I show that, whereas the Muslim issue during Muteesa I concerned how Muslims sought individual autonomy under an Islamic power, the onset of colonialism transformed it into how Islam and Muslims subsisted under a non-Muslim power. The chapter discusses the relationship of Islam and Muslim communities to the colonial state. I reveal how the colonial administration aspired to construct a new type of state project that created both a bifurcated state and a '*multifurcated*' society; colonial governance created a political majority and the Muslim community became the minority. Owing to earlier experiences in governing Islam and Muslims, British colonial authorities were concerned about the threat of Islam as ideology and therefore took measures to limit its advancement. I show that colonial governance of Islam and Muslim communities took two phases: the formative and the transformative. The former involved a set of measures geared towards curtailing the advancement of Islam and Muslims especially in the early years of colonial administration. In the latter phase, Islam was allowed a quasi-public stance because the colonial administration had stabilized and British authorities sought to accommodate Islam and Muslims for various reasons. I show in this chapter that colonial governance posed questions about the interpretation of Islamic sources and Muslim life. As we will see, some events occurred during this period, which gave the colonial authorities the pretext to influence the contents of Islamic practices and the bounds of Muslim life. Yet Islam was not totally absent from the state: the authorities propped up Muslim elites to represent the masses to the state and thereby accorded a quasi-public role for Islam. Consequently, the state's use of Muslim elites fragmented the Muslim minority because it created a leadership vacuum from within the masses thus enabling new Muslim authorities to emerge. As new elites articulated different aspirations that resonated with the plight of Muslim masses, intra-Muslim wrangles emerged and they played out in sites such as masjids (mosques) and Maulid festivals. I highlight these emerging conflicts in the debate regarding how native Muslims responded to colonial governance and undertook conscious efforts to limit the social-political and economic impact of their status as a political minority. The chapter shows however that colonial governance of Islam and Muslims also provided an opportunity for Islam to spread using such practices as the Maulid festivals. Although the colonial political structure frustrated many Muslims, some saw opportunity to participate in non-government forms of employment.

Chapter 4 reveals how the first regime of Apollo Milton Obote (1962–71) accommodated Muslim issues alongside another emerging problem: the nationality question. As a leader who sought to undo the negative impact of ethnic and tribal politics animated by colonial governance, Milton Obote imagined an independent Uganda with national, secular power as the first face of authority, and so religious and ethnic identities were pushed into the private space. Yet, faced with the challenge of governing Buganda, he took a pragmatic approach to politics and looked to Islam and Muslims as an opportunity to support his political interests. Faced with a resurgent Ganda nationalism agitating for secession from Uganda, Obote appealed to the Muslim identity. He begun by founding a national association, composed of Muslims loyal to his camp, which would be beneficial to him. Although Islam transcended race and nationality, the Muslims were without a political party and also looked to national politics as an opportunity to escape political oblivion. Obote's choice of Muslim Ganda leaders revealed the critical place of urban Buganda from which power radiated to rural areas. As he cultivated a public role for Islam and Muslims he ended up fragmenting the Muslim community as multiple camps emerged to protect themselves from state overtures. As a consequence, intra-Muslim violence occurred when Muslim organizations fought to control particular spaces.

In Chapter 5, I show how Islam and Muslims acquired political patronage due to the religious identity of Idi Amin, a Muslim president. I argue in this chapter that, unlike Obote I (1962–71) who looked at nationality as a matter of residence, for Idi Amin (1971–79), the nation was strictly black and therefore all those considered aliens had to return to their 'homes'. I analyse how this perception informed the expulsion of Asians in 1972. Following the international backlash after the Asian expulsion, Idi Amin was ostracized from the Western donor community and therefore looked to Islam and Muslims, at home and abroad as a way to bolster his rule. The chapter reveals that Amin courted Islamic ideology and Muslims for two major reasons: first, to gain political support after the international backlash following the Asian expulsion and, second, to end Muslims' historical marginalization in Uganda. Succinctly, Amin's Asian expulsion invited Western political backlash that forced him to court Arabs and Muslims more generally. At home, he sought out Muslim unity for political support. Although Muslims reaped the social-political benefits of Amin's regime, the biggest economic share went to his ethnic group. This state patronage destabilized the historical balance of power both internally within the Muslim factions and externally with the Christian groups. As a wave of violence targeted Muslims during

Amin's ouster, the general Muslim population became targets of political violence orchestrated by anti-Amin forces. The chapter also shows how the Uganda Muslim Supreme Council (UMSC) became the institutional legacy of the Amin regime, which successive regimes used to their advantage to influence Muslim issues in Uganda.

In Chapter 6, I discuss the re-articulation of Muslim issues under Yoweri Museveni's National Resistance Movement (NRM) regime by providing a historical analysis of Islamic reform in Uganda. As noted earlier, government leaders insinuated that ADF was responsible for the murders because they identified the alleged group leadership with 'radical' tendencies anchored in the history of the 1990s reform movement in Uganda. The chapter revisits the debate involving Salafism/Tabligh reform movements among Muslims. The shift of the Islamic reform movement from the language of *nasiha* (advice) to *naqd* (critique) disorganized the *dawah* (propagation) movement and led to intra-Muslim wrangles that conditioned an environment that invited violent state intervention in the Muslim community. Intra-Muslim acrimony led to splinter groups some of which (e.g. the ADF) claimed to seek reform of the state as the antidote to historical Muslim marginalization. As the state intervened in various Muslim spaces to check the violent potential of reformist Muslim elitism, new Muslim leaderships emerged to challenge the established power and status of particular centres of Muslim organization.

Chapter 7 reveals how the murder of Muslim clerics in Uganda became possible owing to existing historical forces involving multiple actors, Muslim and non-Muslim. The chapter situates the immediate cause of murders within the context of Muslim representation under NRM statecraft (governance). The chapter shows that the desire of the state to court the Muslim public continued an intra-Muslim debate that bred an anti-NRM stance. It describes how the desire to dismantle the Muslim minority leadership, in favour of a state-supported majority that would deliver the Muslim vote within the context of the 2016 national elections, intensified intra-Muslim strife. When the anti-NRM Muslim minority was identified with a history of armed resistance (ADF) towards the state, violence was the outcome.

The Conclusion (Chapter 8) of this book highlights some key issues that this study brings to the fore regarding intra-Muslim relations and their broader relationship with non-Muslim political authorities.

Scholarly debates

Colonial governance of Islam and Muslims

Debates on the governance of Islam and Muslims emphasize the desire of the Muslim subject to aspire for autonomy, on the one hand, and the interest of political authorities to intervene in Muslims' lives. As an autonomous person, an individual seeks to undertake their daily personal and social responsibilities according to their understanding of religious injunctions. The differences in the interpretations of Islamic injunctions, however, lead to various practices, some of which can reflect desires for different ambitions that aspire for political change. These differences in religious practices invite the state to cultivate an interventionist role for itself within Muslim society. Using legal edicts, political strategies and tactics, the state proceeds to transform the social life and also the ambitions of legal subjects. The outcome is a variegated Muslim society whose participants not only possess different interpretations of Islam but also aspire to different futures as embodied in their actions.

In British colonial history, the crisis of empire following the 1857 Sepoy Mutiny in India, forced British colonial actors to devise strategies of intervening in society against the official mantra of non-intervention. British colonial agents in India saw the diverse interpretations of Islam and practices of Muslim autonomy as pointers towards potential instability. Linguistic and ethnic diversity, among Muslim groups living in many Indian cities, such as Bombay (Mumbai), was such that it could not be collapsed together into an 'indistinguishable and uniform religious community'.[4] The dynamic and numerous ways in which diverse Muslim groups interacted within and among each other contradicted the colonial presumption of a monolithic Muslim group that behaved in a uniform way. To overcome this problem of Muslim ethnic and linguistic diversity, the colonial state constructed a Muslim 'community' by a legal edict, the Anglo-Mohammedan Law, which intended to limit the political ambitions of such a diverse Muslim public. Using that law, diverse Muslim groups could only endure if they confined their activities to what the colonial authorities had rendered as the private domain. As British colonial authorities formulated religion to mean a set of practices restricted to the inner recesses of individual conscience and communal custom, individuals and communities were thus required to conduct themselves in ways that

---

[4] See Green, Nile (2011), *Bombay Islam: The Religious Economy of the West Indian Ocean, 1840–1915,* Cambridge University Press: New York, pp. 3–4.

promoted their social mores as circumscribed from the political sphere.[5] This variegating effect of colonial governance on Muslim society was however not merely a reaction of the subject to colonial power; it was the very outcome that power intended to produce. By devising social interventionist strategies and tactics that shaped the attitudes and aspirations of hitherto autonomous Muslims, British colonial agents set up India as the key laboratory for strategies of governing Islam and Muslims elsewhere. Faced with the difficulty of governing diverse ethnic and religious identities, the colonial state implemented a divide-and-rule policy that eventually carved political minorities out of a constructed majority.

British colonial governance of Islam and Muslims in Uganda followed the Indian experience as it sought to cultivate an interventionist role for the state in society. To govern such an ethnically and religiously diverse group of people, the colonial administration enforced a set of strategies and tactics. To control and stabilize foreign minority rule over native majorities became the 'native question'[6] and the policy of indirect rule was the *primary* response to that question. Indirect rule had also been formulated in India after the 1857 Sepoy Mutiny to forestall the tide of imperial decline.[7]

To recalibrate imperial rule, governance would be discrete, hidden and subtle if it allowed the 'natives' to govern themselves through an agency system, using their own native institutions and elite representatives (chiefs). There were many chiefs representing the diverse ethnic groups in Uganda. The solution was to create a formal native institution that would govern using the customary law of the people in a region, as opposed

---

[5] See Hussin, Iza R. (2014), *The Politics of Islamic Law: Local Elites, Colonial Authority and the Making of the Muslim State,* Chicago University Press: Chicago, p. 32.

[6] See Mamdani, Mahmood (1996), *Citizen and Subject: Contemporary Africa and the Legacy of Late Colonialism*, Fountain: Kampala, p. 16.

[7] See e.g. Mantena, Karuna (2010), *Alibis of Empire: Henry Maine and the Ends of Liberal Imperialism,* Princeton University Press: Princeton, p. 12. Mantena argues that the logic of native institutions was to 'refract responsibility' by displacing the sources of 'imperial ideology, power and authority' from the metropole to the colony. In practice, indirect rule would continue 'imperial domination' after the cessation of direct rule, but in this case the defence of empire was predicated on an arrangement that would construct imperial domination as a lesser evil to 'leaving native societies to collapse on their own'. The adjunct to the colonial Governor was to become the native ruler and the attendant structures of authority as the 'alleged elsewhere' that were ideologically constructed to defer and disavow 'moral and political responsibility' on the part of the colonialist.

to having one uniform code for numerous native communities in a state. As in India, the solution to the challenge of diversity was to construct a hybrid legal regime that enabled uniform subjectivity. In Uganda, indirect rule generally bifurcated society between the settler and the native.[8] This occurred when the state shifted policy from the language of exclusion (civilized vis-à-vis uncivilized) to that of inclusion (cultural difference), which bred pluralism and difference that culminated in a legal hybridity designed to govern cultural difference.[9] As an institution, the customary native authority became the tool that colonial authorities used as a distraction to hide their real intention of constructing a governable native subject. These native institutions enabled a cost-effective, socio-cultural and political economy of rule that augmented direct interference, which had been hidden in new tactics of statecraft but not discontinued.

The role of native agency within colonial structure should not however be considered as homogenous; following the logic of the colonial state to fracture native agency through multiple identities such as race, tribe and religion, the native was differentiated by particular social dispositions such as religion and ethnicity. So, internal differentiation was the *secondary* response to the 'native question'. In this way, colonial governance shifted from being a bifurcation to a '*multifurcation*'. Colonial governance of Islam and Muslims demonstrated this reality. Learning from its earlier antecedents such as India, Malaya and North Africa, British colonial governance circumscribed Islam by advancing its social element and precluding the emancipatory potential of its political aspects. At the same time Muslim autonomy became suppressed when the state propped up Muslim elites to represent the masses. As various circumstances emerged to produce new Muslim publics, the multifurcating effect of colonial statecraft within Muslim society became complete. With minimal exceptions, the agency of the subject was bounded by the very structure of the state that had produced the diverse Muslim community. This variegating effect allowed a particular form of politics to emerge, stabilize and eventually reproduce political minorities in various locations such as Egypt and India.[10]

---

[8] Mamdani, *Citizen and Subject,* p. 16.
[9] See Mamdani, Mahmood (2012), *Define and Rule: Native as Political Identity,* Harvard University Press: London, p. 43.
[10] For the emergence of political minorities in Egypt see Mahmood, Saba (2016), *Religious Difference in a Secular Age: A Minority Report,* Princeton University Press: Princeton; for India, see Devji, Faisal (2011), 'The Idea of a Muslim Community: British India, 1857–1906' in Maussen, Marcel, et al.

10 ISLAM IN UGANDA

Regardless of location, the construction of national minorities was politically intended to create excuses for state intervention in society. A national minority generally forms whenever a certain group of people shares a cohesive identity built on social characteristics and therefore over time recognizes the fact of its marginalization within a state.[11] The fact that a minority status forms when subjects register hierarchical subordination to other subjects within the same state makes this a political status. Minority is therefore a political tag signifying continuous subjectivity in a much longer and historical process that congeals in itself historically distinct forms of marginalization. These historical episodes of marginalization also build into the day-to-day state practices and social relations, which become the focal point for a set of practices that drive group-response to ensure its survival.[12]

The construction of the Muslim as a national minority in Uganda therefore began with the colonial state when it constructed a rationale of governing socially differentiated groups. This amalgamation of society according to different traits such as tribe, race, religion and ethnic group reified difference among the native population and constructed new markers of social identity such as religious affiliation, hitherto considered trivial. In Buganda, as the next chapter shows, the introduction of Christianity and its fusion with political influence towards the end of the nineteenth century allowed religion to become a factor in determining access to political office and how this could, in turn, distribute new social goods like formal education in the colonial state. Having been defined as threats to the colonial state, Muslims became a political minority. Although many writers on Islam and Muslims in Uganda[13] have emphasized the ways in which

---

(Eds), *Colonial and Post-Colonial Governance of Islam: Continuities and Ruptures,* Amsterdam University Press: Amsterdam, pp. 118–21, p. 121.

[11] Mahmood, *Religious Difference in a Secular Age,* p. 54.

[12] Ibid., p. 65.

[13] Such as: Kaliisa, Anas Abdunoor (1994), 'Leadership Crisis Among Muslims of Uganda (1850–1993)', Masters Dissertation, Kampala: Makerere University; Kanyeihamba, George W. (1997), *Reflections on the Muslim Leadership Question in Uganda,* Kampala: Fountain; Kasumba, Yusuf (1995), 'The Development of Islam in Uganda 1962–1992 with Particular Reference to Religio-Political Factionalism', Masters Dissertation, Makerere University: Kampala; Katungulu, Haruna Jemba A. (2012), 'Religion and the Search for Peace and Reconciliation in Buganda', PhD Dissertation, Makerere University: Kampala; Katungulu, M.M. (1968), *Islam in Buganda,* translated into English by Mr. Busulwa, Kampala; 1990); Kiyimba, Abasi (1990), 'The

colonial statecraft led to the socio-economic marginalization of Muslims, they are silent on the fact that marginalization was not an innocent consequence of political praxis but the very outcome of a political project that constructed the Muslim as a political minority. Despite its attempt to deny any form of religious affiliation, British colonial statecraft in Uganda ended up supporting the Anglican variant of Protestantism and therefore entrenched religious inequality within the very structure of the state. This bias is the paramount explanation for the persistence of inequality regardless of the state's pretention to integrate and protect everyone irrespective of her or his identity. When the colonial state undertook to integrate all forms of ethnic identity in Uganda to construct one unified country, it relegated Islam to the private domain without undertaking similar treatment to the Christian groups. These were allowed all manner of socio-political mobilization in preparation for self-government.

Secularism

The idea of the secular state has been proposed as a practical solution to states experiencing civil strife arising from religious pluralism. The secular principle works on the logic that the state cannot have a religion. Or, in other words, no single religious group within a state must be allowed to dominate the religious interests of other groups.[14] But the idea of the secular has deeper roots, embedded in Western Christianity. The secularization of the Western mind began in an attempt to establish multiple faces of authority. The state constructed after 1648 in Westphalia became the 'first face of authority'[15], and its first edict was to remove religion from the public and relegate it to the private domain. This separation of religion from politics helped ensconce the sovereignty of the state over society and territory. As claims over political legitimacy were unchallenged, secular statecraft became the new template for political authority in Europe. The secular transformation is however owed to two developments that worked in tandem: first, the capacity of ideas to shape people's social identities; second, the capacity of ideas to function as a basis for social power. Both

---

Muslim Community in Uganda through One Hundred and Forty Years: the Trials and Tribulations of a Muslim Minority', *Journal of African Religion and Philosophy,* Vol. 1, No. 2, pp. 84–120.

[14] See Asad, Talal (2003), *Formations of the Secular: Christianity, Islam, Modernity,* Stanford University Press: Stanford.

[15] Philpott, Daniel (2001), *Revolutions in Sovereignty: How Ideas Shaped Modern International Relations,* Princeton University Press: Princeton, pp. 30–31.

developments worked to convert people to identities that would, in turn, 'mould political interest'.[16] Alongside this political transformation also emerged an intellectual revolution that could therefore conceive of the human person as amenable (or resistant) to subjectivity. Through the alterable character of identity, people continued to identify with particular issues not only because of their intrinsic appeal but also because the new forms of identity (whether religious, racial, social or cultural) became the very instruments to access social-political-economic benefits. Ideas become important because those who purvey them (entrepreneurs of ideas) can persuade and convert other people to believe and modify their practices, which in turn become the basis of new forms of identity. This form of elite power over society was desired by the modern state because subjectivity can easily be attained through representation.

The secular attempt to provide 'political neutrality'[17] within the context of conflict arising from religious pluralism was however controlled because political praxis continued to privilege specific religious groups and restrict others in the public sphere. As Saba Mahmood has shown, the politics of the secular state continued to reproduce religious inequality because it allowed the dominant religion to delineate 'national identity and public norms'.[18] This in effect created a religious minority with all the attendant marginalization that could accrue from such a status. Following Saba Mahmood, my scholarly position is that post-colonial secularism in Uganda could not dissolve the Muslim minority status because it was still locked within the state structure that undergirded historical religious inequality. For the creation of a political minority was the very rationale of the secular state as it gave it the justification to continue state intervention within social spaces.[19] The history of Uganda's political experiences point to this very rationale.

As multiple sites of authority were historically mobilized to augment a centralizing state structure, their integration into a nation-state during the colonial era presented a serious challenge, arising from the contradictions within forms of social power they represented. As some ethnic

[16] Ibid.
[17] See e.g. Taylor, Charles (1998), 'Modes of Secularism' in Bhargava Rajeev (Ed.) (1998), *Secularism and Its Critics,* Oxford University Press: New Delhi, p. 32; Bhargava, Rajeev (1998), 'What is Secularism For?' in Bhargava, *Secularism and Its Critics,* Oxford University Press: New Delhi, pp. 492–6.
[18] Mahmood, *Religious Difference in a Secular Age,* pp. 1–2.
[19] Ibid.

groups like the Baganda claimed a special political dispensation in the form of federal government within the larger state, religious identity was animated as a basis of political praxis. These contradictions presented significant challenges to statecraft and governance; post-colonial leaders responded in multiple ways. Obote I declared Uganda a secular state and mobilized Muslim support in the attempt to dislodge Buganda's recalcitrance. Although Idi Amin perceived the nation-state to be 'black', this came in the context of appealing to Islam and Muslims to legitimize his rule. For the National Resistance Movement (NRM), citizenship was attached to residence and Muslims were required to integrate themselves within the new structure. In diverse ways therefore successive regimes in Uganda cultivated a role for Muslims' minority status. In this way, the secular appeal in Uganda ended up maintaining the historical power of Christian groups that continued to dominate and influence the national political agenda.

Islam, secular governance and Muslim diversity

Scholarship on Islam and Muslims in Uganda[20] has imagined a monolithic Muslim response to its minority status. Historical assumptions that viewed Islamic practices as having similar traits across time and space[21] conditioned such scholarship. The assumptions of old anthropology have felt the strain of intense criticism because they failed to acknowledge the diverse ways in which Muslims understand and practise Islam. Ernest Gellner and Clifford Geertz failed to adequately conceptualize the considerable 'diversity in the beliefs and practices of Muslims'.[22] Such diversity amounts to what Talal Assad calls a 'discursive tradition', which could be discerned by identifying the historical variations in political structure and the different forms of Islam linked to it.[23] The discursive tradition takes the

---

[20] See for example: Kaliisa, 'Leadership Crisis Among Muslims of Uganda (1850–1993)'; Kanyeihamba, *Reflections on the Muslim Leadership Question in Uganda*; Kasumba, 'The Development of Islam in Uganda 1962–1992'; Katungulu, 'Religion and the Search for Peace and Reconciliation in Buganda'; Katungulu, 'Islam in Buganda'; Kiyimba, 'The Muslim Community in Uganda through One Hundred and Forty Years'.

[21] See e.g. Geertz, Clifford (1968), *Islam Observed: Religious Development in Morocco and Indonesia,* Chicago University Press: Chicago; Gellner, Ernest (1981), *Muslim Society,* Cambridge University Press: Cambridge.

[22] See Asad, Talal (2009), 'The Idea of an Anthropology of Islam', *Qui Parle,* Vol. 17, No. 2., pp. 1–30, p. 5.

[23] Ibid., p. 10

primary sources of Islam (Quran and Sunnah) as the 'correct model',[24] in other words the domain of orthodoxy. This, however, can be understood differently across time and space because after the end of revelation from the Prophet Muhammad (PBUH), Muslims are left with learned jurists whose interpretation of the primary sources depends on various considerations based on different conceptions of the truth. The domain of orthodoxy is a site of prescriptive power and what becomes considered as orthodoxy can be a prescription of those who possess the social authority that is capable of excluding unfavourable or contradictory claims. As Shahab Ahmed argued, the domain of orthodoxy can become nothing other than staking an 'exclusive claim of authority' on what Islam is thereby prescribing and restricting alternative claims to truth.[25]

What has become understood as Salafism claims an unbroken link with the beliefs and practices of the Salaf Salih (pious predecessors). The Salaf principle claims that Muslims must believe and practice Islam as the pious companions of the Prophet Muhammad (PBUH) did. In other words, the degree to which a person/community follows or departs from the 'authentic' acts of the pious predecessors is the measure of a person's Muslimness. In trying to locate Muslimness in a pristine Islamic past, Salafist doctrine interprets Islamic history without regard to ruptures in the long historical links it seems to deploy. Although Salafist doctrine makes a strong argument that recognizes what does not change, there are many aspects that change. After all, *ijtihad* (continuous exertion) is a fundamental principle of legal interpretation in Islam. Although the primary sources provide a prescriptive aspect, they alone do not define Muslimness *in toto* because orthodoxy is not an innocent act; it is an outcome of a complex process by which prescriptive power authors its idea of truth in a double movement that excludes its conception of untruth. The critical ingredient in this process is the *intention* of the prescriptive power that operates on the primary sources. For the very fusion of power with its conception of claims to truth forms the core of the discursive tradition in Islam. In the contemporary moment, these processual dynamics of Islam and Muslim life are situated, however, at the historical juncture of Islamic traditions and social-political constructions such as secularism, which also attempt to influence and direct Muslim authority. As Shahab Ahmed emphasized, the primary sources of Islam must be related to the changing dynamics of Muslim generations across time and space, especially the way in which

[24] Ibid., pp. 21–2.
[25] Shahab, Ahmed (2016), *What is Islam? The Importance of Being Islamic,* Princeton University Press: Princeton, pp. 271–3.

Muslim communities construct new vocabularies and discover, through *ijtihad*, what Muslimness means. Such an approach can help us to conceptualize unity in both its diversity and contradictions and to capture the totality of all practices that claim affinity with Islam.[26]

Sources, concepts and methodology

This book deploys the murders of Muslim clerics in the 2010s as the entry point to understanding the Muslim minority question in Uganda. An initial review of the literature revealed these were not the first Muslim murders in Uganda. At the end of Idi Amin's regime in 1979, many Muslims were murdered, an act described as a 'bloodbath' in which security agents of the current government were involved.[27] There were a series of Muslim murders under Milton Obote's first presidency as well (these episodes of Muslims' murders are analysed in Chapters 4 and 5 dealing with the Obote I (1962–71) and Amin (1971–79) regimes respectively). This history caused me to wonder whether the state was always implicated in such murders, even up to the present regime. Further research revealed that the colonial moment witnessed no systematic pattern of murders directed at Muslims. Yet, as I read further, literature detailing 'Muslim martyrs' during the reign of Muteesa I in pre-colonial Buganda came to light. I became convinced that the cleric's murders needed to be approached as an academic inquiry into the broader historical questions that shaped the social-political and economic life of successive governments, and Muslims' place in it.

To begin my inquiry, I chose a genealogical approach as opposed to a linear historical explanation based on origins of the Muslim question, since genealogy focuses on the myriad events that operate to influence particular phenomena both in their micro and macro aspects. Instead of searching for the historical origins of the Muslim question, I examined the conditions that made particular practices possible, conditions that enabled the construction of particular 'value judgements', the value that they possess and the conditions of their 'growth, development and displacement'.[28] Genealogy enables us to establish 'descent' – understood as affiliation to a group sustained by bonds of blood or social strata – so as to tease out the subtle, singular and sub-individual marks that might possibly intersect to

---

[26] Shahab, *What is Islam?* pp. 80–81, 104.

[27] Kiyimba, Abasi (1989), *Is the 1979 Muslim Blood Bath in Bushenyi History?* Kampala.

[28] Nietzsche, Friedrich (1998), *On the Genealogy of Morals*, translated by Douglas Smith, Oxford University Press: Oxford, pp. 5–8.

form a network. While difficult to unravel,[29] since a broad array of other conundrums (such as nationality) have interwoven to influence the lives of Muslims in Uganda, the continuance of these inextricable linkages across time allowed me to establish what were the unique traits and influences of the Muslim issue from similar influences of, say, nationality. In this way, I have been able to tease out aspects – those similar and different – that related to my inquiry and thus to identify the specific events that influenced the position of Muslims within the state.

My unit of analysis was the human body because it is the site of past experiences, including stigmas, desires and errors, which join and engage one another to compound 'insurmountable conflict'.[30] As a surface where inscribed events perpetually integrate within a dissociated self, the human body becomes a site imprinted by history and 'the process of history's destruction of the body'.[31] Focusing on the question, 'what does a Muslim identify with?' revealed the various signs of power inscribed on the body of the Muslim individual, as a site of power owing to the ideology with which such a body claims to identify. Descent focuses on particular moments that 'emerge' within history. The concept of emergence designates 'episodes' in a series of transformations across historical time such that what gets teased out is not an 'uninterrupted continuity' but a series of constructions that persist under new forms. The points of emergence are multiple and lead to diverse interpretation of meaning, due to the substitutions, displacements and systematic reversals. This variety of meaning seems natural because the interpretive process itself seeks to violently appropriate a system of rules that attempt to impose a direction, bend it to a new will, enforce participation in a different game, so as to subject it to secondary rule.[32] Here, the role of genealogy is to record interpretation of events that appear as stages in the historical process.

This book begins with the pre-colonial era in Buganda, followed by the colonial, the Obote I, Amin, Obote II and NRM eras. I thus move through the successive forms of state projects in Uganda, focusing on the social-political and economic contexts within which Muslims' expressions of Islam were situated. Each period produced a unique set of circumstances from which social-political praxis evolved. However, I did not consider periods as a way of segmenting time but rather of transiting ideas whereby

---

[29] Foucault, Michel (1977), *Language, Counter-Memory Practice: Selected Essays and Interviews,* Cornel University Press: Ithaca, p. 145.

[30] Ibid., p. 148.

[31] Ibid.

[32] Ibid., pp. 151–2.

political praxis mutated into something that demanded new social subjectivity, when particular transformations manifested sufficiently far-reaching effects such that the new period repudiated significant parts of the preceding social order.[33] In seeking to understand the transition of ideas in the various periods, I looked at both micro and macro indicators of Muslim issues, thus allowing for a multi-sided ethnography with attention to fleeting changes, ostensibly trivial events, seemingly petty details, the 'mundane and the experiential'.[34] Here the Muslim issues were investigated in relation to varying forms of statecraft where different processes of agency continue to shape Uganda's history. At the micro level, Muslims' articulation of Islam has historically produced an internal politics that invites state intervention. The masjid, for instance, is now identified as a space beyond its ritualistic meaning as a site of prayer. Many discursive practices such as the *khutba* (Islamic sermons) and *darasa* take place within the masjid. In its double role as a site of discourse to perform representation and as a space to inscribe power relations, the masjid has thus become a 'site of conflict'.[35] Through these various roles embedded in its space, it has enabled 'close-up' ethnographic investigations with various respondents. It also produced documents such as property deeds, eviction notices and purging notices, among others, on which power was inscribed. Only by elucidating questions of politics and power not only at the micro level but also at the macro level of social-political settings can we really understand Muslim practices and their relation to other forms of power, religious or secular.[36] Both informal and formal politics involve various individuals and groups whose political performances display particular traits that genealogically emanate from particular locations, becoming 'authoritative and normative' in regard to legitimating or contesting Muslim experiences'.[37] Thus, the

---

[33] Jacques, Le Goff (2015), *Must We Divide History Into Periods?* Translated by M.B. DeBevoise, Columbia University Press: New York, p. 2.

[34] Clancy-Smith, Julia (2011), 'Ruptures? Governance in Husaynid-Colonial Tunisia, c. 1870–1914' in Maussen, Marcel, et al. (Eds) (2011), *Colonial and Post-Colonial Governance of Islam: Continuities and Ruptures,* Amsterdam University Press: Amsterdam, p. 69.

[35] Ibid.

[36] Soares, Benjamin (2016), 'Reflections on Muslim-Christian Encounters in West Africa', *The Journal of the International African Institute*, Vol. 86, No. 4, pp. 673–7, p. 679.

[37] Soares, Benjamin & Osella, Filippo (2009), 'Islam, Politics, Anthropology', *Journal of the Royal Anthropological Institute,* Vol. 15, No. S1, pp. S1–S23, p. S2.

attempt of Ugandan leaders in various epochs to champion their idea of 'good' Muslims in support of their political projects highlights the kind of 'authoritative' discourses that have attempted to influence Muslims in the epochs of both 'Islamic' and 'secular' authority in Uganda.

On the macro level, the state's desire to check and direct the ambitions of Muslim leadership has historically enabled different kinds of politics. By teasing out indicators of state influences it is possible to see how state power inflences Muslim agency. Historical changes occur at both the micro and macro levels, and these cannot be described in the same way at both levels since a different history is being written on each of the two levels.[38] Both must be problematized and examined so as to reveal the intentions and inherent internal differentiations, the various forms of connections, the hierarchies of importance and the several networks of determination.[39] Within this relational framework, this investigation moves from considering the Islamic discursive tradition[40] towards understanding the apparent incoherence, the limits of the discursive tradition and the causes of the transformations that have served as new 'foundations', and how to re-conceptualize the transformations that translated into contradictory Muslim practices.[41] This study thus speaks to new ways of approaching both old and new sources[42] at both the micro and macro levels. Materials obtained from research at both the micro and macro level have been read 'against their grain', that is, against the social and political conditions that produced them.[43] To avoid extrapolation, I have focused on the various 'analytic shifts, practical concerns and political projects', which produced particular materials and the 'truth-claims they documented'.[44]

Conceptual lenses are critical to understanding the Muslim question. The concept of the discursive tradition in Islam has been used to refer to discourses that seek to instruct practitioners regarding the correct form and purposes of historically established practices – which uses the Quran and

---

[38] Ibid.

[39] Ibid.

[40] Asad, 'The Idea of an Anthropology of Islam', pp. 19–21.

[41] Ibid.

[42] Comaroff, Jean & John (1992), *Ethnography and the Historical Imagination*, Westview Press: Boulder.

[43] Stoler, Anna Laura (2002), 'Colonial Archives and the Arts of Governance: On the Content in the Form' in Hamilton, Carolyn, et al. (Eds) (2002), *Refiguring the Archive,* Kluwer: London, pp. 83–5.

[44] Hamilton et al., *Refiguring the Archive,* pp. 87–90.

Hadith as sources for Muslim practices.[45] I found this concept useful for my inquiry because it not only supports how the primary texts form the foundation of any attempt to interpret Islam but also suggests that not all Muslim practices derive from the primary texts; thus we can have diverse and contradictory meanings embedded in Muslims' practices that are still Islamic. By teasing out the coherences and incoherences of Muslim actors, I sought to understand the explanations for the coherence and also inquire into various social, political and economic conditions that constrain Muslim lives.

I also found the concept of a religious field[46] important to my analysis, indicating a space of interaction between practices spanning multiple religions. This was conceived as a way to study Muslims and Christians using one analytical framework owing to the long history of such inter-faith dialogue looking at the similarities, differences and conflicts, and I considered it useful to my research because Muslims in Uganda relate with both Christians and non-Christians. Integrating such analysis in my work did not mean that I read Islam and Muslim practices using the conceptual lenses of Christendom. Rather, I sought to qualify the ways in which Muslim discursive coherence is dialectically linked – in either limited or broad ways – by its relationship to non-Muslim power. Identifying the indicators of religious syncretism and religious pluralism among Muslims and non-Muslims helps us to appreciate the social-cultural performances of day-to-day practices of 'doing religion' and 'being religious'.[47] Using the concept of a religious field revealed the way in which Islam and Muslims in Uganda have always interacted in a region containing non-Muslim belief systems, and day-to-day practices of all beliefs have in many ways impacted on Muslim practices. While non-Muslim practices[48] have in some cases been detrimental to Muslim advancement, they have in

---

[45] Asad, *The Idea of an Anthropology of Islam,* pp. 20–21.

[46] Bourdieu, Pierre (1991), 'Genesis and Structure of the Religious Field', *Comparative Social Research: A Research Annual*, Vol. 13, pp. 1–44.

[47] Meyer, Birgit (2016), 'Towards a Joint Framework for the Study of Christians and Muslims in Africa: Response to J.D.Y. Peel', *The Journal of the International African Institute*, Vol. 86, No. 4, pp. 628–32, p. 629.

[48] Larkin, Brian (2016), 'Entangled Religions: Response to J.D.Y. Peel', *The Journal of the International African Institute*, Vol. 86, No. 4, pp. 633–9, pp. 633–4; Obadare, Ebenezer (2016), 'Response to "Similarity and Difference, Context and Tradition, in Contemporary Religious Movements in West Africa" by J.D.Y. Peel', *The Journal of the International African Institute*, Vol. 86, No. 4, pp. 640–45, p. 640.

other respects supported Muslim progress and Islamic growth. Such oscillation between friendship, enmity or indifference has been at the centre of Muslim relationships with non-Muslim society and states for the periods under inquiry. Teasing out the intricacies of such relationships has enabled a fuller appreciaton of the ways in which non-Muslim experiences affected the discursive field of Muslim life.

The Islamization of the pre-colonial political community in Buganda marks the first period of the study. The question of which sources better explain the nature of the social-political-economic context of Buganda and its encounter with Islam is vexed. Many sources on Islam's entry in Uganda focus on its foreign 'origin', coming to Buganda in the early 1800s.[49] Although the question of *origins* is important because it enables us to perceive the social-cultural-religious practices that refer to the Quran and Hadith, my focus on genealogy as a method of inquiry allows us to appreciate principles that claim affinity with Islam but which *predate* the entry of the Quran and Hadith in Buganda. As will be seen, Baganda believed in Katonda (literally, Creator) and many of their social practices such as polygamy[50] predate the entry of Islam in Buganda; and these practices were indicators of *fitrah* – the natural inclination in man. Yet the sources on the Islamization of Buganda assert that Islam is fundamentally Arabian and thus geographically foreign to Uganda. Claiming that Islam is an 'outsider' religion would also make Muslims outsiders as well.[51] If the history of Muslims in Uganda must encompass the social-cultural-political-economic lives of all who claim to identify with Islam as a faith, it demands understanding the genealogies of Islam,

[49] Musoke, D.R. (1917), *Ebifa Mu Buganda*, No. 120. Buddo; Ssekimwanyi, Abdallah (nd) (*Ebyafaayo Ebitonotono ku Ddiini Y'ekiyisiraamu Okuyingira mu Buganda*); Kkulumba, Ali (nd), 'Ebyafaayo by Obuyisiraamu mu Uganda'; Gomotoka, J.M.T. (1940), 'Makula, kye Kitabo kye Bika Ekilangira Ky'oloyo lwe Buganda', microfim at Makerere University, Kampala; Miti, J.K. (nd), *Ebyafaayo bya Buganda*, Kampala; Gray, John Milner (1934), 'Mutesa of Buganda', *Uganda Journal,* Vol. I, No. 1, pp. 22–49; Mukasa, Ham (1938), *Simuda Nyuma*, S.P.C.K.: London, Vol. I; Katungulu, *Islam in Buganda*; Kakungulu, Badru & Kasozi, A.B.K. (1977), *Abasimba Obuyisiraamu Mu Uganda*, Equator Books: Kampala; Gee, T.W. (1957), 'A Century of Muhammadan Influence in Buganda 1852–1951', *The Uganda Journal*, Vol. 22, No. 2, pp. 139–50.

[50] Many Baganda men took on several wives until Islamic teachings limited them to four.

[51] Manan, Ahmed A. (2016), *A Book of Conquest: The Chachnama and the Muslim Origins in South Asia,* Harvard University Press: London, p. 2.

INTRODUCTION   **21**

which allow us to embrace the emergence of new and diverse sources for understanding Islamic practices.

This book engages with multiple sources to respond to the questions raised in each chapter. The early works of explorers, missionaries and colonial administrators, what Valentin-Yves Mudimbe termed 'the colonial library',[52] have been critical to understanding colonial administrative governance. Covering a number of periods in Uganda's history, and the separate political projects they engender, I found that the sources of one particular era could be limited in interpreting the political praxis of another. While the documents of early Ganda writers supported by oral traditions and early European chroniclers,[53] for instance, allow us to understand the pre-colonial social-political-economic structure of Buganda, they are limited in illuminating the substitution of the Ganda political structure with colonial statecraft after 1900. Here, the colonial library compensates. Similarly, the limits of the colonial library in understanding post-colonial governments beginning with Obote and Amin meant engaging with other sources such as the post-colonial government archive and ethnographic fieldwork.

The sources of the pre-colonial era provide oral accounts for the foundations of Buganda. Writers such as Ham Mukasa, Apollo Kaggwa, Musoke Zimbe, Gomotoka and others witnessed many events that occurred during the second half of the nineteenth century. These local historians' use of oral traditions was not as exacting as it has become in the contemporary era. Coming from a Christian background, they were partisan historians who formed a past that articulated a Christian future in which the Muslims' role would be marginal. Many saw Islam as an inferior forerunner to Christianity.[54] Musoke Zimbe's account of Buganda history for instance depicts a lively Christianity biased against

---

[52] See Mudimbe, V.-Y. (1988), *The Invention of Africa: Gnosis, Philosophy, and the Order of Knowledge,* Indiana University Press: Bloomington.

[53] Gomotoka, *Makula*; Miti, *Ebyafaayo bya Buganda*; Roscoe, John (1911), *The Baganda: An Account of Their Native Customs and Beliefs*, Barnes & Noble: New York; Mukasa, *Simuda Nyuma*; Zimbe, Musoke B. (1939), *Buganda ne Kabaka*, Kampala; Kaggwa, Sir Apollo (1971), *The Kings of Buganda,* trans. Ssemakula Kiwanuka, East African Publishing House: Nairobi; Tucker, Alfred R. (1908), *Eighteen Years in Uganda and East Africa,* E. Arnold: London.

[54] See also Falola, Toyin (2005), 'Mission and Colonial Documents' in Phillips, John Edward (Ed.), *Writing African History,* University of Rochester Press: Rochester, p. 271.

Islam. Missionary accounts also deride Islam and Muslims, and paint Christianity and Europeans in a better light.[55]

Missionary documents cover many subjects and use a variety of media, including reports and official correspondence. Early materials such as those of Bishop Tucker, and Church Missionary Society (CMS) correspondences, focused on conditions for the spread of Christianity and therefore contain extensive information on the lifestyles of Uganda peoples and the situation regarding Islam.[56] Many missionaries' records are contained in their diaries, reports and journals. In using these, I focused on writings on Islam and non-Muslim relations. *The Church Missionary Gleaner* documented stories of successful conversion to Christianity and how this was lessening the Islamic advance in Uganda.[57] Missionary reports also include adverts calling for more 'ministers' to come to Uganda to advance the Christian cause, presenting Uganda as the bastion of Christian ascendancy in East Africa and as a bulwark against Islam.[58] Islam is presented in some records as a fundamentally violent belief system while Christian missionaries are the humanitarian agents of a civilization that Islam threatens.[59]

The colonial library includes reports, periodicals, manuals, investigative inquiries, gazettes and other private collections that concerned administration as well. It also includes private diaries and books belonging to colonial officials, including residents, governors, secretaries, district commissioners, chiefs and many others. Some diaries, books and materials have been considered extensively since they concern the very existence of the colonial state. Annual colonial reports (Blue Books) contain the essentials of colonial policy. Captain Lugard's manuscripts on indirect rule have revealed the logic and rationale of colonial statecraft.[60] Many

---

55   Daniell, E.S. (1913) 'Our Great Opportunities in Uganda', *The Church Missionary Gleaner*, p. 170.

56   *The Church Missionary Gleaner*, 1 August 1913, pp. 121–2.

57   'Mohammedanism hard hit', *The Church Missionary Gleaner*, 1 February 1913, p. 23.

58   'How to Stop the Advance of Islam', *The Church Missionary Gleaner*, 1 March 1913, p. 37.

59   Harding H.G., 'How to Win the Moslem', *The Church Missionary Gleaner*, 1 March 1918, p. 35; Cook, Howard J. 'Christ or Mohammed? Uganda and the Regions beyond', *The Church Missionary Gleaner,* 1 May 1918, pp. 68–9.

60   Lugard, Frederick D. (1968), *The Rise of Our East African Empire: Early Efforts in Nyasaland and Uganda*, Frank Cass & Co.: London, Vol. II; Lugard

of the documents in the colonial archive provide abundant information on the colonial era, regarding the state's relationship with Muslim leadership, their perception of Islam and how to contain it.[61]

European perceptions of the African continent, formed even before the encounter with Africans and persisting under colonialism, tainted early anthropology. Such designations as 'Dark Continent' were born at the moment when European power sought to 'flood' Africa with 'light' to abolish 'savage customs' and move towards 'civilization'.[62] Yet, the discourse of civilization was itself anchored in a language that intended to subject, include and exclude, while voicing and silencing 'African' values.[63] But this was the result of a series of forces operating in the European space – for instance, the anti-slavery movement, the impact of the explorers and the merger of racist and evolutionary doctrines in the social sciences – which combined to give the European public a widely shared view of Africa that demanded imperialization on moral, religious and scientific grounds.

The myth of the 'dark continent' had a double consequence. It enabled, on the one hand, both a secularized and depoliticized speech that considered itself as universally acceptable, scientifically established and therefore no longer open to theoretical or political opposition or criticism. It occluded, on the other, the objective character of the conquered person as possessing values worthy of documentation.[64] There is a fundamental critique that arises from these insights. To the extent that European sources obliterated African knowledge structures towards grounding their imperialist ideology, what would be the continuing relevance of using such sources and materials in the study of the Muslim question in Uganda, for instance? Of course, this is not to present the

---

(2005), *The Dual Mandate in British Tropical Africa,* Routledge: London; Perham, Margery (1960), *Lugard: The Years of Authority 1898–1945,* Collins: London.

[61] Lugard, *The Rise of Our East African Empire,* Vol. II, pp. 423–4.

[62] Brantlinger, Patrick (1985), 'Victorians and Africans: The Genealogy of the Myth of the Dark Continent', *Critical Inquiry,* Vol. 12, No. 1, pp. 166–203, p. 166.

[63] Brantlinger, 'Victorians and Africans', p. 167; see also, 'Among Moslems and Pagans', *The Church Missionary Gleaner,* 1 February 1913, p. 23.

[64] Brantlinger, 'Victorians and Africans', pp. 167–8'. See also Chadwick, Owen (1975), *The Secularization of the European Mind in the Nineteenth Century,* Cambridge University Press: Cambridge, pp. 14–15.

colonial archive as a total monolith devoid of internal contradictions and differentiations, or whose interpretation is static and unchanging. Rather, to alert us to the question that if the European gaze on Africa considered the 'superiority of European civilization' as the fundamental marker of difference with African systems, what could be our interest in using such perceptions? I contend that regardless of the interpretative conclusions of a particular source, they are relevant because they reveal the *attitudes* of the European mind and how it perceived African people generally, Islam specifically and Muslim individuals particularly. The sources in other words speak to how European knowledge structures *thought* about Islam generally and Muslims in particular. The value of these sources lies in how they enable new *interpretations* to be made about meanings of particular practices.

Generally, the value of the colonial archive as a source in studying contemporary problems lies in the shifting character of the archive. In various ways, the interpretation of the archive is not a constant or static activity: it is changing all the time due to the equally shifting 'technologies' of preservation and use; the archive is 'porous to societal processes and discourses',[65] including those relating to individual power choices. It differentiates the 'official representative' of such power from the individual researcher who also exercises personal discretion in deciding which interview transcripts get published or shared with the public.[66]

Some chapters of this study have used 'commissions of inquiry' as source materials for the various epochs. When President Museveni promised a commission of inquiry to investigate the first murdered Muslim cleric in 2012, he was following a method inherited from the colonial state, which marked commissions as 'tactics of delay', and more.[67] In the colonial era, commissions of inquiry were deployed in order to inquire what society knew about emerging issues and use such social facts to produce new truths. Emerging crises became opportunities for state intervention in diverting what authorities considered dangerous political outcomes. Colonial commissions of inquiry were categorized according to the degree of secrecy the authorities deemed necessary to place on some information. Although some information was considered officially secret, other details were categorized as either secret, very secret or confidential. These

---

[65] Hamilton, Carolyn, et al. (Eds) (2002), *Refiguring the Archive,* Kluwer: London, p. 7.

[66] Ibid., p. 10.

[67] Hamilton et al., *Refiguring the Archive,* p. 95.

designations called for special protection.[68] Comparing archival material to ethnographic inquiry shows that information was not as secret as it was actually considered to be. Secrecy is a highly relative concept. When I began my inquiry, I believed that information regarding the cleric's murders was held in secret and could hamper the research. However, ethnographic research revealed that what was perceived as secret was actually known to many sheikhs in the leadership of the Tabliq (the Ugandan sect of Sunni Islam that identifies with Salafism). What is more those who participated in meetings with the government to discuss forms of violence targeting opposing factions passed the information on to non-participating sheikhs. Similarly, ethnographic research into the returning Uganda People's Defence Forces (UPDF) contingents of peacekeepers from Iraq and Somalia reveals that what was secret to the person in Uganda regarding the dealings of the state abroad was not a secret to the returning soldier – especially regarding such issues as officers' corruption and the complexities of the war on terror.

Tools of social media, such as audio and video recordings provided information that I could not otherwise access from some respondents. Audio recordings also enabled me to corroborate information of which some respondents denied knowledge. Using audio recordings for data collection demonstrates the way in which new media technologies have enabled the liberalization of Islamic knowledge. Some sheikhs give and disseminate fatwas (religious rulings) using multiple media platforms, which has also enabled mass education and increased literacy but also resulted in further fragmentation of Muslim authority. Recordings received from former ADF rebels provided insight into how rebel commanders used *darasa* and *khutba* to revive spiritual commitment to rebellion. Recordings of Jamil Mukulu in the 1990s and 2000s revealed the *thinking* that informed the violent turn made by the Tabligh, while later recordings detail the transformation and eventual collapse of the rebellion against the NRM regime. These recordings were corroborated by group discussions and interviews held in July 2016 with former ADF rebels, who provided much of the information contained in Chapter 6. Their names have been withheld to protect their identities; the state has arrested and turned many of their colleagues into state agents. I was able to access these individuals through sheikhs whom they respected, who also remained anonymous to me, only after repeated urgings that I was not a state spy coming to inform on them.

---

[68] Hamilton et al., *Refiguring the Archive,* p. 99.

Divisions, murders and accusations

As highlighted in the opening paragraphs of this chapter, leadership wrangles have existed in the Muslim leadership for over twenty years between the Kibuli[69] and Old Kampala factions.[70] Between 2012 and 2016, this division took a violent turn that culminated in the death of Muslim clerics and other personalities. On 21 April 2012, Sheikh Abdul Karim Ssentamu, a prominent Muslim cleric in Uganda, was assassinated a few metres from Masjid Noor, William Street, Kampala, where he usually responded to questions from the Muslim audience. In June 2012, Hajji Abubaker Abbas Kiweewa Kigejjogejjo, a prominent Muslim leader and businessman, was also assassinated in Kyanja, Kampala. More killings followed: Sheikhs Maganda and Yunus Abubakari Mudungu both of Bugiri, Eastern Uganda, August 2012; Abdu Jawali Sentunga, Imam of Namayemba Salaf Masjid, in Bugiri, Eastern Uganda, September 2012; Sheikh Abdu Rashid Wafula, of Mbale, Eastern Uganda, May 2015; Sheikh Dr Abdul Kadir Muwaya, the leader of the Shia Sect, murdered in Mayuge, Eastern Uganda, 24 December 2014; Sheikh Mustafa Bahiga, the Kampala District Amir of Jamaat Da'wah Salafiyyah, 28 December 2014; Sheikh Ibrahim Hassan Kirya, the Spokesperson of the Kibuli-based faction, 30 June 2015: Major

[69] On the history of Kibuli, see Solzbacher, Regina (1969), 'Continuity Through Change in the Social History of Kibuli', *Uganda Journal*, Vol. 33, No. 1, pp. 163–74.

[70] This division has been the focus of several studies. For instance, Kaliisa, Anas Abdunoor (1994), 'Leadership Crisis Among Muslims of Uganda (1850–1993)', Masters Dissertation, Kampala: Makerere University; Kanyeihamba, George W. (1997), *Reflections on the Muslim Leadership Question in Uganda*, Kampala: Fountain; Kasumba, Yusuf (1995), 'The Development of Islam in Uganda 1962–1992 with Particular Reference to Religio-Political Factionalism', Masters Dissertation, Makerere University: Kampala; Katungulu, Haruna Jemba A. (2012), 'Religion and the Search for Peace and Reconciliation in Buganda', PhD Dissertation, Makerere University: Kampala; Katungulu, M.M. (1968), *Islam in Buganda,* translated into English by Mr. Busulwa, Kampala; 1990), Kiyimba, Abasi, 'The Muslim Community in Uganda through One Hundred and Forty Years, pp. 84–120; Kasozi, A.B.K. (1985), 'The Uganda Muslim Supreme Council: An Experiment in Muslim Administrative Centralization and Institutionalization (1972–82)', *Journal Institute of Muslim Minority Affairs*, Vol. 6, No. 1; Kayunga, Simba Sallie (1993), 'Islamic Fundamentalism in Uganda: A Case Study of the Tabligh Youth Movement', Centre for Basic Research, Kampala, Working Paper No. 37.

Sheikh Muhammad Kiggundu, a member of the Salaf faction and a serving officer of the UPDF, 26 November 2016.[71]

Rumours have circulated within the Muslim community of other prominent clerics who have died under mysterious circumstances. Such deaths have included those of Sheikh Abdul Hakim Ssekimpi, the Deputy Supreme Mufti of the Kibuli-based faction, who died at Kibuli Muslim hospital on 21 July 2012, and, in April 2015, Sheikh Zubair Kayongo, the Supreme Mufti of the Kibuli-based Muslim faction, who had gone for a week-long conference to Dar es Salaam, Tanzania, and passed away in its Aga Khan Hospital. Other sheikhs who received death threats – either assailants shooting at their homesteads or multi-media verbal recordings and telephone calls – include Sheikhs Haruna Jjemba Katungulu, the leader of a breakaway Salaf faction, who survived gunshots at his home and Najib Ssonko, another member of the breakaway Salaf faction who also survived gunshots. Others within the same faction, who have been threatened with death and marked on lists, include Mahmood Kibaate and Umar Swidiq Ndawula. On 12 September 2016, Prince Kassim Nakibinge, the head of the Kibuli-based Muslim faction intimated that he had also received death threats and that he had been added to a list for elimination.

Depicting all of the above murders as similar could be misleading, however: in some respects, they are different. Speaking to respondents and victims' families in Eastern Uganda revealed that Sheikh Abdu Rashid Wafula may have been murdered due to land wrangles involving his family and that the timing of his death, and the fact of his Muslim identity, may have coincided with the wave of murders targeting Muslim clerics. In an environment of Muslim fear, popular belief attributed his murder to a more sweeping explanation.[72] Also, the murder of Dr Sheikh Abdu Kadir Muwaya in Mayuge, the leader of the Shia Sect in Uganda, is allegedly not connected to the deaths of Muslim clerics, since the other deaths have mainly been of Sunni Muslim clerics who largely subscribe to the Salafi sect.[73] What linked these deaths was the method of elimination, committed by assailants riding on motorcycle taxis (locally called 'bodabodas'). As the murders continued unabated, concerned Muslim leaders tasked the state authorities with explaining the cause.

When part of the Muslim community[74] voiced their concerns about the murders, the state responded that members of a rebel group, the Allied

---

[71] See 'Muslim clerics who have been killed', *Daily Monitor*, 26 November 2016.

[72] Focus Group discussion (hereinafter FGD), Mbale, 1 December 2016.

[73] Ibid.

[74] E.g. Chairperson of Uganda Muslim Youth Assembly (UMYA), Professor

Democratic Force (ADF) were responsible for the murders;[75] President Museveni and his then Inspector General of Police, Kale Kayihura, supported this explanation.[76] Although the state's counter-insurgence efforts managed to infiltrate some of the ADF and turn its fighters into state agents to spy on fellow Muslims, the state was only able to incarcerate Jamil Mukulu, the group's leader, when he was deported from Tanzania, where he had been arrested in May 2015. The clerics' murders had continued even after his arrest, and many wondered if Jamil Mukulu possessed the material resources and organizational capacity to continue killing clerics even after his incarceration. Others questioned whether he was in fact responsible for the murders that occurred before his arrest in May 2015. Yet, in a set of recordings obtained from former ADF fighters, Mukulu is heard giving *darasa* (lecture) sessions in the rebel camps in the eastern DRC. In a session recorded in 2012, days after the assassination of Sheikh Abdul Karim Ssentamu, Mukulu denies any involvement in the murder of Ssentamu, regardless of how he detested his ways: 'even when they abused us, and tried to kill us, we did not kill them. And we had the guns and the capacity to do it. Why has Ssentamu passed away when the state admired his work of preaching against jihad?'[77] When the killings continued even after the arrest of Jamil Mukulu, the Muslim community found the state's explanations insufficient. Conversations surrounding the murders continued to generate more questions. During Muslim discussions in *darasa* and *khutba* (sermons), sheikhs allied to various camps continued to speculate as to who was committing the murders, why they continued and how the state security apparatus had failed to halt them.

Abasi Kiyimba called on state police to account for the pattern of killings targeting Muslim clerics. See Mukisa, F. 'Killings: Police, Muslim leaders clash', *Daily Monitor,* 7 January 2015.

[75] The Allied Democratic Front (ADF) was a rebel group founded by Muslims led by Jamil Mukulu, a former seminarian who converted to Islam in 1996 to fight the government of President Museveni. See 'Police link killing of Muslim leaders to ADF rebel group', *Daily Monitor,* 31 December 2014. 'Museveni blames Sheikhs' killing on ADF', *Daily Monitor,* 1 July 2016; at three separate funeral ceremonies for the murdered Muslim clerics in Uganda, the commander of the Uganda Police, Kale Kayihura, purveyed this narrative.

[76] 'Police link killing of Muslim leaders to ADF rebel group', *Daily Monitor,* 31 December 2014. 'Museveni blames Sheikhs' killing on ADF', *Daily Monitor,* 1 July 2016.

[77] Jamil Mukulu recordings, 2012. Audio files kept in the personal archives of various clerics.

In the context of the fear and grief that engulfed Ugandan Muslims, another explanation emerged to counter the ADF's from within the Kamoga-led Salafi faction.[78] As we have seen, Kamoga's faction within the Tabliq group argued that the murder of Muslim clerics was part of the United States' global 'war on terror' and not limited to Uganda alone, and linked the Ugandan murders with a wave of killings targeting Muslim clerics in neighbouring Kenya.[79] According to them, the ADF could not be responsible for killing Muslim clerics in Uganda since the same thing was happening in Kenya where the ADF did not operate. Other sheikhs within Kamoga's faction argued that Israel was targeting Muslims in Nigeria, Kenya, Tanzania and elsewhere.[80] Sheikh Murtadha Bukenya gave this response to the statements made by the Kibuli faction, on 29 December 2014 (at the congregation to prepare for the burial of Sheikh Mustapha Bahiga). Muslims in Uganda could not kill each other, said Bukenya, 'this is the work of the enemy' (referring to the state of Israel).[81] Although others supported his explanation,[82] they could not answer the fundamental question as to why Israel would choose to eliminate only clerics allied to one camp. The link to the 'Zionist' explanation was popularized, however, by an *Al Jazeera* investigation that revealed how the Kenyan security agencies were using a 'rule book' borrowed from 'Israel and Britain', who trained the Kenyan anti-terrorist squads that confessed to murdering Muslims.[83] While the 'Zionist' explanation might have some currency among those whose focus is the ongoing wave of global murders of Muslim clerics linked to the 'war on terror'[84], it decontextualizes the local experiences

---

[78] This narrative was the topic of a discussion called at Masjid Noor, William Street, Kampala, to rebut claims that Kamoga's group was working with assailants involved in the murder of Sheikh Mustapha Bahiga, 30 December 2014.

[79] 'List of Muslim Clerics killed in two years in Kenya', *The Star*, 11 June 2014. See also Deacon, Gregory et al. (2017), 'Preaching Politics: Islam and Christianity on the Kenyan Coast', *Journal of Contemporary African Studies*, Vol. 35, No. 2, p. 2.

[80] Sheikh Murtadha Bukenya, Masjid Noor, William Street, Kampala, 30 December 2014.

[81] Ibid.

[82] Sheikh Mahad Mbaziira, Masjid Noor, William Street, Kampala, 30 December 2014.

[83] See 'Inside Kenya's Death Squads', *Al Jazeera Investigations*, 8 December 2014, www.youtube.com/watch?v=lUjOdjdH8Uk (accessed 19 May 2016).

[84] On the discourse regarding the global war on terror, see, for instance, Mamdani, Mahmood (2004), *Good Muslim Bad Muslim: America, the Cold*

and dehistoricizes local responsibility and accountability for particular acts. Transcending reactionary explanations such as those attributing the murders to 'Zionist' and 'ADF' groups, this book shows that the answer to the murders and the other episodes of violence experienced by Muslims is to a broader historical Muslim question. By linking issues about Islam and Muslims with the various articulations of political power in Uganda's history, this book shows that different political actors cultivated a role for Islam and Muslims within the state and influenced Muslims' life and the form of response to their governance.

War, and the Roots of Terror, Fountain: Kampala, pp. 3–4; Mamdani (2010), *Saviors and Survivors: Darfur, Politics and the War on Terror*, CODESRIA: Dakar; Escobar, Pepe (2009), *Obama Does Globalinistan*, Nimble Books: Michigan, p. 11; Escobar (2014), *Empire of Chaos*: The Roving Eye Collection Vol. I., Nimble Books: Ann Arbor; Escobar (2006), *Globalistan: How the Globalized World is Dissolving into Liquid War*, Nimble Books: Ann Arbor, p. 46; Ali, Tariq (2008), *The Duel: Pakistan on the Flight Path of American Power*, Scribner: New York; Roy, Olivier (2008), *The Politics of Chaos in the Middle East*, Columbia University Press: New York, pp. 75–80; Hobsbawm, Eric (2008), *On Empire: America, War, and Global Supremacy*, Pantheon Books: New York; Zizek, Slavoj (2005), *Iraq: The Borrowed Kettle*, Verso: New York, pp. 2–4; Schwartz, Michael (2008), *War Without End: The Iraq War in Context*, Haymarket: New York; Said, Edward W. (1978), *Orientalism*, Pantheon Books: New York, p. 12; Düsterhöft, Isabel K. & Gerlach, Antonia I. (2013), 'The Successes and Failures of the Interventions of the European Union, the African Union and Neighbouring Powers in Somalia', *Sicherheit und Frieden*, Vol. 31, No. 1, pp. 18–23, p. 21; Menkhaus, Ken (2009), 'They Created a Desert and Called It Peace (Building)', *Review of African Political Economy*, Vol. 36, No. 120, pp. 223–33, p. 224; Pape, Robert A. & Feldman James K. (2010), *Cutting the Fuse: The Explosion of Global Suicide Terrorism and How to Stop It*, The University of Chicago Press: Chicago, pp. 19–23.

CHAPTER 2

Islam in Pre-Colonial Buganda

This chapter will discuss the Islamization of Buganda in the pre-colonial era, when the discursive formations,[1] that is the discourses and vocabularies of Islamic sources and Muslim practices, began to permeate Ganda society. Situating Islam in the social-cultural-political context of the state, I argue that Muteesa used Islam as an ideology to centralize royal power vis-à-vis other competing centres of Ganda power. Islam offered both internal and external benefits to the ruling elite at the time. Internally, Muteesa attempted to use Islam as a new ideology to surpass the Ganda religious system of shrines and public healers, and their influence over political authority. Externally, Islam would cement Muteesa's relationship with other Muslim powers such as those of Egypt and Zanzibar which had different interests in Buganda. It allowed him to strengthen his control over the caravan trade linked with Zanzibar and at the same time positioned Buganda as a Muslim polity against any real or potential Egyptian takeover. The caravan trade provided opportunities to acquire advanced military weaponry, which Muteesa's armies could use to defend Buganda's interests and also undertake internal reorganization of the Ganda polity.

As we will see, Muteesa's attempt to use Islam to transform Buganda met with only partial success. Although Islamization placed the Kabaka as the patron of both Islam and Muslims, and established elite Muslim chiefs who would enforce Muteesa's Islamization project, it met with resistance from Buganda's people and the Christian parties who entered Buganda in the last part of Muteesa's reign. The subsequent killing of Muslims and non-Muslims brought about a phase of violence, which

---

[1]   Michel Foucault describes a discursive formation as occurring whenever one 'describes statements, systems of dispersion, concepts, thematic choices, correlations, positions and transformations'. The conditions under which the 'elements of this division' are subjected he calls the 'rules of formation'. Foucault (1972), *The Archaeology of Knowledge,* Tavistock Publications: London, pp. 42–3.

ISLAM IN UGANDA

demonstrated the limits of Muteesa's use of Islamization as a political strategy. The forces that hindered him set the stage for a political battle for the control of power in Buganda. The onset of religious competition for the control of political power constructed religion as a new form of social-political identity in Uganda.

The chapter is organized into three sections. The first describes the social-cultural-political context of Buganda before its encounter with Islam and the emergence of political power in pre-colonial Buganda to provide a background to the context within which Islam emerged. Describing the Ganda religious system as a way of life that impacted on the social organization and the articulation of political life is the initial step to understanding why and how far Muteesa deployed Islam to transform Buganda. Many Ganda social-cultural beliefs and practices gelled with the introduction of Islam, and the attempt to transform these practices had implications that continued through the successive periods under study. To avoid decontextualizing concepts, this section uses many Ganda concepts whose meaning cannot be easily translated into English. The second section describes the attempts of Muteesa to Islamize Buganda. As well as showing how Muteesa used Islam as a way to focus his power, it also demonstrates the challenges it found, as reflected in the murder of Muslim martyrs under his reign and the conversion of formerly Muslim elite chiefs to Christianity. The third section of this chapter describes the onset of religious wars and the struggle for political power as the major consequences of religious pluralism in Buganda. What I term religious competition demonstrates the nascent stages of both Islam and Christianity as forms of social-political identity in Uganda.

Political power in pre-Islamic Buganda

The word 'Buganda' comes from the root word '*ŋanda*', which basically connotes kinship relations. The larger geographical unit is Buganda; the people are Baganda and their language is Luganda. Their social-cultural values are generally called Ganda. Scholarship has shown that political authority in Buganda has been constituted historically around a community founded on a social-cultural-religious ethos that supported the political institutions. Writers on political institutions in Buganda have differed on the location of political power. Some writers have argued that ultimate power resided with the kingly authority.[2] Other writers have argued that

---

[2]   See Kaggwa, Apollo (1971), *The Kings of Buganda,* translated and edited by Kiwanuka M.S.M, East African Publishing House: Kampala, p. 1;

there were other centres of power that exercised influence over Ganda society, besides the king.[3] These centres of power and influence included palaces of queen mothers and princesses, spirit mediums in non-royal shrines, and other female/male personalities who played multiple roles in the social-cultural-political dynamics of Buganda.[4] Historical accounts for the emergence of political authority in pre-colonial Buganda are therefore multiple and diverse, and depend on the various decentralized sites of power that produced separate histories. As will be demonstrated, there are junctures of centralization whereby separate histories tend to emerge around a particular centre of power in displacing others. These instances of centralization are what concern me here. In what follows I describe how Muteesa used Islam as an ideology to reorganize Buganda as a polity because his guardianship over Islam and Muslims placed him at the pinnacle of the whole Ganda structure beyond the reach of other competing centres of authority. As a religion that recognizes no other deities but Allah, Islam, for Muteesa, offered an opportunity to transcend Ganda cultural beliefs in multiple deities, implying that Muteesa aspired to his political authority stemming from the One God to whom he was accountable as opposed to the multiple gods who exercised various influences.

The kabakaship, or kingship, has been identified as the foremost institution of political authority in Buganda. Etymologically, 'kabaka' means 'small representative/delegate'. Its usage connotes an individual held in low regard. According to Ganda oral traditions, 'kabaka' designated a small representative but it was not limited to human leaders. Oral traditions claim that before Katonda (God) sent Kintu (whom Baganda regard

---

Kiwanuka Ssemakula (1972), *The History of Buganda, From the Foundation of the Kingdom to 1900,* Africana Publishing Corporation: New York; Kabuga, C.E.S. (1972), *History of the Kingdom of Buganda: Birth of the Late King Kintu and the First Kintu*, trans. from Luganda into English by James Wamala, p. 2.

[3] See Kodesh, Neil (2010), *Beyond the Royal Gaze: Clanship and Public Healing in Buganda,* University of Virginia Press: London, pp. 10–11; Kodesh (2008), 'Networks of Knowledge: Clanship and Collective Well-being in Buganda', *The Journal of African History,* Vol. 49, No. 2, pp. 197–216, pp. 200–201; Musisi, Nakanyike B. (1991), 'Women, "Elite Polygyny", and Buganda State Formation', *Signs: Journal of Women in Culture and Society,* Vol. 16, No. 4, pp. 757–86, p. 780.

[4] See also Hanson, Holly (2002), 'Queen Mothers and Good Government in Buganda: The Loss of Women's Power in Nineteenth-Century East Africa', in Allman, Jean et al. (Eds) (2002), *Women in African Colonial Histories,* Indiana University Press: Bloomington, p. 219.

34   ISLAM IN UGANDA

as the founder of the Buganda kingdom) to become '*kabaka owoomubiri*' (kabaka of the flesh), *lubaale* (divinities/spirits) resided in and allegedly ruled Buganda for many generations and were called '*bakabaka abempewo*' (spiritual kabakas).[5] Baganda describe Katonda in words such as '*mukama*' (all powerful), '*lugaba*' (provider), '*ddunda*' (guardian), '*liisoddene*' (all seer); they built palaces called *amasabo* (special shrines, from the verb, *okusaba*, request, where 'requests' are made). The spiritual Kabakas were believed to have come from butonda (place of creation, following the verb kutonda, to create). They also had palaces built for them wherein they would provide intercession between human beings and Katonda.[6] When Kabakas of the flesh replaced their *lubaale* counterparts, royal and commoners' ancestry converged; the belief in the common heritage of butonda (divine place of creation) sustained it. The designation '*abaana ba Kintu*' (descendants of Kintu) confirmed both royals and commoners as belonging to a similar ancestry and it gave them historical legitimacy and authority over various institutions.[7]

Ganda histories also acknowledge *bakabaka abempewo* (spiritual kabakas), which confirms that there were two sorts of Kintu who were significant for different audiences across various locations. The spiritual Kintu occupies a less familiar place because a historiography that sought to reproduce an intellectual politics about Ganda statecraft suppressed him. Yet Kintu as a *musambwa* (spirit) existed and 'serviced' various shrines as spiritual entities towards which many communities directed various practices 'designed to ensure continued prosperity and abundance'.[8] These collective ritual practices allowed wider networks of alliances that stretched across shrines in other locations. This very fact points to a different intellectual reading of the Kintu narrative.[9] This variety of religious allegiance shows that Baganda believed in different spirits and practised their rituals in different non-royal shrines. As spirit mediums also possessed a degree of political influence over adherents, we can conclude that Ganda subjectivity over the Kabaka's power was not total but rather subjective to different

---

[5]   See also Tabawebbula, Kivubiro (1998), *Ebintu By'abaganda Eby'ekinnansi N'ennono Zaabyo, Mu Mirembe Gya Chwa N'egya Muwenda Mutebi (Baganda Material Culture Since 1900, An Indigenous Interpretation),* PhD Thesis, Flinders, p. 99.

[6]   Today, one palace at Bulamu, Kasangati in Wakiso district is still frequented for this purpose.

[7]   Tabawebbula, *Ebintu By'abaganda Eby'ekinnansi N'ennono Zaabyo,* p. 99.

[8]   Kodesh, *Beyond the Royal Gaze,* pp. 27–9

[9]   Ibid., p. 39.

circumstances and occasions. As will be demonstrated in the following section, the entry of Islam in Buganda brought nearly universal rituals and practices that all adherents were required to follow, which allowed the Kabaka to utilize it as an opportunity to overcome the control and influence from spirit mediums and other forms of religious allegiances.

Ganda social-cultural structure was organized around *bika* (clans; *kika*, sing.,), *kabaka* (representatives), *lubaale* (divinities), *butaka* (ancestral lands) *masilo* (palace shrines), *biggwa* (shrines), *nnono* (beliefs in hierarchy, eternity, ancestry and customs, burial rites, succession, warfare, marriage).[10] The basic unit of social organization was the institution of *kika* (clan), headed by an *omutaka* (clan head; pl., *bataka*). Writing about nineteenth-century Buganda, Richard Reid has argued that the Kabaka had increasingly become dictatorial and was eroding the traditional powers of the *bataka* (clan heads).[11] This increasing erosion of *bataka* powers had a deeper history. Initially, the *butaka* institution was the social-political base of Ganda society. Ganda oral traditions show that particular families descended from the founders of particular *bika*, who belonged to special locations called *butaka*, derived from the noun *ttaka* (soil/land/earth). *Obutaka* connotes ancestral land where the founders made their homeland.

The *kika* was organized hierarchically. The *luggya* (ancestral courtyard of an *enju* [household]) formed the basic unit; followed by a *lunyiriri* (lineage), *mutuba*, *ssiga* and *kasolya* (council of clan elders). Each family unit was represented to a higher level of the structure by its head. *Obukulu* (seniority) designated the arch representative chosen from a group of other representatives. To cement spiritual ties among clan members residing in various localities, the *butaka* institution also had its *lubaale* and other smaller spirits for which clan members built shrines to request assistance in small matters. *Biggya* (family burial grounds) and *biggwa* (shrines) were considered important spaces for invoking ancestral spirits. Some smaller spirits were contained in *nsiriba* (amulets), which were worn either in the waist or arms, believed to protect the bearer from both spiritual and human mischiefs. Baganda believed that, upon human death, the *muzimu* (spirit) did not die, unlike the body, which disintegrated into earth. '*okwaabya olumbe*' (last funeral rite) was practised a few months after human demise to chase death out of the deceased's house and to mark the end of the mourning period. The *omusika* (heir) was also presented to the rest of the family (clan relatives) to signify the rebirth of the deceased's children to

[10]   Tabawebbula, *Ebintu By'abaganda Eby'ekinnansi N'ennono Zaabyo*, p. 71.
[11]   Reid, Richard J. (2002), *Political Power in Pre-Colonial Buganda: Economy, Society & Warfare in the Nineteenth Century*, Fountain: Kampala, p. 80

her/his heir. Clans used *abakongozzi* (spirit mediums) to invoke ancestral spiritual presence. These Ganda divinities worked through mediums and as a consequence transferred 'real power to human beings, who had the means of harnessing their life forces'.[12] Ganda assimilation practices allowed *basenze* (latecomers) to be controlled by spirit mediums when the former beseeched territorial beings for wellbeing and success in the new territory; the latter asking for material items like goats, barkcloth and ghee, among others.[13] These rituals made spiritual mediums political actors in their own right and therefore competed, to a lesser or greater degree, with kingly political power.

As the basic unit of the *kika*, each household was duty-bound to inculcate social mores in its inhabitants. The hierarchical structure of the *kika* was replicated at the household level. Ganda norms emphasized self-enforced morality in maintaining the social-cultural integrity of the community; if one uttered obscenities in public, they could be imprisoned for weeks.[14] Whereas women could only be married to one man at a time, Ganda marriage customs allowed polygyny for men, as many wives as his 'material and sexual' prowess permitted.[15] Inside the household, particular practices revealed the internal power relations. A husband's seat belonged to him alone. Whoever occupied it without his permission faced reprimand. If a wife sat in it she could be sent back to her in-laws for a definite time until she was ransomed with a goat (*okugatta*). Men had special eating and drinking gourds (*olwendo*). Although household power relations depict men as overly dominant over the women, this is far from reality. Women held much power and influence; they could decide many issues in the homestead ranging from such simple matters as which second wife the husband could bring to complex matters like choosing an *omusika* (heir). Young members of each household had to respect their elders. As a head of the household, the man represented his family in clan meetings at various institutional levels. Family discipline was organized around concepts like *empisa* (connoting rules, regulations, etiquette, behaviour, et cetera, its meaning depending on the context of its use). Relatedly, *ekitiibwa* was used to connote, respect, honour, dignity, loftiness and hierarchy. Socially acceptable morals were described by the words *obuntu bulamu*, meaning good behaviour, politeness, honesty, trust, et cetera. Cordial and generous attitudes directed at one's guests or acquaintances were considered

[12] See Kodesh, 'Networks of Knowledge', pp. 197–216.
[13] Kodesh, *Beyond the Royal Gaze*, p. 78.
[14] Kiyimba, Abasi, *Stereotypes,* p. 103
[15] Ibid, p. 69

invaluable. Within the household, hygiene was considered a priority. Good hospitality, modesty and tidy presentation designated one as *omuntu mulamu*. When a guest arrived in a household, a fowl or goat could be slaughtered to demonstrate the deep reverence the host had for their guests. Food was always covered in baskets (made from dried reeds); *obuyonjo* (basic hygiene) was encouraged in all spheres. *Obweetowaze* (simplicity, humility or modesty) were the currency of family members. Many of these Ganda practices described above gelled with the formal introduction of Islam during Muteesa I's reign, which impacted heavily on the continued relevance of Ganda social-political structure. When the primary sources of Islam – Quran and Hadeeth – entered social discourse, they shifted the focus of social authority from the households, shrines and spirit mediums and directed it towards the Islamic edicts, the masjids and the sheikhs, and Muteesa's palace where *darasa* and *khutba* were conducted in the first built masjid. As Islamic edicts preached good morals, brotherhood, care and love for parents, social discipline, charity and good social mores, this vocabulary fell on familiar territory. As Islamic religious practices replaced the fundamental rituals of Ganda religion, Muteesa realized the need to control and direct the potential aspiration for Muslim autonomy. He was at first successful in this endeavour but later met resistance from various centres. Yet, it should be remembered that his reorganization of Buganda was not the first. Previous kings had managed to overcome obstacles to their political ambitions. A description of political transformations highlights this issue.

Political organization in Buganda sprang from its social-cultural organizations. The founding *ssaza*s (territorial units) in Buganda were three: Mawokota, Busiro and Kyaddondo; *butaka* institutions governed them.[16] Before Kintu's revolution (late 1200s), in which he fought Bemba and restored peace to Buganda, the proto *bataka* had been considered as having a lot of power. The challenge stemmed from the fact that some *bika* wielded more power than others. Initially, '*bika nnansangwa*' (proto clans) were five: Ffumbe, Lugave, Ŋŋonge, Njaza and Nyonyi. The power and influence of their *bataka* varied to an extent that conflicts would emerge. To stave off conflict, the *bataka* conceived of an institution to enable power parity. They imitated the spiritual kabakas (*bakabaka abempewo*) and constructed an institution of the human kabakaship, as a small representative to their council meetings. This Kabaka (small representative) had power to

---

[16] Ssemakula, *The History of Buganda*, chapter 4.

38   ISLAM IN UGANDA

the degree the *bataka* allowed. When Reid argued[17] that the social-political organization of Buganda positioned the Kabaka as the 'absolute' head of society whose word was 'law', he was speaking about the settled practices of the nineteenth century. On the eve of the European encounter, the Kabaka had become overlord over Buganda. Even this did not warrant the title of 'absolute' ruler. Let me illustrate this point.

Since the *bika* were the custodians of Ganda social-cultural practices and also disciplined communities through the various institutions, they exercised immense power and influence over the affairs of Buganda. *Bataka* delegated some power to the Kabaka and were not subordinate to him. Some scholars situate the watershed moment as beginning in the reign of Mutebi (1611–44) who greatly centralized power through particular acts. Mutebi stripped the *bataka* of their privileged hold on the *bika* and by this act shifted social, cultural and religious allegiance from the *bataka* to the Kabaka. The erosion of *bataka* power was so comprehensive that the Kabaka took over the *lubaale* worship in the *amasabo* and the *biggwa*; he became the chief mediator of all spirit mediums in Buganda. The Kabaka acquired many *mbiri* (palaces, from *lubiri*, sing.) scattered around Buganda, which acquired special status.[18] Other scholars situate the erosion of *bataka* power in the reigns of Kabaka Kimera (1314–74) and Muteesa I (1854–84). The period of this transformation is said to have been the late thirteenth and early fourteenth centuries when Buganda witnessed an invasion from Bunyoro. Kimera is believed to have been of Bito (one of the royal houses of the Bunyoro kingdom) origin and he arrived from Bunyoro with seven more clans. Kimera's period witnessed the introduction of particular artifacts and also the transformation of various Ganda institutions. The production of iron works, especially iron hoes and spears, intensified and supported the increase in agriculture, hunting and the defence of territories. The intensification of iron smelting enabled the manufacture of weapons of violence. Consequently, the powers of the existing clans were curbed and their lands were confiscated directly by the Kabaka who also demanded that each clan become linked to him through marriage and the performance of specific ritual or honorary menial services.[19] Kimera introduced social differentiation in Buganda by ordaining special titles for his descendants: *balangira* (princes) and

---

[17]   Reid, *Political Power in Pre-Colonial Buganda*, p. 98.

[18]   Sathyarmurthy T.V. (1986), *The Political Development of Uganda: 1900–1986,* Gower: Aldershot, p. 75.

[19]   Musisi, 'Women, "Elite Polygyny", and Buganda State Formation', pp. 767–70.

bambejja (princesses) whom he distinguished from the bakopi (commoners). Kimera constructed a new rank of chiefs – bakungu (mobilizers, from the verb okukunga) who apparently supported him in his power fights. Kimera instituted rules that forbade bakungu from directly meeting him lest they could plot to overthrow him.[20]

Kimera proceeded to depoliticize the clan by appointing clan members in his bakungu chiefly ranks, thus cutting out the mediatory role of hierarchical clan leaders and immensely weakening clan control over their members. The new recruits left their natal lineages for full-time service in the institutions overseen by the Kabaka, which did not however negate their continued ties to the respective clans. With this restructuring, Kimera was able to construct a new collaborating category of servants that depended on and identified exclusively with the Kabaka's powers. Their functions included collecting and storing tribute, relaying messages, performing ceremonies and carrying out other special tasks that the Kabaka and his chiefs assigned them.[21] The recruits looked to their new appointments as an opportunity to rise beyond their expectations under the clan system, and they relished taking on responsibilities formerly held by the clan heads. The consequence here was that kinship ceased to be the sole basis for social organization as well as the principle locus of economic and territorial-political organization.[22] Such an expanded bureaucracy intensified militarism especially since not all clan heads were willing to surrender their 'historical' entitlements. The outcome was that society came to be differentiated between a new breed of bureaucrats, royals and the commoners and the latter became subordinates to the new social structure.[23] Bika land and the bataka entered political oblivion when the Kabaka created new territorial divisions – such as the ssaza (county) to replace the butaka clan boundaries with ssaza chiefs who administered them. The Kabaka used his bakungu to confiscate clan lands, which became their properties, commoners could access it by entering into patron-client relations based on the promise of cultivation and tribute. With the control over land concentrated in the hands of a ruling minority (the bakungu and the royal family), the clan lost the political influence to 'collect, redistribute, and control communal resources', especially land, and influence over the clan members.[24]

20   Ibid.
21   Ibid., pp. 767–70.
22   Ibid.
23   Ibid.
24   Ibid.

40   ISLAM IN UGANDA

Nakanyike Musisi has argued that the political consequence of a depoliticized clan structure in Buganda was that social relations came to transcend clan differences and coalesce around ethnic, cultural and linguistic commonalities within one polity (Buganda), all in the 'common service of the king, who became Buganda incarnate'.[25] This statement is difficult to accommodate especially when she locates other centres of power that continued to influence political power in Buganda. We should emphasize instead that within the system of Ganda political authority, the Kabaka's political influence was preponderant over other centres of Ganda power under particular contexts and circumstances. A look at some of these can illustrate this point. Other institutions and personalities in Buganda operated to balance and check the power of the Kabaka. Their political influence meant that the centralization of power in Buganda was not total, it was a matter of degree, and depended on the context and circumstances. These institutions and personalities are however to be understood as part and parcel of political power, which *collectively* operated to constitute political authority in Buganda. From the outset, Ganda norms and customs constrained the personal and official actions of a particular Kabaka. Apollo Kaggwa's King Lists cites one Kabaka Kagulu (r. 1674–1704) who was deposed and killed by his subjects for, among other things, his coercive work regime.[26] Ganda traditions mention two cases of short-lived female rule: one Queen Nnakku was appointed a caretaker ruler when her husband Kabaka Chwa Nabakka (who reigned in the fourteenth century) disappeared. Another Queen, Nnannono, was appointed in a caretaker leadership role when her husband Kabaka Nnakibinge (r. 1494–1524) was killed in war.[27] Queen Nnannono allegedly waited for the birth of the child she carried hoping it would be a boy to succeed the throne; she delivered a baby girl instead.[28]

The personality of the queen mother and the institution she represented also provided a strong check to balance the power of a particular Kabaka.[29]

---

[25]   Musisi (1991), 'Women, "Elite Polygyny"', p. 771.

[26]   Kaggwa, Apollo (1971), *The Kings of Buganda,* translated and edited by Kiwanuka, M.S.M, East African Publishing House: Kampala, pp. 62–6.

[27]   Kiyimba, Abasi (2001), '*Gender Stereotypes in the Folktales and Proverbs of the Baganda',* PhD Thesis, Dar es Salaam, p. 103.

[28]   See also Reid, Richard (1997), 'The Reign of Kabaka Nakibinge: Myth or Watershed?' *History in Africa,* Vol. 24, pp. 287–98, pp. 289–92.

[29]   Schoenbrun, David Lee (1998), *A Green Place, A Good Place: Agrarian Change, Gender, and Social Identity in the Great Lakes Region to the 15th Century,* Kampala: Fountain, pp. 192–3; Schoenbrun, (1996), 'Gendered

Queen mothers worked as rulers by 'supporting, advising, defending, protecting, punishing and nurturing' Kabakas, in ways that performed duties that 'mothers did for their sons'.[30] Like the Kabaka, the queen mother had her own palace, situated on a different hill separated by a stream of running water, signifying both the dividing and uniting qualities of water, which meant that the queen mother had a separate institution from the Kabaka but at the same time made contact with his court when need arose. She did not leave her court to visit the Kabaka but he instead made visits to her and could send a messenger to inform her if he were unable to attend their meetings.[31] The queen mother possessed various estates spread out in different locations of Buganda, which gave her material independence from the Kabaka's court. Her retinue of servants were for her palaces and not for the Kabaka. She received tribute and made distributions to servants; her lands were free from Kabaka's taxation and neither could his officers plunder them. Her authority mirrored that of the Kabaka: she appointed officials, allocated them land on her estates and these collected and sent her tributes. Her officials did not have to obey the Kabaka; it was like a separate government.[32] Kaggwa has stated that a woman became a queen mother when her son became a Kabaka. More importantly in the process of enthroning a new Kabaka, a mother would build up a coalition of benefactors to support her son as the next Kabaka vis-à-vis the sons of a different wife. Such a woman would mobilize either within her clan or outside it by appealing to influential chiefs and other allies that would provide a broad base. Queen mothers would protect their vulnerable sons – such as when Muganzirwazza protected the would-be Kabaka Muteesa I by starving some sons of Kabaka Ssuuna to death – and by appealing to the resources and her coalitions who would in turn receive material benefits from the Kabaka.[33] Queen mothers were not only kingmakers but could also withdraw their support from a particular Kabaka in a balancing act. Kaggwa cites the example of Kabaka Jjunju (1734–64) who lost his reign by performing acts that displeased his queen mother Nanteza, who then supported a rebellion that brought his second son, Ssemakookiro, to power.[34] This balancing act ensured that a queen mother could deploy

---

Histories between the Great Lakes: Varieties and Limits', *International Journal of African Historical Studies,* Vol. 29, No. 3 (1996), pp. 461–92.

[30] Hanson 'Queen Mothers and Good Government in Buganda', p. 220.

[31] Ibid., p. 221.

[32] Ibid., pp. 221–2.

[33] Kaggwa, *The Kings of Buganda,* pp. 118–9.

[34] Ibid., p. 92.

42 ISLAM IN UGANDA

violence to check her son's behaviour in the name of preventing greater violence. Ham Mukasa emphasized that without a queen mother a Kabaka would not have a person to check his evil behaviours.[35]

Besides the queen mother, other female personalities also possessed political influence in Buganda. In what she termed 'elite polygyny', Nakanyike Musisi has described a situation whereby *abakyala* (elite women) such as *bakembuga* (Kabaka's wives) and princesses were in control of important chiefs in Buganda. The position and title of a Kabaka's wife would determine her influence among the chiefs. The Kaddulubaale (first wife) for instance had five chiefs under her control, including the Kangawo, the county chief of Bulemeezi; the Kabejja (second wife) had eleven chiefs under her, including two county chiefs, the Mukwenda of Singo and the sekiboobo of Kyaggwe and the chief tax collector. Put together, the forty-two titled wives of the Kabaka were in control of about eighty-six chiefs.[36] Nakanyike Musisi credits the reasons for the influence of elite polygyny in Buganda on the 'continued use of kinship and marriage alliances as a means of political and economic control'. Other reasons included their capacity to transcend the gendered division of labour and perform work usually specified for men, providing the Kabaka with a clan, and constituting the major force of a succession battle.[37] Kaggwa has shown however that these women were allowed to collect taxes from specified chiefs and also plunder those who fell from grace.[38]

Other elite women like the *bambejja* (princesses) possessed political influence. Bambejja also possessed their own estates and a retinue of chiefs and other servants and could in particular ways be independent of the Kabaka. They were addressed as 'Ssebo' (sir) (this designation continues to date)[39], allowed to use language otherwise considered obscene (*okuwemula*), they could enter into relations with men of their choice except begetting children, were allowed to roam Buganda without restrictions,

---

35 Mukasa, Ham (1934), 'Some notes on the reign of Muteesa', *Uganda Journal,* Vol. I, no. 2, p. 128.

36 Musisi, 'Women, "Elite Polygyny"', p. 780.

37 Ibid. Historically the Kabaka does not come from any of the clans in Buganda. Yet, the fact that he could mobilize his many wives to perform various duties allowed for a semblance of organized structure akin to the clan to emerge, serving his interests.

38 Kaggwa, *The Kings of Buganda,* p. 135.

39 I encountered a Mumbejja (Ganda princess) during the course of my fieldwork and was ashamed when I called her 'Nnyabo' (Madam) until my 'fixer' apologized for my ignorance.

and could be bowed down to during greetings. These privileges allowed them independence from the Kabaka. At the coronation of a new monarch, one queen sister acted as *lubuga* (spirit medium), which symbolized that his sister also shared in the obligation entrusted to the Kabaka. Princesses could also support the Kabaka in different ways. When a Kabaka realized the healing power of a particular spirit medium that had political influence over people, he could court it as an alternative form of authority so as to improve his legitimacy through the support of such strong priests and spirit mediums. Since some spirit mediums and healers presided over a network of shrines and activities that could translate into violence (such as dethroning a recalcitrant healer), they proved that Kabakas and royal members could not claim 'complete command' of such activities.[40] Fear of such power led a Kabaka to send particular princesses to live in the vicinity of a particular shrine and spy on its activities: this was connected to the Ganda tradition of imbuing women with public healing complexes such as offering youthful women to important spirits as 'wives'. When Kabakas dedicated princesses – already restricted by their inability to marry or reproduce socially recognized offspring – to the service of a particular shrine, they 'sought to direct the collective energies and authority associated with shrine complexes towards the royal center'.[41]

The above discussion of political power in Buganda demonstrates that political authority sprang from multiple spaces in which the Kabaka had come to play a dominant role. These multiple layers of power, authority and influence within Buganda's structure provided a challenge to Muteesa I because he could not easily overcome the kind of checks and balances they contained without becoming totalitarian. Although previous Kabakas had tried to undertake significant centralization by usurping some of the power held outside the royal court, the entry of Islam presented Muteesa with a unique opportunity. As the Ganda religious system contained multiple spirit mediums and shrines that prevented leaders from transgressing on various spaces and territories, Islam provided an expansive ideology to transcend limitations presented by the Ganda religious system. As will be seen below, Islam would allow Muteesa to claim a divine right to authority, which came from the One God, as opposed to the many gods in the Ganda structure, which could justify whatever totalitarian practices he could undertake. Islam also provided benefits in form of commodities of trade and trading partners from Zanzibar who dominated the caravan

[40] Kodesh, *Beyond the Royal Gaze*, pp. 19, 155.
[41] Ibid., p. 157.

trade from the East African coastal cities. Some of the commodities in the caravan trade included arms and ammunitions, which could be used to build advanced armies to defend Buganda against internal and external enemies. Islam also provided a status. By claiming affinity with Islam, Muteesa positioned Buganda as an Islamic state and therefore prevented any hostile takeover from the Khedive Ismail of Egypt who wanted to control the area surrounding the source of the Nile river. As will be seen in the following section, the benefits that Islam offered for both internal organization and external relations far outweighed the benefits of the Ganda religious system in Muteesa's eyes. This is why Muteesa's Islamization project marked one of the greatest centralizations of power in Buganda's history. The entry of Islam in Buganda, the consolidation of the benefits from the caravan trade and the Islamization of Buganda, put Muteesa at a higher status of political statecraft within and outside the region. Although Kabaka Ssuuna II was the first Kabaka to learn about Islam, he ignored it for various reasons. His successor, Muteesa, however realized Islam's value as an ideology that would enable him to transform his power within and outside Buganda. Let us first see how Muteesa deployed Islam to reorganize Buganda.

Muteesa's attempt to Islamize Buganda

The attempt to Islamize Buganda begins with Mukaabya Walugembe Muteesa, Ssuuna's successor, and it marks the discursive formations of the Muslim question in contemporary Uganda. Describing the attempts of Kabaka Muteesa I to Islamize Buganda, this section argues that Muteesa looked to Islam as an ideology to centralize his power because of the benefits it would bring, both internally and externally. Internally, Muteesa would use Islam as the new religion to surpass the Ganda religious system of shrines, public healers and their political influence over society. Islam would also enable him to greatly centralize his power and influence over the remnants of *bataka* power and the other centres of Ganda power and influence. These multiple centres of Ganda power, authority and influence were an obstacle to Muteesa's greater centralization. Islam presented a unique opportunity because the principle of the One God, Allah, transcended any claims to spirit mediumship and the attendant allegiances such claims engendered. Externally, Islam would cement Muteesa's relationship with other Muslim powers such as Egypt and Zanzibar that had different interests in Buganda. It would cement his trade links and control over the caravan trade with Zanzibar and at the same time position Buganda as a Muslim polity and secure it against any potential Egyptian takeover. The caravan trade provided opportunities for advanced military arms and the conscription of a standing army that would enable Muteesa to internally reorganize the Ganda polity. This centralization would enable him consolidate his grip onto power, reorganize society and act as a bulwark against the looming foreign colonial designs. Islam would, in other words, make Buganda join the league of established Islamic states like Zanzibar and Egypt.

With Islam working as an ideology for Muteesa to centralize his power, one would think that this put Muteesa in a dilemma whereby Islam put a single powerful God in control of the Kabaka. As shall be seen later with the coming of Christianity, Islam was functional to political ends, just as was Muteesa's later claim to convert to Christianity. Islam in Buganda did not operate in a vacuum, it worked alongside other political realities. The role of Islam in Buganda is similar to that it played in the Sultanate of Dar Fur, one of the Sudanic states, during the seventeenth and eighteenth centuries. As Mahmood Mamdani has lucidly shown, three institutions supported the centralization of royal power in the Sultanate of Dar Fur. The first was the development of an estate system in which the king granted individual estates, which eroded the clan control over land. The second institution was the slave system from which the royal army was recruited to provide the king with independence from and supremacy over chiefs. The third was the institutionalization of Islam as a court ideology.[42] The first and third institutions were also similar to what Muteesa did for Buganda. As in the Sultanate of Dar Fur, the political realities in Buganda were such that the king had begun to approve private land estates to individuals, and that Islam would serve him as a court ideology for particular purposes. Islam in Buganda would justify and legitimate royal power against the claims of clan-based chiefs. It would enable a new breed of Muslim elites around the king to counter old chieftains. The ideology would support the founding of a new Islamic community to provide a solid basis for society to counter kin-based/clan-based modes of social solidarity. Islam would also provide an opportunity for economic expansion by attracting long-distance trade and co-opting traders and Islamic teachers from other Muslim territories.[43] As in the Sultanate of Dar Fur, Islam would situate Buganda within a wider Muslim world in which Muteesa would feel secure against the possibility of invasion from a Muslim state like Egypt.

[42] Mamdani, *Saviors and Survivors*, pp. 133–4.
[43] Ibid.

Scholarship[44] has shown that formal Islam entered Buganda in 1851, brought by Arab[45] traders from Zanzibar. These came to Kabaka Ssuuna's palace and began to teach him Islam to the extent that he had learned about four chapters of the Quran before his death. Historians[46] have noted that Ssuuna was less interested in Islam as an ideology but more in the other benefits brought by Arab traders especially the trade in guns and ammunition. This trade further gave Ssuuna advanced weapons that equipped Buganda's army, further eroding *bataka* power and authority.[47] Upon Ssuuna's demise in 1856, Muteesa replaced him. The new Kabaka soon realized the potential of Islam beyond its material benefits. As the Kabaka, Muteesa was the first layer of power, authority and influence in Buganda and so articulations of Islam begun in Muteesa's court before they reached the masses.[48] When the Arabs taught Muteesa, he, in turn, would pass on the information to his chiefs and subjects. The Arab teachers at Muteesa's palace taught the Shaafi[49] school of Sunni Islam[50] especially about the existence of the One God, Allah, who created the first generations of human beings from Adam and Eve.[51] The Arabs informed Muteesa that they used to teach his father Ssuuna about Allah the King of kings who

---

[44] Ssekimwanyi, *Ebyafaayo Ebitonotono ku Ddiini Y'ekiyisiraamu Okuyingira mu Buganda*; Kkulumba, 'Ebyafaayo by Obuyisiraamu mu Uganda'; Gomotoka, J.M.T. (1940), 'Makula, kye Kitabo kye Bika Ekilangira Ky'oloyo lwe Buganda', microfim at Makerere University, Kampala; Miti, *Ebyafaayo*.

[45] Although 'Arab' designates a member of the Semitic race of the Arabian Peninsula, it has become a fluid category, beyond its linguistic and ethnic meanings. I use it here as a 'political' statement that speaks more to the 'assertion' than as 'imposition' of power. See Mamdani, S*aviors and Survivors*, chapter 3, 'Writing Race into History', p. 118.

[46] Katungulu, *Islam in Buganda*, p. 1; Musoke, *Ebifa Mu Buganda*; Kakungulu & Kasozi, *Abasimba Obuyisiraamu Mu Uganda*; Miti, J.K. (nd), *Ebyafaayo bya Buganda;* Mukasa, *Simuda Nyuma.*

[47] Ssemakula, *The History of Buganda.*

[48] Kasozi, A.B.K. (1976), *The Process of Islamisation in Uganda 1854–1921.*

[49] Islamic *fiqh* (jurisprudence) is named after the teachers' founding schools. The first four Imams are Shaafi, Hanbali, Malik and Hanafi.

[50] Gee, T.W., 'A Century of Muhammadan Influence in Buganda 1852–1951', *The Uganda Journal*, Vol. 22, No. 2, p. 140. The Shaafi school of Sunni Islam represents one of the four great Sunni Imams. The Shaafi school is named after Abu Abdillah Muhammad ibn Idris al-Shaafi (c. 767–820 CE), the first contributor to the principles of Islamic jurisprudence.

[51] Katungulu, *Islam in Buganda,* p. 1; Kakungulu & Kasozi, *Abasimba Obuyisiraamu Mu Uganda.*

would cause people to die and then resurrect them from their graves.[52] Muteesa found this astonishing and wondered about the reality of death and resurrection from the grave. His teachers reminded him that Allah's power encompassed everything among the known and the unknown.[53]

Muteesa's discourse with the Arabs about the Quranic views on the story of creation, the journey of the human soul after death and, the day of resurrection challenged his prevailing perceptions of God, humanity and extinction, as explained under the Ganda religious traditions. As a Muganda, Muteesa knew the existence of Katonda (Creator), but he believed other spirits interceded on Katonda's behalf. Muteesa knew that human beings died and were buried in graves. He did not understand this religious monotheism that Arabs had inserted in the sea of Ganda religious polytheism. Undeterred, he continued to listen to more teachings about Islam and in the process befriended many Arabs, who began to participate in his politics as chiefs, clerks and scribes.[54] Gradually, Muteesa commanded his chiefs to read and practise Islam. The masses in Buganda also obeyed what the chiefs did. The *kiragiro* (order, command) to 'read' Islam ushered in one of the most fundamental social revolutions that any Kabaka had ever had to undertake.[55] As was seen in the previous section, Baganda possess an expansive religious system spread out in their homesteads, communities and in the royal household. When Muteesa ordered the chiefs and masses to read and practise Islam, the masses were suddenly required to abandon or suspend their existing religious systems, or integrate them into the Islamic tradition. Muteesa's order shifted people's affinity with their spirits, mediums, shrines and other cultural institutions and directed it towards Islamic beliefs, rituals and practices. This social transformation was so pervasive that it enforced a new form of social discipline.

Early Ganda writers, many of whom were palace pages in the later years of Muteesa's reign, including Ham Mukasa, Apollo Kaggwa, Zimbe, Gomotoka and Miti,[56] initially embraced Islam but would later convert to

---

[52] Kakungulu & Kasozi, *Abasimba Obuyisiraamu mu Uganda,* p. 5.

[53] Ibid.

[54] Ibid., p. 6. noting thus: 'For example one Arab, Bukeri, supported Muteesa in writing his letters. Masoud Reslmin bin Suleiman was one of Muteesa's scribes, who wrote many letters on the Kabaka's behalf. Bo Ibrahim, Johar, Idi and Ramadhan, were Muteesa's comedians. There were also other Arabs who served Muteesa in various capacities.

[55] Gray, John Milner (1934), 'Mutesa of Buganda', *Uganda Journal,* Vol. I, No. 1, pp. 22–49, p. 22.

[56] Gomotoka, *Makula*; Miti, *Ebyafaayo bya Buganda*; Mukasa, *Simuda*

48 ISLAM IN UGANDA

Christianity. They have recorded Muteesa's Islamization of Buganda. As Kabaka's chiefs were obliged to stay close to the palace due to the fear that they could stir rebellion in the countryside, they were the first target of Muteesa's Islamization campaign. He commanded them to study the Quran and to listen to the Islamic teachings from the Arabs. He summoned them to the palace at Banda and told them about Islamic teachings on religious monotheism, saying that Allah was one, the Powerful, 'Hakibalu' (Akbar), and that the spirits were not His equal. Following this persuasion, Muteesa commanded the chiefs to study the Islamic religion, thus inducing them to do so both in anxiety about its promise and in fear of inciting his fury – as later events were to reveal.

A new group of Muslim elites emerged to enforce Muteesa's orders. Influential chiefs in the palace including Katikkiro Mukasa, Ssaabakaaki Musisi, Ssaabawaali Basudde, Omuwanika Kyankonyi, Mukasa Kauta, Mutebi Omutabuuza, Ssembuzi Wakibi, among others, took to Muteesa's command with a determination that culminated in the spread of Islam through Buganda. Once the Kabaka's command was relayed, it spread through the various social spaces including farms, bars, markets, village courts, county meetings and funeral ceremonies. The reading of the Quran was quite exacting to some of his officials. One Mmandwambi, from Kyaggwe, failed to learn the lines that begin the opening chapter of the Quran: '*Bismillahi Rahman Rahim, Alhamdu Lillahi Rabbil-alamin*'.[57] Since Muteesa would summon his officials to recite in his presence what they had learned, the official instead renamed his wives after these Quranic verses and once summoned to Muteesa's palace to recite, he would quickly call out to his wives to remind him by their new names. One wife he had named 'Simidaayi', to the second, 'Lwakimaani', to the third 'Lwakiimi', the fourth, 'Kamudulira' and the last 'Labbiraami'.[58] Learning Arabic was as easy for Muteesa as it was difficult to many of his officials. He came to realize this and encouraged them to do their best. To his subjects, Muteesa made Quranic learning a personal choice except for other aspects that he felt were the distinguishing symbols of Islam.

To substitute the Ganda rituals of *kusamirla* (sanctifying and seeking assistance from supernatural spirits), Muteesa ordered the saying of the five daily Salat (prayers) in Buganda. Here, people were redirected from the shrine to the masjid as the new site of worship. Prayer could not be

---

Nyuma; Zimbe, *Buganda ne Kabaka*; Kaggwa, *The Kings of Buganda*.

[57] These are the transliterations of the opening verses of the first chapter of the Quran, called Al-Fatiha.

[58] Kakungulu & Kasozi, *Abasimba Obuyisiraamu Mu Uganda*.

performed without a ritual bath, however. Like the Ganda rituals of washing the body with special herbs to cleanse oneself before or after entering a shrine, Islam also requires its adherents to cleanse themselves and perform ablution before prayer. This regime of sanitation and hygiene was substituted and transformed. Muteesa made it mandatory for every home in Buganda to have a washing stone to clean the feet when proceeding to Salat as one performed ablution. Although many people embraced Islam and willingly implemented Muteesa's orders, many other homesteads did not and mounted these stones as a public display of Islam yet in fact they hated it. Those homesteads without washing stones were designated homes of '*abakaafiri*' (unbelievers in Islam). In trying to advance a new social convention, a derogatory term was created to stigmatize whoever refused to follow the new practices.

Since Salat had been made mandatory, Muteesa chose to lead by example. He constructed the first masjid in his new palace at Nnabulagala near Kasubi, as both a space of worship and education. Throngs of new pages came to learn about Islam, and Muteesa led the Salat. He began to congregate the Jumuah (Friday Salat) and his subjects would promptly follow him, since they were expected to obey his commands and avoid earning his displeasure. Muteesa founded a new department, Kizikiti, which was concerned with Muslim affairs, headed by Edward Mukasa (he later left Islam). The youthful Apollo Kaggwa and Yona Wasswa were some of the first caretakers of the Masjid. Muteesa had received a flag with a crescent and star from the Arabs as a symbol of his Muslim identity, which was hoisted daily in front of the Masjid. The flag and its emblems became the new symbols of the emerging Muslim state that Muteesa was building. One of Muteesa's servants named Choli hoisted this flag at the various palaces Muteesa built at Nakawa, Munyonyo-Salaama (peaceful abode), Nabulagala-Kasubi, Kinaawa-Kabojja and others.[59] What we see here is that a new ritual practice of prayer is replacing an old one, and for many people, the Ganda ways were not abandoned at all, but rather displaced and driven to the private domain; thus many people begun to construct fences around their shrines hidden behind their homesteads from public view. Something else is going on however. The construction of a *masjid* and corresponding departments is institutionalizing Islamic traditions in Buganda in a way that goes beyond the personal nature of Ganda shrines that were safeguarded by mediums and other custodians. With Islam, Muteesa is constructing a new way of life based on fundamental principles

[59] Zimbe, *Buganda ne Kabaka*, p. 18.

50 ISLAM IN UGANDA

that undergirded common but also diverse practices, although this diversity was not initially appreciated and when it was, it became the source of violence, as the next section reveals.

Muteesa ordered the observance of the Islamic calendar, which was identified with fasting during the holy month of Ramadan. He made his initial fasting in 1867, but failed to fast the following Ramadan due to his military campaigns, although he made up for the fast upon his return. To ensure the observance of fasting Ramadan, Muteesa appointed a Ramadan force to investigate the recalcitrant subjects. One of the members of the fasting police was a man called Kakolobooto who went about searching for Ramadan offenders but was himself once caught eating in Ramadan: he was tied up and taken to his superiors. Muteesa spread the Islamic greeting, Assalaam Alaykum (peace be upon you) and its response, in Buganda and taught his chiefs how to pronounce it. Failing to pronounce the correct version, many conjured up 'Salamaleko, Yee Salamaleko dekimu Salaam'.[60] Muteesa also changed the custom on inheritance to the effect that a non-Muslim would not inherit their father's estate. As the previous section mentioned, Ganda inheritance customs (*obusika*) allowed a male to inherit his father's estate. The heir was also identified as continuing the lineage of the deceased. When Muteesa ordered that non-Muslims could not inherit from Muslims, he met opposition from traditionalists.[61]

Muteesa transformed Ganda burial customs. The Islamic belief in resurrection after death forced his rethink of the burial method of the Kabakas. Historically, Ssekabakas (deceased Kabakas) were buried after dismembering: the head was separated from the body and the jaws from the skull. These parts formed the contents of a new shrine, where okusaba (requesting) took place. Muteesa considered this burial method crude for a body that would be resurrected. He therefore ordered all subsequent burials to be done in the Islamic way, which involved wrapping the deceased in pieces of *mbugo* (fabric made from *mutuba*/fig tree) and burying them whole without dismembering body parts. He also commanded that all the jawbones of the dead Kabakas should be exhumed and reburied with their bodies; he willed that upon his death, he should be buried in the Islamic way to enable a quick resurrection of the body. Muteesa transformed animal slaughter to ensure that all animals in Buganda were slaughtered according to Islamic etiquette so as to be halaal (permissible) to eat. Before

---

[60] Katungulu, *Islam in Buganda*.
[61] This was a large group led by chiefs who felt Muteesa's Islamization commands were eroding Ganda customs. They kept their misgivings silent to avoid earning Muteesa's displeasure. See Zimbe, *Buganda ne Kabaka*, p. 56.

the coming of Islam, animals met a very brutal death, which Muteesa felt was repulsive to the human eye; some animals would be beaten on the head till dead. He selected one of the Arabs, Choli, to oversee his abattoir and other chiefs ensured that his palace consumed halaal meat.[62] Around 1875, during the Ramadhan fast, Muteesa declared Islam the official religion of Buganda. He strictly enforced conversion to Islam, Salat, *saum* (fasting) and halaal slaughter; whoever refused to practise the injunctions had disobeyed the Kabaka. Everyone was required to submit to Muteesa's version of Islam, and many who resisted the Kabaka's Islamization policy were executed in various places, the biggest number occurring at Nkumba, where *lubaale* worshippers were killed by burning, spearing and drowning, for refusing to read Islam, which they said was difficult to learn.[63] After these executions, the fear of death gripped Ganda subjects, who converted (or pretended to convert) to Islam en masse.

In instituting Islamic beliefs and ritual practices, Muteesa saw in Islam the potential to unify religious systems in Buganda as he sought to substitute Ganda religious practices with Islamic ones. Unlike the Ganda religious systems, which differed in various aspects depending on which shrine or spirit medium one attended, the fundamental principles of Islam such as belief, prayer, fasting, pilgrimage to Mecca, cuisine and burial rites, among others, seemed uniform and could therefore become the basis of enforcing discipline in a hitherto differentiated and diverse Ganda religious system. Islam was only later discovered to have internal differentiation as well, so that Muslims came to differ. Muteesa was ignorant of this in the beginning. As the patron of Islam and Muslims, Muteesa was able to command and demand allegiance from a mass of Muslim adherents in Buganda. Although he could previously command the same allegiance as Kabaka, claiming affinity with Islam provided an edge of discipline that out-competed the allegiance some Baganda owed to the other centres of power, authority and influence. By instilling an Islamic ethos common to all Ganda subjects, Muteesa was able to direct and bend the masses to do his will. As the Islamic practices followed Islamic time based on the movement of the lunar year, Muteesa sought to link the personal rituals and practices of his Ganda subject with those of the community and sync them with those of other Islamic states in the region and beyond. In the hope of joining a pan-Islamic league, Muteesa had to ensure that the whole of Buganda believed and practised Islam.

[62] Kakungulu & Kasozi, *Abasimba Obuyisiraamu Mu Uganda*, p. 9.
[63] Zimbe, *Buganda ne Kabaka*, p. 18.

52 ISLAM IN UGANDA

Having instituted Islamic rituals and practices and declared Buganda an Islamic state, Muteesa looked to the region outside Buganda. He sent envoys to Bunyoro to invite Omukama Kabarega to accept Islam. There is debate as to whether Muteesa sent this Islamic invitation to Kabarega out of altruistic feelings or out of desire to befriend Kabarega for political ends. The latter view was based on the fact that Muteesa had heard about the presence of a powerful 'Kabaka' in Misr (Egypt) who had intentions to expand his kingdom down to Buganda. This view has bolstered the argument that Muteesa intended to invite Kabarega to Islam, as the latter's acceptance would fortify deterrence against any possible threat.[64] Kabarega was already influenced by Egyptian Sudan[65] but regardless of the outcome of the delegation to Kabarega, Muteesa pressed on. He sent Ssaabaddu Omujaasi and Muwanga Ssaabakaaki, with gifts, including, a Salat mat, water vessel, a flag with Islamic emblems and sandals, with the following message:

> I have sent you two teachers … conveying the message of the One God, the Most Powerful over all the spirits, Owner of heaven and earth. It would serve you better to accept this message because there shall come a day of judgment when the dead will be resurrected to account for their souls in God's presence. The evildoers shall be sent to hellfire. Therefore, my friend, it would pain me if you were to dwell in hellfire.[66]

When Kabarega received the delegation and the message it carried, he declined to receive the gifts and told the envoys to return to Muteesa and remind him that he (Kabarega) had his *lubaale* (spirits) who protected him and that the message of monotheism was not logical; that the resurrection he spoke of could bring many adversities, if it did occur; that the hellfire he spoke about would only burn his bones and not his body. Besides, the moment of resurrection would present serious problems for all the living, especially the Kabakas, were it to occur. Kabarega took the 'resurrection' message literally: he wondered about Muteesa's excitement with resurrection since it would rekindle historical political rivalries were it to occur.[67]

---

[64] Gray, *Muteesa of Uganda.*

[65] See Ngendo-Tshimba, D. (2020), *Transgressing Buyira: An Historical Inquiry into Violence Astride a Congo-Uganda border,* PhD Thesis: Makerere University, chapter 3.

[66] Mukasa, *Simuda Nyuma*, p. 22.

[67] Ibid. Kabarega asked: 'why is the Kabaka [Muteesa] happy that people shall be resurrected while alive? Let us ask, if his father [Ssuuna] were to be resurrected, would he accept his son [Muteesa] to remain on the throne? Would

Muteesa was disappointed when the envoys returned with the gifts. He knew that Kabarega had rejected Islam and he told his chiefs that he felt 'sorry' for his 'brother' because he had failed to save him from 'hellfire'.

From the foregoing, it can be seen that foreign Islam entered Buganda through Muteesa's palace from where it spread to the rest of Buganda. The Kabaka's authority over the masses enabled Islam to spread en masse especially since recalcitrance would invite his wrath. Muteesa's Islamization attempt transformed Ganda traditions in important ways. By instituting Islamic monotheism as the official religion of state, Muteesa relegated Ganda polytheistic belief systems to the private realm. Ganda society was required to become Muslim by the command of the Kabaka. His articulation of Islam was supposed to be the standard for the masses to follow. The speed with which Muteesa's commands were carried highlights the respect and honour the Ganda had over the Kabaka. When he decided an issue, all Buganda was supposed to follow. The Baganda translated the word Allah as Katonda (Creator). And as we have seen above, Ganda practices such as polygamy and social discipline also endeared some Baganda to Islam. They did not however consider Islam and Ganda traditions as mutually exclusive because many considered Islamization a formality such that they would continue to worship Allah alongside requesting intercession from Ganda spirits. Religious pluralism was therefore preserved in this way. Muteesa's violent crackdown on *lubaale* worship (Nkumba incident) coupled with his new inheritance rules, intensified people's resistance to Islam as he continued to assert himself through violence.

It is difficult to argue that Muteesa's Islamization of Buganda so comprehensively transformed society that there remained no pocket of practice in Ganda religious systems. And we cannot explain the violence meted out to traditionalists by saying that Ganda religious system was the soft underbelly to Muteesa's Islamization of Buganda. Nor can we argue that Islamization was so radical that resisting it was always met with violence. We have to think of the context in which this kind of violence first arose. This violence against traditionalists arose from the context in which Muteesa intended to enforce his will on the masses, who were required to

---

not Ssuuna execute Muteesa? And does not he know that if the previous Kabakas were to be resurrected he would become a commoner? What about those princes he murdered, would not they remove him from the throne were they to be resurrected...? I am deeply concerned about my brother for jubilating about what could be disastrous for him. For myself, I cannot become Muslim for I would hate being a commoner were my father Kamurasi to be resurrected.'

54   ISLAM IN UGANDA

either become Muslim or at least pretend to do so. Even Muteesa publicly identified with Islam but was on various occasions keen to summon the spirit of Mukasa to cure one of his illnesses, which failed until European medicine was brought to improve his health.[68] What can be seen is that Islam ended up playing a functional role to Muteesa's social reorganization to support a new type of state project that on the one hand removed all sorts of resistance to the Kabaka while at the same time positioning Buganda as an Islamic state for particular benefits. In the following section, I posit that the violence against Muslims emanated from the fact that multiple paths became available for individuals to take. When Christianity entered Buganda, it expanded the religious field that contained Muslims, traditionalists, Christians and others. Religious competition for the Kabaka's favours brought hostility among the different religious denominations. Violence erupted from Muteesa's unwillingness to overcome traditionalism and embrace the ideals he imposed on the masses.

Muteesa executes his Muslim pages

The execution of Muslim pages, totalling about seventy, was just another murder episode since Muteesa's Islamization policy had witnessed the death of many people who refused to either convert or fulfil Islamic practices. Ham Mukasa and Musoke Zimbe reveal that what disturbed many was how Muteesa, claiming to be the leader of the Muslims in Buganda, could kill his own brethren many of whom lived in his palace, prayed in his Masjid, ate the meat he slaughtered and read Islam with him. This section engages with the debate about the context surrounding Muteesa's execution of his pages. It reveals an internal debate regarding a second Islamic renewal (after Muteesa's) in Buganda, which introduced another interpretation of Islam to challenge the Shaafi-leaning Zanzibar teachers. The new Islamic revival from Egyptian Sudan (Turkiya) instructed the palace pages in the Maliki interpretation of Islam. The new Islamic principles they taught the pages informed a new Islamic practice that challenged the role of the Kabaka as the leader of the Muslim community. The pages' desires to break away from Muteesa and establish their own space outside the Lubiri was interpreted as *okuzza oggwannaggomola* (treason). These intra-Muslim debates were however intensified by two other forces: the influential 'traditionalists' who detested the increasing 'erosion' of their customs, and the Christian missionaries. The latter's

---

[68]   Zimbe, *Buganda ne Kabaka*, p. 37.

'civilizing' propaganda contributed to the religious violence that would engulf Buganda. The murder of the palace pages symbolizes the challenges of Muteesa's Islamization policy to permeate society. The limits of the attempt to Islamize Buganda can, however, be found in the entry of Christianity in Buganda. I think the events that unfolded thereafter showed how foreign religions (first Islam and later Christianity) were functional to Muteesa's state designs. Before he could decide to execute his Muslim pages, there was an event that disturbed his mind about the role of religious power in social-political advancement. The entry of Christianity played a critical role in this.

According to Zimbe, Muteesa had learned about Christianity from J. Grant and J.H. Speke who visited in 1862, and from H.M. Stanley who visited Muteesa in the early 1870s while the Kabaka was undertaking an expedition at Nnakalanga in Buvuma. Stanley used his daily meetings with Muteesa to teach him about Christianity. He informed the Kabaka that Christians believed in God but also considered Jesus his son. He also told the Kabaka about the Bible and its capacity to teach human beings about the nature of God. Stanley also mentioned that Jesus had died on the cross, was resurrected and would also return to resurrect all the dead. He mentioned to the Kabaka that all human beings were children of God and it was not befitting for human beings to deal in slavery and slave trade. Zimbe mentions that Muteesa had observed Stanley's friendly character and he did not arrive in Buganda with any slaves at all. These words, as framed by Stanley, impressed Muteesa because, unlike Jesus who died and resurrected, the Prophet of Islam (PBUH) died and was buried and would neither be resurrected nor resurrect other people himself, but this would be done by Allah. Zimbe mentions that these words made an impression on Muteesa because he thought Christianity was better than Islam.[69] The Battle of Nnakalanga took three months during which Stanley had an opportunity to showcase some of the British military stratagems and tactics that helped Muteesa to defeat the Bavuma. Zimbe describes that on two separate occasions, Muteesa's army was near the jaws of defeat until Stanley advised Muteesa on how to prepare and organize the soldiers and weaponry. These tactics worked and helped the Kabaka who was very impressed by the power and organizational capacity of the Europeans. Stanley did not tell Muteesa about the old battle between Islam, represented by the Muslim Arabs from Zanzibar, and Christianity, represented by Stanley and his cohorts. It seems Zimbe neglected to mention the fact

[69] Ibid., pp. 23–6.

that Europeans took every opportunity to advance their interests because we can see Stanley was using Christianity to ridicule Arab participation in slavery and the slave trade but keeping silent on European complicity in the same matter.

Muteesa convened a public meeting upon return from Nnakalanga and summoned the leaders of the Arab Muslims to rebut Stanley's statements. Muteesa had been confused because both the Muslims and Christians claimed to believe in the One God but differed on the personality of Jesus Christ. He therefore wanted the Muslim Arabs to clarify their position about Jesus. When both parties explained their positions, Muteesa noted that both religions were similar. Stanley continued to insist that the Prophet of Islam was just a human being who had also died. The Arabs responded that even Christians believed in Jesus, a human being, who was also circumcised like the Arabs did, but that the Christians attributed divinity to Jesus whom they considered God's offspring, something the Muslims considered anathema to the nature of God. When Stanley stuck to his narrative, Muteesa decided that Christianity was better than Islam. He thereafter commanded Baganda to read Christianity. Stanley made study charts for the English alphabet and begun teaching the chiefs and the masses. As Stanley prepared to exit Buganda, Muteesa requested for missionaries to be sent by the British Queen, and Stanley wrote a letter to that effect.

Zimbe mentions that Muteesa's command for Christianity to be taught led people to reject and despise Islam. This may have happened because people had been forced to become Muslims against their will and those who refused had been murdered in large numbers. Islam was neither rejected nor despised. People instead found an alternative religious denomination that may not have been as exacting as that which Islam required. This may have worked for the laity but not Muteesa, who continued to build mosques and also fasted during Ramadhan. In the main, the entry of Christianity in Buganda did not obviate the need for Islam. Muteesa found both foreign denominations equally as important to his political designs. By accepting Christianity to enter Buganda, Muteesa had witnessed firsthand the technological power of the British during war. Stanley's knowledge and directions in warcraft had helped Muteesa defeat a local adversary. By allowing Christianity to be taught in Buganda, Muteesa positioned Buganda as the repository of new ideas, which could be beneficial in particular circumstances. Requesting that missionaries come into Buganda was an opportunity to befriend a powerful monarch from another country whose ideas were considered advanced. By accepting that both Islam and Christianity be taught in Buganda, Muteesa sought

ISLAM IN PRE-COLONIAL BUGANDA   **57**

to maximize the benefits that accrued from both the Arab Muslims and the Europeans. As the religious field in Buganda expanded from the traditionalists and Muslims to now include Christians, it became a period of religious confusion because Ganda masses had never experienced such a situation because they were required to negotiate multiple religious terrains in the service of Muteesa's will. Required to read and practise Islam, and then commanded to learn Christianity and British ways, many Baganda became disturbed and searched for individual autonomy from the Kabaka. This is the context in which we can understand the violence that engulfed Muteesa's court.

On 2 June 1876, in an action that would shock Buganda and have wide-reaching implications, Muteesa ordered that a defiant faction of Muslim pages, who objected to his promulgation of Christianity, be murdered. The killings at Muteesa's palace had as much to do with the internal pluralism arising from multiple interpretations of Islam as to external forces. As stated above, the forces of traditionalism and Christianity intensified it, leading to a dialectical stimulus in later years. The intra-Muslim debate began with the articulation of the Islamic rite of circumcision. When Muteesa became the leader of the Salat at his palace Masjid, he had a very large following of pages that read Islam and practised it. Although the Arabs had taught circumcision, they had not *stressed* it as critical to the articulation of Islam. Under Ganda culture, the Kabaka would not shed blood. The Ganda practice of *okulanya* (pledging allegiance to the Kabaka) included these words: '*alikukaabya amaziga, ndimukaabya musaayi*'.[70] Although Muteesa had declared Islam the state religion, he did not enforce circumcision on the masses. Two reasons explain this: one, he feared that he would be perceived weak and fail to lead by example, whereby subjects would ask why he was enforcing a rite that he was not willing to undergo. Second, he was concerned that forcing many of his chiefs to circumcise would stir dissent among them, such that they would influence possible rebellion in their counties and dethrone him. Muteesa however did not stop those who chose to circumcise themselves. Muslim historians have mentioned over thirty individuals who accepted circumcision.[71] Ganda writers have disagreed on the specific dates of events surrounding the pages' executions. Ham Mukasa recorded the Muslims'

---

[70] Literally, 'Whosoever shall make you cry, I will make them bleed.' These were part of the words in a whole litany of performances that showed one's love towards the Kabaka, and continues to date.

[71] Katungulu, Kasozi and Kakungulu have all reproduced the list of the first Baganda Muslims to undergo circumcision.

58 ISLAM IN UGANDA

execution under the section '1873' but his dating mentions the expedition to Nnakalanga, which occurred around Stanley's return in March 1875. James Miti's dating mentions the event around the time of Stanley's departure in May of that year and the arrival of Muslim Turks from Misr that stayed in Buganda for two or three months. Ham Mukasa's record mentions that the executions occurred between Stanley's visit and Muteesa's news about the British army officer General Charles Gordon's expedition in Bunyoro (see below). The real issue began when two Muslims arrived from Misr and visited Muteesa's palace. Ham Mukasa and James Miti each provided a narrative of this event.

When they reached Muteesa's court, the 'Turks' (Egyptians) were glad to see symbols of Islamic practice in Buganda. The westward direction of the Lubiri Masjid, as opposed to the east, however, bothered them. After consultations as to this situation, the Turks were informed of the Arabs' advice in its construction. They requested a meeting with Muteesa, who summoned the Arabs, the chiefs and the pages to appear in the palace to listen to the visiting teachers on the next day, when they would be taught the timing of *Al-fajr* (the early morning Salat). In the *dars* the Turks emphasized the importance of the rite of circumcision in Islam. Uncircumcised individuals could neither slaughter animals nor partake in leadership of the Muslim community especially in performing Salat. They emphasized that even if this uncircumcised person were their Kabaka, they were not obligated to obey his leadership.[72] Upon further inquiry, the Turks learned from the palace that Muteesa led the Salat in the masjids at his palaces, slaughtered meat and yet he had declined circumcision. The Turks advised that this was indeed a dire situation, as they had taught in the Masjid, especially since the Quran prohibited any uncircumcised person from leading Salat in the Masjid anywhere. When the Turks asked why Muteesa had refused to follow the Quranic injunctions, the pages replied that he had his authority over the palaces and masjids, spaces where pages had neither authority nor power. The Turks thereafter advised the pages to follow the new teachings they had taught in the *darasa*.[73] With these new teachings, many pages began to abscond from the Masjid activities, refused to eat palace meat and began performing Salat outside the palace Masjid. They argued that as the Maliki interpretation of Islam emphasized circumcision, Muteesa's refusal to undergo that rite made him a *kaafir* (non-Muslim). He was thus

[72] Mukasa, *Simuda Nyuma*, p. 25.
[73] Ibid.

ISLAM IN PRE-COLONIAL BUGANDA   **59**

described as unworthy of leading them in Salat. The pages split from the Kabaka and established their own spaces to express their newly learned Maliki interpretations of Islam.

Muteesa's conversation with one palace page, Mudduawulira (obedient servant)[74] revealed the gravity of the looming defiance. He was reported to Muteesa for two offences: one, he refused to eat the meat from the palace except if he knew a 'true' Muslim prepared it. Second, Mudduawulira was the head of the breakaway faction that split from the Kabaka's Masjid. His conversation with the Kabaka disturbed Buganda:

> Muteesa: Mudduawulira, is it true that you no longer eat meat slaughtered in the palace?
>
> Mudduawulira: Yee Ssebo (Kabaka) [responding with confidence and determination].
>
> Muteesa: Even if I slaughtered it?
>
> Mudduawulira: I cannot eat it, even if you slaughtered it [responding with determination].
>
> Muteesa: Why?
>
> Mudduawulira: Because of Islam and I also follow what it commands and as you Ssalongo[75] also know the Quran prohibits it.[76]

The outspoken character of the servant's responses begins to paint a gloomy picture of the events that would follow. The confidence and determination with which Mudduawulira responded to Muteesa was analogous to the Ganda saying that '*Kabaka avoddwa*' (disgraced), which was tantamount to *okuzza oggwannaggomola* (a grave crime) such as *okulya mu nsi olukwe* (treason). Baganda were astonished to hear of Islamic readers who believed in Allah but did not fear Muteesa. The tone of this dialogue began a precedent that later events would confound. Relatedly, two youthful pages, Mbogo and Sewajwali escorted the Turks as they left Buganda to return to Misr. Ham Mukasa and James Miti are not clear whether or not the youths intended to go up to Misr. When Muteesa received word about them, he was infuriated and immediately

---

[74] He was also the *muadhin* (caller for Salat) in the palace Masjid.

[75] 'Ssebo' means 'sir'; 'Ssalongo' means 'father of twins'. In Ganda culture, however, the Kabaka was considered to own various magnificent names including those given to 'extraordinary' events like fathering twins.

[76] Mukasa, *Simuda Nyuma*, p. 26.

60   ISLAM IN UGANDA

sent messengers to inform the Turks that it was bad practice to leave with his servants without his permission and knowledge. The messengers found the Turks in Bulemeezi (north-western Buganda) and returned the pages to Buganda.[77] Muteesa read this as an act of emigration of two Muslim boys running away from their leader whom they saw as *kaafir*. The combination of various acts of defiance enraged Muteesa.

As the intra-Muslim altercations unfolded, *bakungu* (chiefs) decided to side with Muteesa. He had publicly declared that his pages had lost his trust. Fearing to further enrage him, the chiefs, many of whom had hated Islamic rites, approached the Kabaka and skilfully spread rumours about the seditious and slandering acts the pages did to Muteesa's name. These chiefs were aged men who had found Ramadan fasts very exacting for their bodies. Coupling this with their fear of circumcision, which they believed would kill an old man, they unanimously agreed to paint the worst picture of the Muslim pages and told Muteesa how these had called him a *kaafir*.[78] Muteesa drew up a list of wrongs done against him by the Muslim pages.[79] But there was more. The entry of Christianity also destabilized Muteesa and contributed to the altercation with his pages.

The behaviour of the Muslim pages, as evidenced in the conversation between Mudduawulira and Muteesa reveals a clash between the pages' conviction about the supremacy of Islam over the Ganda religious system. By accepting the fundamental tenets of Islam, especially the unicity of Allah, the pages thought that their allegiance to Islam was preponderant to the demands of any other power such as Muteesa. Yet such defiance, coming from the Kabaka's subjects and directed towards his person, was sure to provoke a forceful response as a way to re-assert the preponderant power of Muteesa over his subjects. The actions of the Muslim pages

---

[77] Ibid., p. 27.

[78] Ibid.

[79] 1. Muteesa is abused for being uncircumcised, that he is a *kaafir* and they cannot accept his leadership of the Salat, better to say Salat outside the Masjid; 2. Kabaka eats haraam meat slaughtered by *kaafir*; he also eats pork; 3. Mudduawulira abused me (Muteesa) that he could not eat meat I slaughter even if I am Kabaka; 4. Mbogo and Sewajwali were trying to emigrate from Buganda, calling it *kaafir* territory; 5. Muteesa is abused for being uncircumcised, that he is a *kaafir* and they cannot accept his leadership of the Salat, better to say Salat outside the Masjid; 6. They exposed my not being uncircumcised to the Turks and made me unworthy of leadership in Salat; 7. They showed how the Masjid was built in a wrong way. Therefore, they have lost my trust; they are now my enemies. See Mukasa, *Simuda Nyuma*, p. 28.

therefore drew the ire of Muteesa and other sections of Buganda, especially the traditionalists, who wished to see Islam eradicated. Not all the Muslim pages were murdered; some readers of Islam were spared because their behaviour did not provoke Muteesa's ire. The internal debate among Muslims in Muteesa's time would later foreshadow later factions between Muslim groups aligned to prevailing political power, those opposed to it and others indifferent to either group.

Christianity comes to Buganda

As mentioned in the previous section J.H. Speke and J. Grant had called at Muteesa's palace in 1862, but it was Stanley's visit in the early 1870s that instigated the entry of Christianity in Buganda, and the execution of the Muslim pages. Stanley arrived when Muteesa was preparing for an expedition to Nnakalanga, and agreed to go with him. It was there that Muteesa heard about Christianity. His interest had been roused by what Muteesa heard in the Islamic teachings about the status of Jesus in the Quran, where he had read that Christ was the son of Mary and also a descendant of Israel. When Muteesa went to the Arab teachers for further explanation, they 'failed to satisfy his interest and even denied knowledge'.[80] When Muteesa insisted, he was informed that indeed there was Jesus Christ, whom the Christians called 'son of God' but Muhammad 'is not a son of God but only a messenger'.[81] Muteesa was informed that the readers of the Christian religion were the whites. When he discoursed with Stanley, the latter recommended his servant, Darlington Mufta to respond to Muteesa's inquiries and used his Kiswahili skills to translate about five books of Prophet Moses from the Old Testament, naming them '*Somo La Kwanza*'. After this publication, Muteesa summoned his officials and discoursed with them as to which religion they would follow, since he had discovered a new religion of Jesus Christ, 'the true son of God'. The new religion did not require circumcision.[82] With the publication of the Pentateuch in Kiswahili (*Somo La Kwanza*), Muteesa was confusing Buganda and the Muslims.[83] How could he lead Salat in the Masjid

---

[80] Musoke, D.R. (1917), *Ebifa Mu Buganda*, No. 120. Buddo, p. 7

[81] Ibid.

[82] Gee, 'A Century of Muhammadan Influence', argues that Stanley had also played on Muteesa's fears that the Arabs were 'bad' men who would circumcise him by force but Christianity did not circumcise.

[83] The Kiswahili Pentateuch provided Buganda with an alternative religious text intelligible to the Baganda since some already knew that language.

62 ISLAM IN UGANDA

yet he had summoned his chiefs and intimated to them his desire to follow Jesus Christ? The sparks began to fly when Muteesa went to the Masjid to explain some of the translated books of the Pentateuch and found some of his 'disciplined' ('good') pages there. Three other pages now entered the Masjid dressed in tunics. The pages already gathered in the Masjid moved away from Muteesa towards the three newly arrived pages. The newly arrived pages, however, stormed out in anger for what appeared to be evidence of the suspicion that Muteesa was reading Christian teachings inside the Masjid. Muteesa himself also rushed out, then summoned his chiefs to prepare for the execution of the defiant faction of Muslim pages. Ham Mukasa and D.R. Musoke have recorded the executed number as seventy at the court, along with many others around Buganda.[84]

Why did Muteesa execute the Muslims? Did the defiant Muslim faction threaten his throne? Was it the influence of the chiefs who secretly hated Islamic rites and therefore leaped at the opportunity to display their loyalty to Muteesa by contributing to the elimination of his opponents? Was it the influence of the Christian entry in Buganda that challenged Muteesa's understanding of monotheism that influenced his actions to remove defiant pages that he no longer needed since he had discovered another equally powerful religion? Or was all this the outcome of Muteesa's use of religion to achieve political ends? Two important incidents occurred in Bunyoro, after the Muslim murders, which provide some explanations to the 'why' question.

Muteesa had intimated to his chiefs that he had dreamed of white men coming to 'eat'[85] his country. Around the same time, he heard that General Charles Gordon (a British army officer and administrator) was planning to attack Kabarega. He immediately summoned his chiefs to advise on the available choices, fearing that Gordon would proceed to Buganda after overrunning Bunyoro. It was agreed that they write a letter of friendship to the 'Kabaka of Misr'. The chiefs reminded Muteesa that there were no learned envoys to carry the message as he had executed them; and it was

---

As a text, it became equal to the Quran as a religious authority in people's consciousness. That Muteesa allowed two religious texts to enter religious circulation was confusing to Baganda because they could not imagine that he could advance both Islam and Christianity at the same time.

[84] Musoke D.R. (1917), 'Okukangavvula kwa Kabaka Mukabya Muteesa eri Abavubukabe' in *Ebifa Mu Buganda*, 120, 7–9.

[85] Literally, acquiring a position of power. The meaning from Muteesa's dream was that White men would conquer his country. See Pulford, Cedric (1999), *Eating Uganda: From Christianity to Conquest*, Ituri: Banbury.

important that they send two letters, one to Charles Gordon, who would ensure their audience with the Khedive of Misr.[86]

It is in Muteesa's response that we discern his intentions for the murder of the Muslims. As the chiefs wondered which of the remaining 'taught' (educated) men they could send to Bunyoro, Muteesa replied: 'Worry not, let us write nonetheless. And look around for some of the remaining readers that we can send. Besides, I am also still reading. Those men I killed angered and enraged me when they abused and demeaned me.'[87] To Muteesa, any form of Islamic interpretation had to be articulated within the framework of respect for established power and authority. As Kabaka, his power fused with other aspects of authority: he was both the religious leader of Muslims and the head of his political community. The maintenance of order and discipline thus required that dissent could not be accepted in such a volatile context where disrespect to the Kabaka was not only treasonous but could break the social fabric of Ganda society. Ganda institutions were founded on hierarchical discipline and respect for power and authority across all levels.

Why did Muteesa associate with Christianity when he had ordered the Islamization of society? Two letters to Charles Gordon highlight some explanations. According to Mukasa's records, the purpose of the letters was to befriend the 'Kabaka of Misr' who would plead to the 'Bazungu' (the white people) not to take over Buganda. The letter to Gordon read thus:

I have written this letter to you and sent you a leopard skin, a bark cloth and a shield, the national attire of Buganda. Ssebo, I implore you to accept the envoys that I have sent to visit the Kabaka of Misr because I would like to befriend him. As for me Muteesa, I am learning the English way [Christianity].[88]

The letter to the Khedive was different in tone and read like this:

Ssebo, I have written this letter to inform you that I am the Kabaka of Buganda. I have sent you a leopard skin, bark cloth and a shield, the attire of Buganda. I want to befriend you. This country is also yours. If there is

[86] Mukasa, *Simuda Nyuma*, p. 28.
[87] Ibid., p. 29, emphasizes that 'Muteesa did not hate Islam after the incident of the Muslims' execution. He was still convinced in his soul that God was true; there would be a day of resurrection; his heart was still concentrated on knowing God.'
[88] Muteesa to Gordon cf. Mukasa, *Simuda Nyuma*, p. 30

64 ISLAM IN UGANDA

any trouble in future, I seek your protection. I am here truly reading the Islamic religion. Signed, Muteesa, Kabaka of Buganda.[89]

Gordon had already known of the letters even before they reached him. His response to the envoys was thus:

Muteesa has said in his letter that he is reading Christianity, yet he is interested in befriending the Kabaka of Misr: how can he do that when he has just executed Muslims? Yet he emphasizes that he is studying Christianity, and his envoy to Misr is Muslim. So, what is the basis of Muteesa's message to the Kabaka of Misr? And Muteesa calls himself 'English' that he is learning English, does not he know that England is a country like Buganda and Bunyoro and not a religion?[90]

Muteesa's intentions in pledging allegiance to two religious identities disturbed Gordon. Yet, Muteesa's dream had intimated a looming threat of conquest over Buganda. Attenuating these potential threats required alliances with countries other than Arab power. Pleading to the English would convince them to rethink attacking a 'Christian' Buganda while pleading to the Khedive would guarantee the same result of intervention to protect a 'Muslim' Buganda. It is clear that Muteesa's letters show his desire to befriend both Misr and England so as to offset their colonial designs. The coming of the Christian missions to Buganda marked the entry of a new religious dynamic in Buganda's political atmosphere. Zimbe mentions that when Muteesa discovered an internal differentiation in Christianity, he was disturbed because these schisms threatened his delicate balancing of religious denominations. When members of the CMS arrived in 1877, Muteesa was overjoyed as they also came with new technologies like the printing press. These were stationed at Nnateete (about three miles south-west of Mengo, the capital of Buganda). When, in 1879, members of the Roman Catholic mission arrived and were stationed in nearby Rubaga, Muteesa was disturbed because he wondered whether both versions of Christianity were built on the same fundamentals. The Anglicans denied that they were similar to the Roman Catholics. Internal bickering and jostling for Muteesa's favour became apparent as many Ganda chiefs and other elites crossed sides. Even Muteesa intimated his desire to be baptized in the Anglican way and marry one official wife as he had left Islam, only for Katikkiro (Prime Minister) Mukasa and close chiefs to advise against it. The chiefs

[89] Muteesa to 'Kabaka of Misr', ibid.
[90] Ibid.

ISLAM IN PRE-COLONIAL BUGANDA   65

noted that for Muteesa to become baptized would make him patron of the Anglican religion and bring religious strife since every other religion would also fight to bring him to their side. After this advice, Muteesa advised and cautioned that every person was free to follow their religion of choice.[91]

Conclusion

A few issues can be discerned from the events described in this chapter. Before the entry of Islam, political power, authority and influence in Buganda were constituted under various layers that supported the institution of the Kabaka. Various ruptures had transformed the authority of successive leaderships. As Buganda was founded on religious ideas that supported its material structures, Islam entered Buganda and found a fertile ground whereby many Ganda practices such as family discipline and marriage practices could gel with Islam. Although Islam's entry pre-dated the reign of Muteesa, he recognized its potential as an idea to reorganize society due to the internal and external benefits that would accrue. Muteesa attempted to Islamize Buganda by institutionalizing particular Islamic practices that cumulatively made Buganda to appear an Islamic state. This was the seminal moment that founded discourses about Islamic belief and practices in Buganda. As discussed above, Islam differed from from the Ganda religious system because its claim to monotheism provided uniform practices. Although there was internal differentiation in Islam on non-fundamental principles, as Muteesa discovered with the incident regarding the 'Turks' and the palace pages, he did not know this at first. Islamization met resistance from various sections and the murder of Muslim pages was not the only such incident. *Lubaale* worshippers had been murdered because they refused Islam. The attack on Muslim pages occurred within the context of a widening religious field containing traditionalists, Muslims and Christians. As Muteesa recognized the potential role of Christianity in social-political advancement of Buganda, he began courting British missionaries as a vehicle to earn the good pleasure of the English monarchy, at the same time claiming affinity with Islam. These acts of statecraft and foreign diplomacy confused certain sections in Buganda who did not know what to choose. The murder of Muslim pages occurred because various sections in Buganda began to search for religious autonomy away from the Kabaka and actually began to take these

[91]   Zimbe, *Buganda ne Kabaka,* pp. 44–5.

ideas seriously beyond Muteesa's politicking. Unfortunately, the manner in which some individuals, like Mudduawulira, responded to this desire for autonomy was confrontational to the person of the Kabaka and treasonous. As Muteesa himself noted, the pages had demeaned and disgraced his person.

What is clear however is that the entry of multiple Christian denominations in Buganda widened the scope of religious competition for the patronage of the Kabaka, and inter-religious rivalry ensued. Although the religious system in Buganda had been a matter of social-political identity, the entry of Islam and Christianity increased the religious field in Buganda. Such religious pluralism fragmented society as the masses begun to identify with different religious groups leading to social-political conflict. When the religious wars of the 1880s emerged, British imperial intervention sided with the Anglican Christians. The entry of formal British colonialism then introduced a new power dynamic that transformed Ganda society and the Muslim question in tremendous ways. It is to the colonial governance of Islam and Muslims that I now turn.

CHAPTER 3

Muslim Communities in the Colonial Era

This chapter focuses on the colonial governance of Islam and Muslim practices in Uganda. It argues that the state's supervision of Islam and its control over the Muslim masses reproduced colonial state power at various zones of interaction with Muslim society, leading to the emergence of elite authority to link Muslim society to the centre. I describe how colonial governance occurred in two phases: the formative and the transformative.

In the formative phase, the Muslim question was about securing the state from Muslim threats emanating from two sources. On the one hand, a resurgent Muslim quest for political power reflected in the experiences of the religious wars in the 1890s convinced the British of the need to contain Islam and the Muslims. On the other hand, the fear of Islam as an ideology was also part of the experiences of earlier British colonialism, outside Uganda. This formative phase informed the geographical positioning of Muslim groups between Protestants and Catholics so as to check Muslim practices, thereby making Muslims the neutral arbiters between the Christian groups. By playing a neutral role in balancing the Christian groups, colonial power also accommodated the Muslims.

In the second, transformative phase, the colonial state instituted tactics of administrative governance that would undergird a stable political structure. Having positioned the Muslims in that particular territory, the state limited the public role of Islam to the activities of Muslim elites that it propped up to represent the Muslim masses. In the formative phase, questions such as 'who are the Muslims?' 'where are they located?' and 'who represents them?' were subsets of the broader Muslim question. Since the colonial state governed society through what Mahmood Mamdani has called a bifurcation, the settler Muslim community was considered to be under civil law and Islam was accorded a public standing due to the international patronages of the Islamic communities involved. For the native Muslim, however, Islam was pushed to the domain of the larger customary native authority, which however allowed a special version of Muslim law to govern private matters like marriage, divorce, inheritance, et cetera.

I extend Mahmood Mamdani's notion of the bifurcated state to show that 'the native' was not a homogenous category but, rather, differentiated. Although customary law attempted to homogenize the native under one set of laws to govern such diversity, the Muslim question demonstrates how the institution of the customary native authority was a contradiction in terms. When the state identified Muslim elites to represent the masses, it constructed another layer of custodianship and authority over the Muslim masses that were in many respects different from the official customary authority under which the native Muslim was assumed to belong. This additional layer of authority created what I call a *multifurcated* society. As a consequence, it suppressed Muslim autonomy and invited multiple responses from the native Muslims. Tensions emerged from within the Muslim groups that spoke to various issues: theological interpretations of Sharia law as reflected in the Juma-Zukuuli schism (see penultimate section of this chapter), the management of 'Muslim' land (especially Designated Mosque Sites) and its micro-politics, and the desires of some Muslims to partake of various economic opportunities. These contradictions produced diverse and multiple Muslim alliances. Although the state engaged some of these through the Muslim elites, it showed no interest in some Muslim alliances whose members accepted to participate in the economy as butchers, drivers and janitors. Other Muslim alliances took opportunity in their inferior situation to begin Maulid festivals that became sites of intra-Muslim politics. Although Muslim scholarship in Uganda has considered colonial governance of Islam and Muslims as the darkest time of Islam in Uganda, it was ironically the period in which Islam witnessed its largest spread. Colonial governance of Islam and Muslims varied during the whole colonial period from 1894–1962. As colonial control was uncertain and unstable in the first twenty years of colonial rule, this uncertainty also affected the Muslim groups. The stabilization of colonial rule in the later periods allowed Islam and Muslims to stabilize and grow as well.

Historical antecedents in the governance of Islam and Muslims

The management of religious groups under British colonialism did not begin in Uganda. Since Sub-Saharan Africa only became a target of later colonialism in the second half of the nineteenth century, it saved tremendous time to apply the ideas borrowed from similar experiences elsewhere. As another colonial project, Uganda was subjected to similar policies in the governance of religious difference and diversity. As a structure of political authority, the colonial state was an imposition from without. Its life however witnessed various adjustments to the structure of local political authority so as to realign it with colonial power. Lacking the capacity to destroy institutions of native power, the colonial state chose to 'exploit' the 'inherent ambiguities' in ways that allowed them to direct local institutions towards 'more favorable functions and effects'.[1] Regardless of the adjustments, practical necessity and the experiences of early British colonialism laid the blueprint for political praxis in the new dominions.[2] The historical context of the Muslim question under coloniality begins with the Anglo-Mohammedan Law under British imperialism in India, where British officials constructed a body of 'knowledge about Muslims, Islamic law and how to govern Muslim societies'. India worked as a laboratory that produced the experiences that were exported to other colonies, especially Malaya, Egypt, Nigeria, Sudan and East Africa. This network of imperial governance of Muslims was however not a monopoly of the colonial state; Muslim traders, travellers and other interested parties also contributed to it.[3] The influential role of British colonial power in regulating these social networks cannot nevertheless be understated.

The Indian colonial experience of Muslim governance reveals that the Muslim 'community' was a colonial construct. The destabilization of royal authority and its replacement with settler authority allowed colonial statecraft to separate Muslims from political authority. It 'made the Muslim community a site of competition between different groups, elites and laymen'.[4] The struggles between elites in regard to Muslim representation under the colonial state revealed that the power of different actors was relative; all were contingent upon each other.[5] In this way, the local conditions shaped Muslim identity as much as the powers of the colonial state and its global experiences with Muslims.[6] These outcomes between

---

[1]   Mahoney, James & Thelen, Kathleen (Eds) (2010), *Explaining Institutional Change: Ambiguity, Agency, and Power,* CUP: Cambridge, p. 18.

[2]   Mamdani, Mahmood (1996), *Citizen and Subject: Contemporary Africa and the Legacy of Late Colonialism*, Fountain: Kampala, p. 38.

[3]   Hussin, Iza R. (2014), *The Politics of Islamic Law: Local Elites, Colonial Authority and the Making of the Muslim State,* Chicago University Press: Chicago, p. 20.; See also Bishara, *A Sea of Debt*, p. 20; Bose, *A Hundred Horizons*, pp. 6–10.

[4]   Devji, Faisal (2011), 'The Idea of a Muslim Community British India, 1857–1906', in Maussen, Marcel, et al. (Eds), *Colonial and Post-Colonial Governance of Islam: Continuities and Ruptures,* Amsterdam University Press: Amsterdam, p. 111.

[5]   Hussin, *The Politics of Islamic Law*, pp. 12–13.

[6]   Ibid., p. 19.

70 ISLAM IN UGANDA

Muslim elites and the colonial state had enduring implications on Muslim religious and cultural identity; the transformation of Muslim relations with colonial power cultivated a new role for Muslim institutions in the state, the state a new role in religion.[7] Dialectical influences emerged. A new 'confluence' of ethnic group and Muslim identity, and a new 'vision' of Islam that was more patriarchal and state-centred than in the pre-colonial era. Consequently, representative Muslim institutions and discourses of Islam became centralized under the control of elites.[8]

India was not, however, the only laboratory of colonial governance of Islam. French experiences with its Muslim populations in Africa (Algeria, Tunisia and West Africa) also influenced British Muslim policy in Sudan, Nigeria and Uganda. French concerns about Islam and Muslims in Algeria and Tunisia stemmed from the response of groups of Muslim elites to various issues, including naturalization laws. In French Algeria, indigenous Muslims could only become French citizens by first renouncing their Islamic 'personal status'. Here, marriage, inheritance and other issues regarding private life would be governed in the domain of French civil law alone. Tunisian nationalists equated this demand to apostasy from Islam.[9] Elite groups like the *Jeunes Algériens* (Young Algerians) advocated for French naturalization on easier terms and a host of other reforms using peaceful means such as visits by Algerian Municipal Councillors in Paris in June 1912. Various Muslim protests such as those regarding military conscription, aroused French fear of Islam.[10]

What India was to British Tropical Africa, Algeria was to French West Africa. Christopher Harrison has cited Georges Hardy, a one-time Inspector of Education in French West Africa stating that Algeria was the laboratory for 'political and economic doctrines' applied in the French domain.[11] The violence it unleashed has been described in blunt words.[12] In Senegal, colonial policy revealed mixed debates: the 'normal' practice

---

[7] Ibid., p. 21.

[8] Ibid.

[9] Derrick, Jonathan (2008), *Africa's 'Agitators': Militant Anti-Colonialism in Africa and the West, 1918–1939*, London: Hurst & Co., pp. 26–7.

[10] Ibid.

[11] Harrison, Christopher (1988), *France and Islam in West Africa, 1860–1960*, CUP: Cambridge, p. 15, stating that 'it was Algeria that served as a testing ground for political and economic doctrines ...whether for good or for evil ...the mark of Algeria's colonization was to be found in all parts of the French domain'.

[12] Ibid. In the policy of April 1845, one Governor Bugeaud said: 'we have never obtained anything from these people except through force. In vain we have often tried means of persuasion. Either there was no response at all or they

had been to consider Muslims as a 'mere anomaly', but 'political pragmatism' bred accommodation and militated against the norm. Faidherbe, the Governor of Senegal, noted this puzzle in 1854. I reproduce it here because it speaks to the very picture of the accommodation of Muslims during colonial governance in Uganda. He said:

> The Muslim element here is by far the most numerous and active and perhaps also the most useful ... On all sides we are surrounded by Islam. The war we are waging on the lower river is nothing compared to the serious and endless dangers of the Holy War provoked and maintained by Alhadji [Umar] ... What is the class that is the most indispensable to us in Senegal? It is the admirable *laptots* of the river. They are all Muslims. ... If we need volunteers for war with the Trarza or whether even it is a Muslim war as with Alhadji, who is it that responds to our call? The Muslims.[13]

For Governor Faidherbe, regardless of the normal French attitude towards Muslims, the existing conditions of administration called for accommodation in various ways.

Yet, others did not share the Governor's pragmatism; they believed the norm should prevail in Senegal. One M. Carrère believed that 'serious methods should be employed' to efface the marabouts[14] from Senegal by destroying masjids and other spaces such as *qadi* courts where they operated.[15] Faidherbe's critics believed that Senegal was different from Algeria and that there was no warrant for extending 'diplomatic gestures to local Muslims'. The argument was that, unlike Algeria where Islam was the only religion during French conquest, such that it was important to accord it 'respect', Senegal was 'created' by France and this worked against similar 'obligations'. The 'town of St Louis was shaped by France' and only 'gradually' did Islam filter into its 'black population'. Islam 'does not, therefore, have freedom of the town and cannot claim the same rights to those in Algeria. Here...the Muslim as a result of his profound ignorance which his fanaticism has encouraged is absolutely hostile to our ideas, our usages, our language, our customs and our civilisation'.[16]

---

 told us that we would first have to fight and that if we triumphed, then they would submit.'

[13] Harrison, *France and Islam in West Africa*, pp. 11, 13. Emphasis in the original. *Laptots* were African colonial troops in the service of France between 1750 and the early 1900s.

[14] Marabout designates Muslim holy men in Saharan Africa.

[15] Harrison, *France and Islam in West Africa,* p. 12.

[16] Ibid., p. 14.

72 ISLAM IN UGANDA

In the end, Faidherbe's pragmatism won, which speaks to how the character of colonial Muslim policy depended on the presiding governor. As David Robinson has also shown, French colonial administrators sought to found institutions of control that would establish hegemony over the Muslim subjects of empire.[17] A series of policies accommodated the 'good' marabouts and punished the recalcitrant through periodic exiles.[18] British imperialism shared the French concern arising from the political influence of Islam. After a suppressed Mahdi rebellion in Sudan that endeavoured to conquer both Egypt and Mecca,[19] the British were always concerned that 'Mahdist' and 'Pan-Islamic' ideologies would 'distract' 'loyal natives'.[20] Although these concerns arose from experiences involving large Muslim populations, it was not the individuals that were much feared, but rather the Islamic ideologies to which they adhered. Such concerns in majority Muslim areas also spread to minority Muslim regions such as Uganda.

Early British concerns about Islam in Uganda

The success of British imperialism in Uganda was predicated upon confronting the Muslim challenge, understood as the suppression of Islam and its Arab purveyors. Gerald Portal understood this contest well; he championed Christianization as a bulwark to Muslim expansion. It was known that communications frequently passed from the Arabs of Tanganyika and Tabora to the 'fanatical Muslims' at Wadelai and along the White Nile to the neighbouring states. So long as Uganda was under 'European supervision', there was 'little or no danger of those probable disturbances spreading south to north'.[21] Hayes Sadler later echoed this perception.[22] On 30 March 1892, Lugard signed a treaty of 'suzerainty' with Kabaka Mwanga

---

[17] Robinson, David (1999), 'France as a Muslim Power in West Africa', *Africa Today, Vol.* 46, Nos 3–4, pp. 105–27, p. 106.

[18] Harrison, *France and Islam in West Africa,* pp. 49–56.

[19] Theobald A.B. (1951 [1899]), *The Mahdiyya: A history of the Anglo-Egyptian Sudan 1881–1899,* London, p. 14.

[20] Derrick, *Africa's 'Agitators',* p. 27.

[21] Portal to Rosebery included in Portal's Report on Uganda, 14 April 1894. Unless otherwise stated, all correspondence of the colonial officers is referenced from colonial Blue Books, Vols I & II, accessed from the Africana Section of Makerere University library, Kampala.

[22] Sadler, Hayes J. (1904), 'General Report on the Uganda Protectorate', No. 12. p. 17.

to grant Portal's wish. The vanquishing of the Arabs and Muslims on Lake Victoria began this Muslim 'suppression'.

A letter written by an eyewitness of one of the last battles between the Christian factions and the Arab and Ganda Muslim armies near the islands in Lake Victoria symbolized British entry in Uganda:

> The news of this place is that everything is quiet except that there is bad news of the circumstances that took place at Uganda ... the fire of the Europeans got into the dhow loaded with gunpowder; the dhow burn [*sic*] and all the Arabs died. The Europeans then returned and went to Uganda with their own people, and fought with the present sultan of Uganda and the Arabs of the place. The Arabs all ran away ... Now the place is spoiled, and Uganda is in the hands of the Europeans. We do not know what will be the result. The dethroned prince is with the Europeans.[23]

In the letter Zaid bin Juma is describing the scenes of the battle: how the Ganda Christians were strengthened with European tactics and weaponry, which combined to overpower the Arabs and the Ganda Muslims; the burning of all their dhows and explosions of gunpowder and the defeat of Nuhu Kalema ('Sultan'). Ham Mukasa and Zimbe Musoke participated in this war and have given corroborative accounts of this particular incident.[24]

The prelude to what would later become colonial domination over the Muslims in Uganda was decided by the political outcomes of the religious wars in Buganda that culminated into Lugard and Portal's treaties with Mwanga.[25] A brief reminder should suffice here. Upon Mwanga's restoration to the throne in 1889, Protestants and Catholics were both split on how to share power; these disputes were reflected in the nationalities of rival mission stations whereby the English Protestants and French Catholics all favoured their native brethren. These disputes occurred at a time when Britain and France were competing to 'carve up' parts of Africa.[26] British imperialism had taken over from the Imperial British East Africa Company (IBEAC, aka 'the Company'), and Protestant Ganda had perceived it as an opportunity to resuscitate their political

---

[23] Letter from Zaid Bin Juma bin Saalem to Hashir bin Mselem (nd), received in Zanzibar on 13 February 1890, Zanzibar Archives.

[24] Mukasa, *Simuda Nyuma*, pp. 361 ff.; Zimbe, *Buganda ne Kabaka*, pp. 204–8.

[25] *Treaty between the King of Buganda and the Imperial British East Africa Company*, 26 December 1890; *Provisional Agreement between King Mwanga and Sir G. Portal*, 29 May 1893.

[26] Oliver, Roland (1952), *The Missionary Factor in East Africa*, Longman: London.

74   ISLAM IN UGANDA

ambitions vis-à-vis the Roman Catholics in Mwanga's palace. Mwanga and the Catholics, therefore, had perceived the Protestant Ganda and the Company as threats to Buganda's 'sovereignty'.[27]

After their war with the Muslims, the Protestant Ganda were determined to assume a superior position and therefore conspired to acquire all the chiefly offices from the Catholics. These Protestants argued that their war intended to 'establish a Protestant Christian Government' that would realize their ambitions and religious ideology.[28] Later, the Protestants relented and came to an agreement with the Roman Catholics, first at Bulingugwe, and later after the total defeat of the Muslims.[29] Substantively, the implication of these agreements was that the Christians had agreed a political future for Buganda where, Islam and Muslims, if they featured at all, would be distant. If the Christian agreements instigated the marginal integration of Muslims in the Buganda political space, Lugard's treaty with Mbogo at Mwera, Singo, confirmed it.[30] The future of this political space became enshrined in an agreement signed between Mwanga and Henry Edward Colville by which the Kabaka surrendered all his powers to Her Majesty's Representative.[31] The man of the moment was Captain Lugard.[32] It has been argued that the fusion of varying legal codes and belief systems under coloniality went beyond 'layering one system over another' and moved towards fundamental change, which also transformed the 'strategies, attitudes and aspirations' of all those who used it.[33] While it is true that colonial policies emerged from competing varieties of 'often contradictory ideas and doctrines', and that contestation also emerged from various sides, the process of their implementation and execution also witnessed constant alteration in reaction to local circumstances.[34] Policy

[27]   Ashe Robert P. (1971 [1889]), *Two Kings of Uganda: Life by the Shores of Victoria Nyanza,* Frank Cass: London, especially the introduction by Rowe.

[28]   Ashe, *Two Kings of Uganda,* p. xii.

[29]   *Agreements Concluded at Bulingugwe,* between the Protestants and the Roman Catholics, 3 February 1890; *Agreement between the Chiefs of the Protestant and Roman Catholic Parties,* 22 April 1893, witnessed by Gerald Portal and Captain Macdonald.

[30]   *Treaty between Captain Lugard and Nuhu Mbogo,* 1892.

[31]   *Treaty between Henry Edward Colville, Her Britannic Majesty's Acting Commissioner for Uganda, and Mwanga, King of Uganda,* 27 August 1894.

[32]   See Perham, Margery (1960), *Lugard: The Years of Authority 1898–1945,* Collins: London.

[33]   Hussin, *The Politics of Islamic Law,* 32.

[34]   Veit, Bader and Maussen, Marcel (2011), 'Introduction' in Maussen, Marcel.

MUSLIM COMMUNITIES IN THE COLONIAL ERA   75

and its contestations were however results of a particular geographical positioning designed to 'securitize' groups and demarcate the contours of the political field. Law could not operate in a vacuum, but rather on a designated territorial space that delimited the political field of various actors.

The administration of the Uganda Protectorate was based on a legitimate foundation represented by the 1900 Buganda Agreement (the Agreement), which laid out the structure of power between competing centres and the roles of various agents.[35] In many ways, the Agreement was a culmination of negotiations that accrued over a whole decade. Captain Lugard was instrumental in laying the political setting that produced that law, which he perceived as getting rid of known 'threats'. As early as 1890, Lugard had identified Islam and Muslims as threats to the spread of 'European civilization' in Africa: his counteracting lay in constructing 'a line of frontier forts, with an organised system of defence', which were necessary to counter the 'wave' of Muslim 'fanaticism and power' spreading southwards from the north. He was convinced that this wave would inevitably collide with the 'influences' of European civilization already spreading towards the interior of Africa. He imagined a show down. It was not a matter of *if* but *when* 'Islam from the north' and 'British influence from the south and east' met, and the outcome would be vitally important not only to the 'interests of the Company', but to the 'cause of *civilization and Christianity*'. When this occurred, it was imperative that the Company be '*ready* to meet force with force'.[36] When in Uganda, he set about realizing his fortification defence system, beginning with Lugard's Fort at Old Kampala.[37]

To contain the Muslim threat, Lugard reorganized the territorial spaces. He began with a treaty, first with the Christian factions to divide the 'spoils of war', which in this case included counties, chieftainships and arms. Although the chiefs were concerned that guns were easily available to the opposite factions, Lugard stipulated that all arms 'belonging to the Company' be returned, which were guns that he had lent to the Christian factions against the Muslims. He disarmed the chiefs by promising to be neutral in seizing the guns of opposite factions. In the treaty, Lugard ceded the southern Buddu county and an island on Lake Victoria to the Catholic chiefs. They yielded three counties separated by a day's march from each

---

et al. (Eds) (2011), *Colonial and Post-Colonial Governance of Islam: Continuities and Ruptures,* Amsterdam University Press: Amsterdam, p. 11.

[35] *The Buganda Agreement, 1900.*

[36] Lugard to Administrator-General of I.B.E.A.C., 24 December 1890, emphasis added.

[37] This still stands next to the National Mosque at Old Kampala hill.

76 ISLAM IN UGANDA

other so that all Catholics going and coming to Mengo might camp in the estates of their own party, and to avoid friction with the opposite faction. The treaty did not restrict Catholics settling elsewhere in Buganda, so long as they were unarmed'.[38] Ceding Buddu to the Catholics was not an innocent act; it was done in response to an ongoing debate within Buganda.

Whereas some wanted strategically to frustrate Muslim ambitions for political power, political economy influenced others over Buddu. Lugard was learning from the lessons of the wars that defeated the alliance of the Zanzibar Arabs and local Muslims on Lake Victoria. He strategically cut off the possibility of the 'lesser people' (Muslims) from acquiring arms and ammunitions to cause war since Busoga (the region east of Buganda) and Kampala garrisons would check them.[39]According to Zakariya Kisingiri, future regent of Kabaka, Buddu was richer than all the provinces of Buganda and would support a large population, unlike other counties like Singo, Kyaggwe and Bulemeezi that were ravaged by war.[40] Besides, it was big enough to fully accommodate all the Catholics. The Muslims also coveted Buddu for similar reasons. Regardless of the desires of the different groups, Lugard spoke to Mwanga and sought a restitution of all 'their estates at the capital and elsewhere'.[41]

Having strategically blocked Muslims' access to water, Lugard invited Nuhu Mbogo for a pact (the Mwera settlement). He made the Muslims accept Mwanga as Kabaka by promising them a province to settle. Mbogo would also have an estate 'as a private individual' if he agreed to 'entirely resign his position'. To the last condition, Lugard also insisted that Mbogo 'must come to Kampala' and 'place himself in my hands' failing which he (Mbogo) would be seen as 'king' in case of future trouble: 'having had *a* part of Uganda, the Muslims would try to get *all*'.[42] Colonial agreements such as this were not innocent acts. They were moments to demarcate Muslim political space. They served a dual purpose: first, they demarcated colonial violence and its legitimation. Second, they distinguished between chaotic politics and the imperatives of colonial rule (the pragmatism).[43]

---

[38] Lugard, Frederick D. (1968), *The Rise of Our East African Empire: Early Efforts in Nyasaland and Uganda*, Frank Cass & Co.: London, Vol. II, p. 423–4.

[39] Ibid., p. 421.

[40] Kisingiri, Lukiiko Minutes, cited in Lugard, *The Rise of our East African Empire*, p. 423.

[41] Lugard, *The Rise of our East African Empire,* p. 431.

[42] Ibid., p. 438, emphasis added.

[43] Hussin, *The Politics of Islamic Law,* p. 41.

Lugard proceeded to exercise 'considerable diplomacy' in the deliberations with the Muslims regarding the province to settle in. His intention was to propose three comparatively small provinces, which were, when combined, inferior to Buddu. At the meeting, he suggested two of the three provinces and mentioned the third as a 'great concession' so as to delight and provide the 'impression' that they had 'scored a success'.[44]

As the Muslims accepted their position amid Christian factions, Lugard was 'disappointed', on relaying the outcome, that the Katikkiro and the 'Ingleza' (Protestant) chiefs were displeased over his award of provinces poorer than Buddu to the Muslims, noting that they would listen to neither justice, fair play, nor commonsense'. The Muslims accepted Lugard's concessions with the 'worst possible grace', which served him well since they were situated in the middle of the Christian factions. And although apparently anxious to be fair to all, he was not 'eager' to give more than was 'necessary to the Muslims', citing Gerald Portal who had noted that the position of the provinces 'accorded to the Muslims so *cramps them* that *they are not to be feared*, and will probably become absorbed by the Christian factions'.[45]

Lugard's attempts to 'secure' Mbogo to Kampala was intended to denounce Mbogo's 'kingly' status among the Muslims, to 'bring them to the same political footing as the other two factions'; to deny Mbogo and his Muslim faction an opportunity to work with Kabarega in Bunyoro; and ensure that the Muslims would become an internal faction whose importance in Buganda was reduced to maintaining 'the triangular equilibrium' between the competing religious groups. As a 'considerate' diplomat, Lugard surprised even himself. Hitherto, he had been the 'opponent' of Islam in Africa but then as it were mutated to be its 'champion'.[46]

Lugard was no champion, just pragmatic. The hostility of the Christian groups had allowed him an opening to *use* the Muslims as the negotiating platform to deter Christian chaos. To achieve this, he needed to situate the Muslims under his 'control', where he could 'foster' what was best in their 'creed' and 'check' its 'evils'; at a distance, 'the evil may get the better of the good'. Lugard's action was not '*encouraging Islamism*, but rather *controlling* and *limiting* it'.[47] The Mwera settlement thus anchored the 'division of jurisdiction', the struggles over these demarcations and the power they represented. By implication, the treaty reserved a space for the

---

[44] Lugard, *The Rise of our East African Empire,* p. 440.
[45] Ibid. p. 439. Emphasis added.
[46] Ibid., pp. 439–41.
[47] Ibid., p. 442, emphasis added.

state's intervention in its politics – a discrete space for religion and culture, and for an Islamic space separate from the rest of the state.[48] Lugard's 'triangular equilibrium', which sought to accommodate the Muslims, was the logic behind the need for pragmatism. Lugard and his associates endeavoured to show the importance of their power in 'controlling' and 'limiting' Islam.

Other sources however point to facts internal to the Muslim groups, which also influenced the decision to accommodate Islam and Muslims. Abasi Kiyimba has argued that Islam and Muslims were a reality on the Ugandan social-political scene and the Christian groups and their benefactors had to live with them either way. It was therefore better to identify strategies of accommodation than to negate Muslims' existence. Kiyimba ties this reality to three other realities. First, Islam preceded Christianity, and colonial power realized this fact; second, Muslims had increased in population through conversions and natural increase, a fact with which the state had to live; third, the Muslims had put up a formidable fight in the religious wars, which still concerned the British authorities so they needed to find better containment strategies.[49] In words that echoed Faidherbe (Governor of Senegal in 1854) the colonial Governor Harry Johnson confirmed these realities when he said in reference to the Muslims that the British were 'obliged to put up with the existence of people of this faith because they were here before we came' although such accommodation did not include Muslim 'nonsense'.[50] What Johnston meant by 'nonsense' was the Muslim resistance during the religious wars, which served as a reminder that they could be 'difficult to contain' if poorly handled. Johnston knew that Muslims had tasted political power and still coveted it however vanquished they seemed. The Muslim groups therefore became important to colonial power because they could be used to maintain order due to political realities that the state could not ignore.

Lugard met Mbogo in Mwera (Singo County) to negotiate his return to Kampala where he would be treated with 'all honour'. When Mbogo noted that he had given up all 'kingly' rights but wished to stay as a private individual among 'his people' (Muslims), Lugard declined this, arguing that

[48] Hussin, *The Politics of Islamic Law*, p. 41.
[49] Kiyimba, Abasi (1990), 'The Muslim Community in Uganda through One Hundred and Forty Years: The Trials and Tribulations of a Muslim Minority', *Journal of African Religion and Philosophy*, Vol. 1, No. 2, pp. 84–120, pp. 98–9.
[50] Harry Johnston to Provincial Commissioner Busoga, December 1900, Kampala Archives, 1/53 A.

there would be trouble as long as the Muslims still 'regarded' him as their 'king', which would create many 'kings' in Buganda and 'endless' trouble. Lugard gave the agreed provinces to the Muslims and Mbogo accepted to return to Kampala. Although Lugard's intervention had severely weakened Muslims as a political force, Portal believed that even in their inferior position, Muslim 'fanaticism' remained high in comparison to the Christians, so high actually that there were 'perhaps' fewer Muslims than Christians prepared to change their religious affiliation for political benefit. Portal stressed the 'Mohammedan' material disadvantage in 'numbers, organization, and fire-arms' as obstacles to 'becoming an element of *serious danger*' except in an intra-Christian civil war. Portal attempted to deride Lugard's decision of allocating three counties to the Muslims but concluded that it would be 'injustice' to extirpate them, '*a step which I have been urged by high authorities to recommend*'. He realized that Lugard's 'triangular equilibrium' arose from Muslims' strength to 'hold the balance' between the Christian parties. He forecast a bleak future for Islam and Muslims in Africa, predicting that the collapse of the slave trade would lead to poor harvests, emigration and loss of political influence, all of which would combine to 'completely' disintegrate Muslims in Uganda and the region.[51]

As Lugard brought Mbogo to Kampala and took the Muslims to Butambala, Busujju and Kabula, he successfully constructed a Muslim elite whom he separated from the Muslim masses. This separation of the leader from the faction necessitated the need for political representation. It was in this limited role that Islam received public profile. While it is true that Mbogo was a Ganda royal, local political authority did not animate this difference with the *bakopi* (commoners) as much as Lugard and Portal did. Privileging Mbogo's status as a site of power (and also Portal's withdrawal of Muslim lands and ceding them to the Catholics),[52] while blocking others not only intensified power inequalities but also propped up elites as important arbiters between the state and its Muslim subjects. This elite dominance grew out of complex interactions between local elites such as Mbogo and colonial officials like Lugard. The negotiation between Mbogo and Lugard relegated Muslim masses to the periphery of political practice. As the state became the final arbiter of Islam and Muslim articulations of it, elites like Mbogo 'guarded' Islam and Muslim masses. This change explains some of the privileges heaped on Mbogo

---

[51] Portal to Rosebery, 24 May 1893, emphasis added.
[52] Portal to Rosebery, 8 April 1893.

and later Muslim representatives. In the eyes of the state, they had become its servants in managing the Muslim masses. Not all Muslims accepted this new arrangement. Resistance came from various quotas fueled especially by men such as Selim Bey who were actually close to Mbogo.[53] The 'Sudanese Mutiny' provided an opportunity for the new Muslim elites to show their 'loyalty' to the colonial state vis-à-vis the Muslim masses.

The Muslim question as containment: the Sudanese Mutiny

What became the Mutiny of Sudanese soldiers threatened the colonial administration because of the religious identity of the mutineers. These Muslim soldiers had been under Emin Pasha until Lugard took over their command and integrated them into the Uganda Army. There is a debate as to what actually caused this insurrection. Although some colonial reports speak about the 'ingratitude' of the Sudanese soldiers, others observed that the mutineers were actually justified in defying orders due to the poor, often-delayed pay and failure to fulfil logistical pledges on the part of the administration. There is also an internal debate among the mutineers as to why some defied authority, which revealed schisms as to who were ready to support the Protectorate administration and those opposed to it. The end of the mutiny also revealed how the British administrators were prepared to marshal all military and political skill to thwart this 'threat'. One scholar has argued that the brief history of the Sudanese Mutiny needs to be located in the personalities that influenced it. His position is that Selim Bey, who was close to Mbogo, was critical of the Mwera pact and had advised Mbogo to resist the British. His influence as a commander of a military unit spread to some of the soldiers, which established the first moment of anti-colonial revolt from a side identified with the Muslim groups.[54]

When the mutiny commenced, British authorities struggled to explain its cause. Harry Johnston belonged to the side of those who believed that these soldiers were ungrateful to the state. Although the Government had not granted enough pay to satisfy their wants, these Muslims were ungrateful because they had in the first place been 'practically refugees' and should have been 'thankful' to get a 'home' and land to establish familial relations. Regardless of the material explanations, Johnston believed that their Islamic belief influenced a mutinous behaviour. As 'ardent' Muslims focused on 'spreading' Islam amid Christian power, there was a tendency

---

[53] Interview with AK, Makerere University, 24 July 2017.
[54] Ibid.

'already in their minds' as Muslims to become disloyal towards serving 'a Christian Government'. Even their valor and victories owed much to the able and gallant leadership of 'British officers'. Their mutinous behaviour also stemmed from their 'ambitious' officers who conceived the idea of driving out the British and establishing a great Islamic kingdom in Uganda and its neighbouring territories, one which they would either rule directly or through a 'Muganda puppet'. Johnston concluded that sooner or later, it would have occurred quite independently of other grievances.[55] Others felt the mutiny inevitably arose from material failures of British administration in designing measures to either prevent or remedy it.[56] For the mutineers, Janna Billal gave a long account of the cause of the Mutiny in which he identified the delayed low pay and the material wants but stressed that they were 'tired of travelling' since they had been ordered to move (with their families) and quell insurrections in Bunyoro, Nandi, Buddu, 'the Ravine' and elsewhere.[57] The mutiny was later weakened and eventually defeated when the soldiers in Kampala and Entebbe were disarmed,[58] but it was not the character of its suppression that revealed the validity of the particular sides of the debate, rather how it arose in the first place.

Johnston's perception that regardless of material grievances, the mutineers were driven by the desire to found an Islamic kingdom is limited in explaining the context. Part of the response lies in the understanding of military discipline by the agents involved. The professionalization of the military arm of government is a development that coincided with the centralization of violence and the founding of standing armies. Before this, war making was a voluntary occupation and to that extent, military recruitment allowed scope for a whole series of resistances, refusals and desertions, which were 'absolutely ordinary' practices in armies.[59] The transformation occurred when war making moved from being a profession

---

[55] Johnston Harry (1901), 'Report by His Majesty's Special Commissioner on the Protectorate of Uganda', *Parliamentary Papers: Africa*, No. 7, pp. 4–5; see also Stuart, Ramsay, 'The Mutiny in Uganda, 1897–98: A Précis of Events', 9 March 1898.

[56] Portal to Rosebery, 31 March 1893.

[57] Janna Bilal, Spokesman of the Disaffected Sudanese troops speaks to F.J. Jackson, 25 September 1897. 'The Ravine' refers to the Rift Valley in present-day Kenya.

[58] Macdonald to Salisbury, 22 October 1897.

[59] Foucault, M. *Security, Territory, Population,* Lectures at the Collège de France, 1977–78, Ed. Michel Senellart, trans. Graham Burchell. Palgrave Macmillan: Houndmills and New York, p. 198.

82   ISLAM IN UGANDA

to also comprise a particular code of ethical conduct that defined 'a good citizen'.[60] These effects transformed the volunteer into a committed professional soldier within the European military tradition. How far did this compare with the Sudanese soldiers that Emin Pasha and Lugard later managed? What was the philosophy that informed their consent to accept recruitment? How did they understand 'discipline'? Further, was this a 'mutiny', 'desertion', 'end of service' or 'insubordination'? I generate these questions to show that the conflict of conduct inherent in the nature of the relationship that the Sudanese soldiers were called to respond enabled, by its very constitution, a grammatical disparity that disempowered them from the start. We can discern from Janna Bilal that since they always moved with their families, they had believed that they could just tell the Government to choose from other 'Companies' since they were tired of moving to different localities. Their conception of soldiery therefore differed from what the colonial government imposed on to them.

When they insisted on resting, the British soldiers fired against them using the Maxim gun. As they dispersed, the Government called this a 'mutiny'. A series of events followed and the soldiers retreated to their Islamic identity, reaching out to Nuhu Mbogo. This happened when the leaders among them felt they had lost the cause of the fight. They roused their 'brothers' to join the fight, reminding them how they were to die anyway and asked them to look to the hereafter as opposed to the worldly in which there was no 'life'; and looked to Mbogo to legitimate their fight.[61] They immediately sent a letter saluting Mbogo and reiterated his 'kingly' status and signed out: 'we are your brothers. All the Muslims salute you'.[62] One Ganda Muslim also asked Mbogo to join the mutiny although it is not clear for how many others the author spoke.[63]

---

[60]   Ibid.

[61]   Billal Effendi to Native Officers, not dated, stating thus: 'Oh. Brothers, we have to die, there is no life in this world. Major Macdonald fired against us with the Maxim, and we fought them. Strengthen yourselves against the Waganda. Eight British officers fought us, three of them were killed; of us fifty, Suliman Effendi and Mabruk Effendi were also killed. Now we want assistance from you and Sultan Mbogo. Prepare yourselves, oh my brothers, and take possession of Kampala. Now the British Government will fight you. Open your eyes like men, and perhaps we will come to you. At present the fighting is raging hot. Call your brethren, who are in Buddu, Sharp.'

[62]   Officers of Sudanese Mutiny (signed by Mabruk Effendi, Bilal Effendi Amin and, Suliman Effendi) to Mbogo not dated.

[63]   Letter from Muslim Muganda to Mbogo, neither signed not dated, stating,

MUSLIM COMMUNITIES IN THE COLONIAL ERA   **83**

George Wilson had perceived the potential outcome of the situation and guarded Mbogo's residence. What Lugard had called 'control', Wilson termed 'honourable surveillance'. As the Muslim representative, Mbogo was briefed on the situation and was reminded of his duty to support the Government 'seeing that his integrity and the welfare of his sect in Buganda was endangered by some irresponsible co-religionists'.[64] The mutineers' letter reached Mbogo, who read and handed it over to Wilson in whose presence Mbogo's reply was written and in the presence of the Sudanese soldiers opposed to the mutiny.[65]

Whether Wilson or Mbogo personally wrote this reply is difficult to establish but the language it contained must have come from one knowledgeable about the course of proceedings. Mbogo wrote from Wilson's house and his reply reminded the mutinying camp how they had done a 'wrong thing' since they had chosen disobedience, which he detested. Their best option, he continued, was to stop agitating and avoid the disturbance it bred. He noted that they were ignorant of the potential outcome and would regret (he used 'repent') when they saw the consequences of their actions. He was sure that war would come and he quickly chose a side:

> When the fight commences, I will be on the Government side and fight against you. I am not *powerful* to fight the English. I am loyal to British rule and will not withdraw my *obedience* to Government. If you do not listen to ... what I am writing you will be sorry. All your action is bad. I received your letter, and personally took it to Mr. Wilson, and am now replying to you in Mr. Wilson's house. I have been to the coast at Zanzibar, and have seen the *strength* of the British Government and found that I have not the *power* to fight them. You also have not the *power* to fight the British Government. If I had not been to the coast perhaps I might have taken your part. I have seen with my own eyes their *power*, how they in about *half-an-hour bombarded even* Zanzibar. Last of all I advise you to lay down your arms and be obedient. Do not disregard my advice, you will then have an opportunity to bring your grievances to Government; and when you come, I do not wish you to come in a body, because you will then

---

'to Sultan Mbogo salutations, and after salutations: I inform you by letter that five of the Europeans of Usoga have been actually killed. Tell all the 'Mahommedans' that they should get up their strength, and you also should get up your strength. Tell your 'Mahommedan' people to get up their strengths. Salutations.'

[64]   Wilson to Salisbury, 5 October 1897, emphasis added.
[65]   Wilson to Salisbury, 9 November 1897, emphasis added.

84 ISLAM IN UGANDA

repent. This is all I have to say to you. This letter is from Sultan Mbogo Ibn Sultan Suuna.[66]

Mbogo's reply targeted the disparities of power that the mutinous camp actually possessed in comparison to the military, diplomatic and political skill of the British authorities. The whole letter spoke to how British *power* was so formidable that their only alternative was to surrender and obey. Mbogo was the best person to deliver this message, since he had witnessed British military strength in Zanzibar. He could only do that due to his 'obedience', which had been dictated by the nature of his integration into Buganda by Lugard. By the very fact that he had become one of the elite subjects, his British superiors placed Mbogo in a position that compromised his status among some Muslims.

Mbogo influenced others to follow in his stead so as to choose obedience over rebellion. Similar letters followed Mbogo's obedience to the Government from the 'loyal' Sudanese soldiers who reminded the mutinous camp of how 'evil' their actions were; 'Satan' was influencing their actions; and the futility of disobedience and its consequences.[67] This loyal group also sent letters to their counterparts in Buddu, Toro and Unyoro reminding obedience to the British Government and to desist from joining the mutiny, since the Government had improved their welfare and, besides, they could not fight the British whose strength was similar to 'iron' and whose orders were obeyed 'throughout the world'.[68] The four companies in Toro accepted the advice of their colleagues in Kampala as Macdonald noted that they were 'quiet' and 'contented'.[69]

It is not easy to gauge the influence of George Wilson, the Acting Commissioner of Uganda over the internal debate about native Muslims joining the mutiny but Macdonald noted Wilson's 'judgment and skill' in keeping Uganda 'quiet', in spite of being no trained soldier; making sound arrangements for the defence of Kampala; and 'his influence over Mbogo'

---

[66] Mbogo to Officers of Sudanese Mutineers, 19 October 1897. See also Berkeley to Salisbury, 16 May 1898, containing the Report on Mutiny of the Sudanese Troops in the Protectorate.

[67] Letter from Native Officers to Mutineers, not dated; it was signed by: Yuzbashi Abdullah Effendi, Mulazim Tani Ramathan Effendi, Mulazim Tani Bilal Effendi, Mulazim Awal Sabra Effendi and Mulazim Awal Sabaha Effendi.

[68] Native Officers at Kampala to Sudanese Companies in Buddu, Toro and Unyoro; signed by Yuzbashi Abdullah Effendi and Mulazim Ramathane Effendi, not dated.

[69] Macdonald to Salisbury, 12 November 1897.

MUSLIM COMMUNITIES IN THE COLONIAL ERA   **85**

produced the best results regarding the Baganda Muslims, who deserted the Sudanese Mutineers.[70] For his elite influence over the Muslims, the Sultan of Zanzibar decorated Mbogo on behalf of the British Government for his loyalty during the disturbances (mutiny) in the Protectorate.[71] The personality and character of Mbogo has been a divisive issue among Muslims that know this history. In discussions with various Muslim personalities during the course of writing this book, some cast Mbogo as an elite agent hell-bent on appeasing British interests. These believed that British colonial structure prevented Mbogo from joining his co-religionists to support the mutiny. They compared Mbogo to a sellout who had failed the Islamic cause.[72] But others have argued that whoever has criticized Mbogo fails to understand the context that informed his actions and the personality of the man. Mbogo was a careful, collected and calm person who cared for the future of Islam and Muslims in Uganda and the actions that he took worked to strengthen Muslims and carve out a space for Islamic advancement in Uganda. As a powerful agent working within a British structure, Mbogo used the few resources at his disposal to carefully negotiate an outcome favourable to Muslims' interests even though it seemed that Islam had lost out in the Mwera settlement. By refusing to join the mutineers, Mbogo's actions allowed Islam and Muslims to survive and later thrive in Uganda.[73] Meanwhile, Kabaka Mwanga II had 'suddenly and for some unknown cause, left Mengo by canoe to Buddu'.[74]

Ternan made arrangements to secure Buganda by installing Mwanga's son Chwa, already baptized as a Protestant. With Mwanga chased into German territory (Tanganyika) by British forces,[75] Chwa was publicly proclaimed Kabaka with no opposition.[76] With a young, Protestant Kabaka reigning, Muslim containment proceeded, among other settlements, into law (the 1900 Agreement). In the words of Hayes Sadler, Chwa's enthronement vindicated the importance of a Christianized Uganda acting as a bulwark against a Muslim revival in Africa.[77]

---

[70] Ibid.
[71] Berkeley to Hardinge, 12 November 1898.
[72] FGD, Iganga, May 2017.
[73] Interview with AK, Makerere University, 24 July 2017.
[74] Ternan to Salisbury, 9 July 1897.
[75] Ternan to Salisbury, 13 July 1897; ibid, 23 July 1897; Herr von Wulffen, the German commander at Bukoba notified Ternan of Mwanga's imprisonment, in a letter of 22 July 1897.
[76] Ternan to Salisbury, 14 August 1897.
[77] Sadler, 'General Report on the Uganda Protectorate', p. 17.

Framing the Muslim question after 1900: administrative surveillance of Islam and Muslims

This section discusses the transformative phase of colonial governance of Islam and Muslims. Having contained the Muslim threat, the state proceeded to construct an administrative structure that would stabilize colonial government. The administrative structure was intended to surveil Islam and Muslims. Muslim elites became important in playing a custodial role over the masses. Here, colonial administrative governance was undergirded by the violence of enacted laws and ordinances that delineated the boundaries of social relations. Although the colonial state generally governed through a bifurcated system, the customary native authority was actually multifurcated because groups like Muslims were also given a special Muslim law to govern their private affairs. The 1900 Agreement cemented the settled negotiations of the previous decade. As with the Indian experience, the Ugandan Muslim 'community' was born of the colonial moment. Before, Muslims masses had considered themselves the subjects of royal Ganda power on the one hand, while still belonging to their *bika* (clans) on the other. Colonial statecraft separated these Muslim masses from their political authorities and 'made' a community represented by elites, which also became a site of competition between various groups, elites and laymen.[78]

Colonial policy was undergirded by laws such as the Agreement, which legitimated the interventionist role of the state in society.[79] The formal bifurcation of state and society meant that the native was faced with two forms of power originating from two centres. As the colonial state governed the settler community through 'civilized' law, the native authority directed the affairs of the native populations under 'customary' law that was considered static, archaic and uncivilized. In reality, the power of the colonial state also entered the domain of native authority to mediate the formulation of ordinances. As bifurcation became multifurcation, it revealed the contradictory schema of the customary native institution and the deceptive nature of indirect rule as non-intervention. Muslims, for instance, felt subjected to the primary texts of Islamic law, particularly the Quran and Hadith, alongside cultural practices that still bound people. How to navigate around this plethora of identities was the challenge of individuals and groups. The state's solution to this challenge was to forge alliances; Muslim elites were 'chosen' from among the already existing

[78] Devji, 'The Idea of a Muslim Community', p. 111.
[79] Hussin, *The Politics of Islamic Law,* p. 41.

influential personalities.[80] Here, the Muslim question became one of representation. In other words, it was a matter of identifying layers of elites who represented the Muslim masses to the various layers of colonial authorities, both native and central.

The 1900 Agreement was enacted for multiple purposes: to declare the distribution of power among the various centres, establish an administrative structure to support bifurcated government financed from a taxation regime, and found the basis of future social-political relations. In reality however the Agreement resembled a system intended to prop up elite power vis-à-vis others, and looked more like a system of rewards. The award of land estates highlighted this. The 19,600 square miles of Buganda were divided into various proportions awarded to different institutions and individuals. The Christian missionary societies were awarded ninety-two square miles of land as 'private property'. Nuhu Mbogo the Muslim 'chief' received for 'himself and his adherents' twenty-four square miles of land, as individual private property.[81] Unlike for the Christian missions, the Agreement did not allocate any land to the Muslims as a group. Mbogo was also to be paid a life pension of 250 pounds Sterling each year conditioned on his cession of any rights he claimed, which the Agreement had not guaranteed.[82] By allocating land to Mbogo as a Muslim 'chief', the state propped him up as the representative of the Muslim body.

The allocation of land to Nuhu Mbogo has been the subject of immense debate. In referring to Mbogo as 'himself and his adherents', the Agreement was unclear whether it meant close relatives, Muslims belonging to his party or all Muslims in Uganda.[83] A later court decision declared that the land belonged to Mbogo as a 'private' person and not for the Muslim community in Uganda. Mbogo's designated twenty-four square miles comprised Kibuli and Nsambya hills in Kampala but, since he was unable to possess it on time, a dispute emerged between the two Catholic factions: the Verona Fathers and the Mill Hill mission. The colonial state decided to award Nsambya land to the Verona Fathers. Having failed to possess it, Mbogo lost Nsambya land to the Veronas.[84] The legal ambiguity surrounding Mbogo's land bred internal debate among the Muslims to which a partial solution would be provided by allocating ten square miles as 'public' Muslim land, as described in Chapter 4.

---

[80] Maussen, *Colonial and Post-Colonial Governance of Islam*, p. 13.

[81] *The Buganda Agreement, 1900.*

[82] Article 19 of the *Buganda Agreement*, 1900.

[83] Interview with AK, Makerere University, 24 July 2017.

[84] Ibid.

88 ISLAM IN UGANDA

It should be emphasized however that the Muslim identity was not the only determinant of Muslim residence on land. Not every Muslim subsisted on lands given to Nuhu Mbogo or the designated Muslim territories such as Butambala County. Muslims also subsisted on land availed by their relations to ethnic, clan and religious identities. Many non-Muslim chiefs gave land to Muslims through patron-client relations. Muslims also received land as relatives and friends of fellow Muslims. Others subsisted on land because of their ethnic and kinship ties to both landed Muslims and non-Muslims; in many ways, many people did not perceive land through political lenses.[85] Land became a critical resource because of the effect of the Agreement, which had confiscated various lands and given them to the colonial authorities that constructed a landed gentry in Uganda. The intention was to intensify the erosion of *butaka* holdings on land by channelling it to the peasantry, which was more productive in colonial cash crop production.[86] This invited a backlash from an organized *butaka* movement (founded by various clans in 1922) that led to a lengthy court case.[87] Eventually, the colonial government informed Katikkiro Apollo Kaggwa that the *bataka* issue was a Buganda matter in which the central government would not intervene[88], with Kaggwa advised to find a solution to it.

When Mbogo was 'ordered' to live at Nakasero hill (in Kampala), with a few of his adherents, under the watchful and protective gaze of the colonial authorities (Wilson's 'honourable surveillance'), this separated him from his group, leading to two critical consequences: first, it weakened the Muslims who had settled in Butambala by denying them 'royal' leadership to articulate political demands; and second, it split the Muslim faction when a new elite force took advantage of Mbogo's leadership vacuum in rural counties to claim representation. When Abdallah Ssekimwanyi used this leadership vacuum to establish himself as leader of another Muslim faction in Butambala, opposed to Mbogo and his successor (Badru Kakungulu), it began the Juma-Zukuuli disputes, as will be

[85] Ibid.
[86] Mamdani, Mahmood (1976), *Politics and Class Formation in Uganda*, Monthly Review Press: London, pp. 123–4.
[87] Secretariat Minute Paper, no. b 902 on Native Land and other reference to other Papers associated with issues of Bataka Land disputes – Buganda, 1925; Bataka Community (nd), *The Baganda Landholding Community*, Uganda Printing and Publishing: Kampala.
[88] Acting Governor Jarvis, speech to a special meeting of the Lukiiko, October 1926.

shown in the penultimate section of this chapter. Mbogo's acquisition of land, regardless of its private character, had implications on the future of the Muslim question in Uganda arising from the location and tenure of the land in question. Of his twenty-four square miles, Kibuli hill measured three hundred and twenty acres.

Writing on colonial Tunisia, Clancy-Smith has argued that elite representation of Muslim masses became more pronounced in the urban areas. As a linkage of spaces beyond itself, urban areas functioned as nodes linking people to other destinations. The effective management of urban centres as spaces of 'people in motion' was important because such people 'thwart or bedevil state efforts to impose social legal categories that devised to manage population and resources'. This reality meant that colonialism was 'continually in the making since its policies owed much to the 'nagging weight of pre-colonial pasts, to diverse forms of resistance from below'.[89] This urban experience in elite representation was not however limited to Tunisia alone but was widespread in many colonies. The outcomes of such elite representation in urban areas reflected the convergence of diverse powers in creating a new political, legal and moral landscape.[90] For the case of Uganda in the 1900s, Kibuli was transforming into an urban centre as new social demographics emerged to reduce its physical isolation.[91]

Mbogo moved from Nakasero to Kibuli to create space for a new generation of settlers. His new home, however spacious, was poorly located, as it was cut off from the Kibuga by the Nakivubo swamp and from Mengo (native administration) by the Kayunga swamp. To access Mengo, one had to move around the south of Nsambya, which further complicated Kibuli's physical isolation from the urbanizing influence.[92] For tax obligations, colonial law required the cooperation of the landlord but, for accountability, Kibuli was under the jurisdiction of Apollo Kaggwa, the Katikkiro of Buganda. Having re-settled Mbogo at Kibuli, it became important for the Chief Secretary to have knowledge of possible heads of Muslims in other areas. A survey was therefore sent out to various provincial commissioners

---

[89] Clancy-Smith, Julia (2011), 'Ruptures? Governance in Husaynid-Colonial Tunisia, c. 1870–1914' in Maussen Marcel, et al. (Eds) (2011), *Colonial and Post-Colonial Governance of Islam: Continuities and Ruptures,* Amsterdam University Press: Amsterdam, p. 72, 66.

[90] Asad, Talal (2001), 'Thinking About Secularism and Law in Egypt' *ISIM Occasional Paper,* ISIM: Leiden, p. 4.

[91] Solzbacher, Regina (1969), 'Continuity Through Change in the Social History of Kibuli', *Uganda Journal,* Vol. 33, No. 2, pp. 163–74, p. 166.

[92] Ibid.

with one uniform question: was Prince Mbogo the recognized head of the Muslim Community in the various provinces? The Chief Secretary did not intimate the reason for the question but a few explanations are deduced.

Having brought areas outside Buganda under British control, it was important to know the status of Muslim leadership in those areas; second, some of the new immigrants, especially in the Asian settler communities, included Muslim groups belonging to various sects of whose leadership the government was ignorant; third, since Lugard had made Mbogo an absentee landlord in Butambala, it was important to investigate the nature of the Muslim leadership that had sprung up from the vacuum and how to manage it. Later events in the intra-Muslim disputes would reveal this, as shown below. The Chief Secretary's survey received replies that confirmed Mbogo's popularity among the 'Sunni sect of Muslims' among whom he had 'great influence' in the heads of Sunni communities not only from Mbale but as far as Teso and Pallisa eastern Uganda and Lango in the north, and 'as a leading man even at Mombasa' (Kenya coast). The District Commissioner of Eastern Region concluded that he could not ascertain whether Mbogo was the recognized 'head' of the Sunni communities in those areas, but he was influential.[93] This interest in 'Sunni Muslim' leadership arose from the colonial desire to keep 'fanaticism' at bay; a critical matter that informed the grant or denial of privileges such as poll tax exemptions.

Colonial governance and the settler Muslim

As mentioned earlier, the settler population also contained Muslim groups that were internally differentiated. Generally governed under civil law, Sharia was also allowed a quasi-public space in matters that did not threaten the security of the state. The Asian community has a long historical presence in East Africa that ranges from multiple themes including the Indian Ocean as a 'sea of debt', oscillating between merchant businessmen on the coast and indentured workers in the construction of the Uganda railway.[94] This history of Indian Ocean 'economic life' bound the various actors in obligations that had implications on the social dimensions of commerce, especially religious syncretism. The Asian community consisted of

[93] District Commissioner to Chief Secretary, 27 November 1913.
[94] Bishara, *A Sea of Debt*, pp. 20–22; also Gregory, Robert C. (1993), *South Asians in East Africa: An Economic and Social History, 1890–1980*, Westview Press: Boulder, pp. 11–12.

Muslim groups that affiliated with Shias, Khojas, Boras[95] and Ahmadiyya groups. The colonial state feared these Muslim groups for reasons to do with indoctrinating 'fanatical' religious ideologies. Their location under settler civil law compounded this fear, since it placed the Asian Muslims in a privileged position vis-à-vis the native Muslims. For the settler Muslims, Islamic Sharia was accorded a quasi-public presence. The degree of its application depended on the implications of the issues involved, what was acceptable and could be 'accommodated', or what was not.

A case arose in which the Kampala Sunni Muslim Mosque applied for a poll tax exemption for Maulavi Rahmat Ali Khan, the acting Imam.[96] In reply to the application, the Director of Education advised the Chief Secretary on his findings regarding the request. Noting his visit to the School in the Kampala Muslim Sunni Mosque, he concluded that the personality of the Maulavi appeared 'decent enough' but looked like a 'fanatic'. His concern was beyond the actual issue of tax exemptions, which seemed trivial; he was more concerned with the implications of this gesture especially the 'principle' that government should give 'sympathetic support to a missionary movement from India' which was Islamic. He expected the Indians (Muslims) to fight the issue 'to the last ditch', and if successful, this would bring out 'a considerable number of [Muslim] missionaries'. Even this would have been of little concern were it not for the possibility of the introduction of 'sectarian' (read reformist) Muslim 'teachers', which was likely to cause 'friction among the African Muslims', and the 'political trouble that might arise'.

The Director proceeded to advise the Chief Secretary that sound policy required Government to formulate an official stance on *secularizing* the Muslim schools to prevent African children being taught by 'Indian School masters', and suggested that a suitable Muslim of 'Shaafi denomination' be procured from Zanzibar to advise the Provincial Commissioner on Muslim questions and to train Muslim teachers'.[97] The Director did not reveal the intentions of suggesting a Shafii sheikh from Zanzibar to become the government advisor on Muslim questions. We can surmise however that the desire to contain fanatical tendencies led to intervention

---

[95] Khojas and Bohoras are people of Indian descent who migrated to eastern Africa especially during the colonial era. Both belong to the Ismaili sect of Shia Islam.

[96] Fakhar Din to Colonial Chief Secretary, 23 March 1925, Kampala Archives, A.58.

[97] Director of Education to Colonial Chief Secretary, 10 September 1925, Kampala Archives, C. 865.

in communal spaces, which bred spatial divisions among groups. On another occasion, an application to construct a masjid in Jinja by the Ethna Ashari and Khojas communities was denied because of lack of 'leases' for 'non-Europeans'. The refusal letter did not mention that there was a nearby masjid belonging to the Sunni community.[98]

Among the Muslims within the Asian settler community, a debate arose as to what 'true' Islam meant and which sect represented it. A dispute arose from Sunni attempts to close the debate on what 'Islam' is and choose themselves as its representatives. The issue began with the attempts to change its nomenclature, 'Sunni Muslim Community', by which it was known, to the 'Muslim Association'. The Ahmadiyya sect led the agitation and took the matter to the Chief Secretary. In a letter, the Secretary of the Ahmadiyya Movement in Kampala was concerned that the desire of the Sunni community to become known as the 'Muslim Association' was prejudicial and detrimental to the 'various sub-divisions of Muslims' since they pretended to represent the 'different sects of Muslims' yet in 'reality' they were 'interested in their own sect' wherein they denied admission to all the others, who were all 'Muslims'. The Ahmadiyya secretary noted that allowing the Sunnis to become the 'Muslim Association' would deceive the authorities that it was 'responsible' for all Muslim sects yet this was untrue. He thus pleaded with the authorities to force them to revert to their old title (Sunni Muslim Community), thereby 'giving an opportunity to every sect of Islam to lay their grievances individually and not through a unilateral Association'.[99] It would seem that in the closed nature of these new Muslim Asian settler communities, familial and religious bonds were so tight that it was easy to identify who belonged (inclusion) and who did not (exclusion). Thus, the Ahmadiyya feared that the Sunni attempts to create a Muslim Association were equivalent to eliminating the Islamic character of the other sects.

Yet, why the Ahmadiyya came to question Sunni power posturing begs more research. The motto of their movement was inscribed with the words: 'Ahmadiya Movement: The *Only True* Manifestation of Islam in these days' (this author's emphasis). This battle between 'truth' and 'falsehood' was manifested in an issue that seemed trivial yet gigantic for its communal, national and international implications. And it furthered a vocabulary of ridicule regarding 'authenticity'. More critically, it revealed the extent to which the colonial state could accommodate Sharia within

---

[98] Land Officer to Provincial Commissioner, Eastern Province, Jinja, 29 July 1919.

[99] Secretary of Ahmadiya Movement to Chief Secretary, 4 November 1932.

the settler Muslim community. The matter began with the death of Anwar Ahmad, an eight-month child of Doctor Laldin Ahmad, who belonged to the Ahmadiya sect. The matter of his burial was to involve the Ahmadiya Movement in India, the Indian Government, the Uganda Chief Secretary and all his attendants. Under what custom was the deceased to be buried especially because the colonial state had reserved one 'Muslim cemetery' (in Kololo) yet the Muslim sects considered themselves diverse, each practising contradictory principles. The Secretary of the Sunni Muslim Community visited the parents of the deceased and paid his respects but he denied space for the child to be buried in what he considered 'Muslim cemetery' where the Ahmadiyya were excluded.

The attitude of Sunni leadership arose from how they perceived the Ahmadiyya sect; it was not 'Islamic'. On the poster of the Ahmadiyya Movement, below their motto was written the words 'In the Name of Allah ... We praise Him and invoke His Blessing upon His noble Prophet Muhammad and "Ahmad" the Promised Messiah'. The last phrase '"Ahmad" the Promised Messiah' had convinced the other Muslim sects that the Ahmadiyya were outside Islam since, according to them, the line of messengers had ended with Prophet Muhammad (PBUH). When the Ahmadiyya approached the Sunni secretary to arrange the boy's burial, he showed sympathies but declined to allow burial in the cemetery. This enraged the family and the Ahmadiyya members, who issued insults. When the Kampala District Commissioner was approached, the Sunni secretary still insisted that the boy would not be buried in the Muslim Cemetery since the Ahmadiyya were 'non-Muslims'. The secretary of the movement was astounded how the Sunnis could behave in such a manner yet the Ahmadiyya Movement was 'the only true manifestation of Islam so widely known throughout the world', believing that such Sunni behaviour stemmed from 'their ignorance and narrow-mindedness' since the treatment of the Ahmadiyya during the attempted burial was 'most inhuman and unsympathetic'.

Although another Muslim community, the Ethna Ashari Jammat (Twelver Shii) offered a burial place in their line of the same graveyard, the Ahmadiyya declined because they wanted to settle the burial issue in case of future deaths for their members. The Chief Secretary was requested to condemn the action of the Sunni Muslim Community.[100] The news regarding Anwar Ahmad's burial was telegrammed to the Foreign Secretary

---

[100] Secretary, Ahmadiya Association, Kampala to Chief Secretary, 22 February 1932.

94   ISLAM IN UGANDA

of the Ahmadiyya Community in India, who in turn communicated his dismay to the Chief Secretary at Entebbe reminding him that Sunni actions were illegal and painful to the Ahmadiyya Community already declared 'Muslims' by the Indian high courts of Madras and Patna'.[101] It would seem that Sunni recalcitrance was born of the fact that the Ahmadiyya had needed a human court sitting in India to declare their Islamic character, which went contrary to Sunni belief that only Allah declared a community Islamic. Regardless, the burial of Anwar Ahmad sparked off a wave of official conversation about what the Ahmadiyya Association would later call 'Sunni Tyranny'. The Foreign Secretary of the Ahmadiyya Community in India notified the Indian Government who, in turn, sent a telegram to the Chief Secretary in Entebbe requesting a 'brief report' of the alleged incident.[102] The Ahmadiyya Association in Bombay also telegrammed the Chief Secretary in Entebbe reminding him of the Government's duty to protect Ahmadis' rights by reversing the 'Sunni tyranny' of preventing Anwar's burial; that the plea of 'non-Muslim' directed against Ahmadis was 'ridiculous fanaticism overruled by Indian high courts'.[103]

Before the Government could pronounce itself on the matter, the Ahmadiyya Association lodged a formal request for a 'separate graveyard' to bury their dead, which required urgent attention.[104] The matter went to the Provincial Commissioner who undertook a census to discover that the Ahmadiyya Community numbered about thirty members, and was the newest entry into the settler Muslim community. His basic research discovered doctrinal differences as the cause of resentment directed at the Ahmadiyya Community from the other Muslim sects. To avoid conflict, the Provincial Commissioner advised the demarcation of an additional piece of ground, adjoining the Muslim Cemetery that was already subdivided among other communities; and requested that the Kampala Township Authority should consider a further extension to cater for future need arising from the increasing population; the proposed extension to be allocated to the Ahmadiyya sect would be demarcated to include the spot where Anwar Ahmad was to be buried.[105] The Chief Secretary telegrammed the Government of India noting that the Ahmadiyya situation in Kampala

[101] Foreign Secretary Ahmadiyya Community to Chief Secretary Entebbe, 24 February 1932.
[102] Secretary of Ahmadiyya Community to the Government of India, 5 March 1932.
[103] Ahmadiyya Association to Chief Secretary, 7 March 1932.
[104] Mohammedan Secretary to Chief Secretary (received) 7 March 1932.
[105] Provincial Commissioner Kampala to Chief Secretary 14 March 1932.

was 'under consideration';[106] approved the suggestion of the Provincial Commissioner;[107] the Kampala Township Authority approved the site of the proposed cemetery;[108] communicated to the Ahmadiyya sect;[109] furnished the Chief Secretary with a plan;[110] and prepared to publish the information in the Gazette Notice.[111] These sect-based burials were later reconsidered, due to overcrowding: the Kololo cemetery was extended[112] and gazetted as a general cemetery for the burial of all persons of the Islamic faith without regard to differences in sect.[113]

The foregoing debates regarding intra-Muslim disputes gained importance for a number of reasons. First, they concerned a Muslim community that lived under settler law; in various ways, they were privileged since they belonged to the second tier of society (after the Europeans) under an already classified society, regardless of its internal differentiations.[114] Within the settler category, Sharia could be allowed a quasi-public domain in issues that directly implicated the security of religious groups. Second, the Muslims in this settler category were, in many ways, an extension of their groups from India, which allowed them another layer of 'protection' thereby insulating them from any indicators of 'tyranny'. Third, since these groups were extending to Uganda from India, it was desired that the Ugandan government implement colonial policy already reached in India, as in the decision on the Islamic character of the Ahmadiyya. Fourth, as already highlighted, the matters involved were such that could be accommodated and not considered 'heavy' that would require forced dealing with the state, which would, in this case, have escalated the issue with a government that laboured to postulate its humanity. Before engaging the intra-Muslim debate among the native Muslims, it is important to

---

[106] Secretary to Government of India, Code telegram dispatched 22 March 1932.

[107] Chief Secretary to Provincial Commissioner, Buganda, 24 March 1932.

[108] Provincial Commissioner Buganda to Chief Secretary, 25 April 1932.

[109] Executive Officer, Township Authority, Kampala to Ahmadiyya Sect, 23 April 1932.

[110] Ibid, 12 May 1932.

[111] Land Officer to Chief Secretary, 29 July 1932.

[112] Secretary for Social Services and Local Government to The Resident, Buganda, 17 September 1953 and the reply of the Resident on 22 September 1953.

[113] The Public Health Ordinance, Mohammedan Cemetery, Kampala, Legal Notice No. 242 of 10 October 1953, cancelling Legal Notice No. 88 of 1932. Since the dead did not ask for particular graves, this law somewhat prevented the living from representing them.

[114] Mamdani, *Politics and Class Formation in Uganda,* Heinemann: London.

96   ISLAM IN UGANDA

focus on the educational aspect, since it transformed the native subjection to the state.

Education policy and Islam

Education policy also influenced the Muslim question in Uganda especially in how it nurtured a particular way of life by teaching the Muslim students 'secular' knowledge, attempting to ensure that they would abandon their 'fanatical' ideologies and at the same time acquire relevant knowledge that would contribute to the colonial economy. Louis Althusser has identified 'ideology' as an important 'level' of the state structure, alongside others, in his interpretation of the Marxist theory of the state.[115] Engaging the concept of 'respective indices of effectivity', Althusser argues that the ideological state apparatus includes specialized institutions like schools (the educational), which belong to the *public* domain due to the state's desire to direct education.[116] Colonial statecraft also reflected its desire to direct education as a function of stability. In colonial Senegal, the French founded *Medersa* (Madrasa) to 'teach an elite of young Muslims how to speak and write in French and at the same time give the proper views' on their perceived French civilizing role in Africa. In St Louis, a *Medersa* was erected in 1908 to complement existing 'normal' colleges; it was the 'best way of combating the Marabouts'. Beyond being a centre of Islamic learning, it had to reflect the 'French spirit' and also serve as 'the most logical form of education in Muslim country, the only one capable of usefully serving our policy whilst at the same time flattering the vanity of the natives'.[117]

British education policy in tropical Africa reflected this. It aimed at improving the conditions of the people, understood as a transition from 'heathenism' to 'civilization'. As the 'primary concern of Government' it was to become the 'first charge on revenue'.[118] Since the Government had no schools of its own, it had to support those of the missions. In 1912, proposals were made to provide education-improving grants to the three Christian missions. The criteria of this choice owed much to their rendering of 'exceptional and valuable services' in the 'spread of civilization

---

[115] Althusser, Louis (1971), *Lenin and Philosophy and Other Essays,* Monthly Review Press: London, p. 134.

[116] Althusser, *Lenin and Philosophy,* p. 144, emphasis added.

[117] Harrison, *France and Islam in West Africa,* pp. 62–3.

[118] Education Policy in British Tropical Africa, 13 March 1925, Kampala Archive, S.112, p. 4.

and education among the natives'.[119] These grants could however be discontinued when the Government took a direct interest in educational work.[120] When the grants were actually made to the CMS, the White Fathers' Mission and the Mill Hill Mission in the financial year 1913–14, the Government advised that they should be used not only for 'general educational purposes' but also for '*specific purposes*'.[121] What 'specific purposes' meant was to put acquired skills into practice. Although these purposes began with the improvement of local skills like 'mats, basket making and pottery',[122] encouraging industriousness in the people led to the establishment of technical schools.

On the whole, education had to inculcate a comprehensive transformation among society: it had to begin by improving what was 'sound in indigenous tradition'. To this end, education policy recommended that institutions should focus on strengthening the 'feeling of responsibility to the tribal community', 'will power', sensitizing the 'conscience' to moral and intellectual 'truth' while imparting some power to discriminate good from evil or 'reality and superstition'. It was understood that religious teaching and 'moral instruction' in the schools and training colleges had to accord 'equal standing' to the 'secular' subjects that related to the 'conditions of life and to the daily experiences of the pupils' expressed in habits of 'self-discipline' and communal loyalty. These were the 'safeguards' to protect the native 'contact with civilization' from injury and to balance the 'new religious ideas' with the 'constituted secular authority'.[123]

As the colonial state came to stabilize, it became increasingly important to embed its 'regime of compulsions' in institutions that represented 'civility' but whose undercurrent reflected the violent rules that transformed social relations. Education was one such institution. The system of missionary education in formal institutions that was introduced in various areas transformed social relations in many places where the schools were located. In these educational institutions, 'squads of boys' were to be instructed in disciplines, such as agriculture in the 'Government Plantation' to enable 'knowledge of produce culture' particularly, of cotton plantation. Although this contributed to the colonial economy, its effect was also socio-political. Since many of the 'squads of boys' were sons of chiefs,

---

[119]   Jackson to Colonial Secretary, 27 December 1911.

[120]   Chief Secretary to Colonial Secretary, 16 April 1912.

[121]   Harcourt to Jackson, 11 June 1912, emphasis added.

[122]   Colonial Annual Report, Uganda, 1908–09, pp. 18–19.

[123]   Education Policy in British Tropical Africa, 13 March 1925, Kampala Archive, S.112, pp. 3–4.

with the intention of educating a breed of future administrators – and soon sister schools were established for the 'daughters of chiefs' at Gayaza (Kyaddondo), Namasagali (Kyaggwe) and Bwanda (Buddu) – the effect was to transform Uganda society through these 'model citizens'. After the death of Nuhu Mbogo, the state imagined a new representative for the Muslim community. His heir, Kakungulu, had to become a 'model citizen' for the Muslim community, generally, and particularly for its youth.

Education policy influenced the Muslim question especially after the death of Nuhu Mbogo in 1921. Two issues disturbed the colonial authorities: first, how to sustain elite control over the Muslim masses after Mbogo, the Muslim 'chief', had passed on; second, who should be the appropriate individual with the requisite character to provide leadership to the Muslim masses? The answer to the first concern was to prop up another elite to continue Mbogo's role; his son Badru Kakungulu was chosen as the heir to both his father's estate and 'status' as the chosen representative of Muslims. Choosing Kakungulu predetermined the answer to the second concern. As a young prince, it was important that his education focused on the 'secular' knowledge as opposed to a sole emphasis on 'Islamic' knowledge. This had two implications: first, it would bring him closer to 'Western' knowledge and therefore ground 'respect' for the colonial authority as the guardians of 'civilization', unlike his father who 'feared' British means of violence. Second, educating Kakungulu in 'secular' knowledge would influence Muslim masses to consider 'secular' education. The critical factor that informed these developments was the 'growing realization of the urgency of finding alternatives' to naked violence as a tool of colonial statecraft.[124]

Education provided an alternative formula to dealing with the Muslim groups. The education system began with imparting knowledge but with the higher goal of directing the consciences of the 'multitude' in Uganda. The institutions of education were located in the towns (capitals) of particular provinces from which they radiated into the countryside. This urban location was important because the township 'academies' were the sources of the 'sciences and truth' that would spread to the countryside.[125] The impact of these institutions of formal education was extensive. These schools came to represent a new route to social advancement, which was initially attained by negotiating favours for the Kabaka and his chiefs. The Ganda concept of '*okulya obwaami*' (attain a higher social status) is

---

[124] Harrison, *France and Islam in West Africa*, p. 57.
[125] Foucault, *Security, Territory, Population*, p. 14.

identified with this social advancement. As the colonial system intensified the commoditized economy, formal education promised jobs and salaries to its students; these formed a new class of colonial clerks. Consequently, education weakened the social base of Uganda society since youth spent time in school as opposed to learning the 'traditional' ways of their societies.[126] Catholic and Protestant missionaries managed the formal educational institutions, which may not in itself have been a fundamental problem,but when knowledge was designated as 'secular' and fenced off from its 'Islamic' other, it revealed a colonial intention to inculcate Western civilization as opposed to particular versions of Islam.

Kibuli had operated a Madrasa (Islamic school) to teach Quran and other 'Islamic' knowledge. However, the absence of 'secular' institutions at Kibuli so bothered the colonial administration that they founded a primary school there in 1922, one year after the death of Mbogo. The school was intended to impart 'secular' knowledge to Badru Kakungulu, whose earlier education had consisted of Arabic and Islamic studies. Disputes began as to what sort of education Kakungulu was to acquire as he was considered a person of 'social-political importance'.[127] In the end, Kakungulu's 'conscience' was to become 'secularized'. To consolidate its recommendations, British educational policy had stressed the role of 'inputs' (teachers and technical persons) with a particular 'intellectual' 'character' and 'technical' ability to enable 'social progress'. The 'outlook', 'capacity' and 'enthusiasm' of such inputs was critical to attracting the 'best available men, both British and African, to effecting education policy'.[128] As both 'student' and 'leader' of the Muslim masses, Kakungulu was one of the 'best available men'. As the new leader of the Muslim community, his 'secular' education would enable him learn the logic of 'Western civilization' and use his influence to convince Muslim masses to take their youth to the mission schools.

Kakungulu's study at Buddo in 1925 was symbolic. It emerged within the context when the colonial government ceased to consider the Muslims as a 'dangerous' political force able to 'threaten' its interests.[129] At the same time, since Mbogo's status as a Buganda royal had played a

---

[126] Kiyimba, Abasi (2001), *Gender Stereotypes in the Folktales and Proverbs of the Baganda,* PhD Thesis, Dar es Salaam, p. 8.

[127] Kasozi, A.B.K. (1996), *The Life of Prince Badru Kakungulu Wasajja and the Development of a Forward-Looking Muslim Community in Uganda, 1907–1991,* Progressive: Kampala, pp. 47–53.

[128] British Education Policy in Tropical Africa, p. 4.

[129] Kasozi, *The Life of Prince Badru Kakungulu Wasajja,* p. 53.

moderating influence within the Muslim community, it was prudent that his heir continued that role in a new way. Kakungulu would cause Muslims to reflect and consider that 'secular' education was not as bad as thought; one could still be a Muslim and educated as well – although his royal status privileged his stay at Buddo as a Muslim.[130] Regardless of its outcomes, Kakungulu's 'secular' education symbolized an alternative path to a Muslim's advancement beyond focusing on Islamic studies. It allowed the state to reduce the emphasis on Islamic knowledge and Arab language, which was considered as providing a wide arena for Islam, accentuating colonial versions of Islam as focusing on such rituals as Salat, *sawm*, *janaza* (burials), marriages and other ceremonies.

The native Muslim response to colonial governance of Islam

How did the native Muslim respond to colonial governance of Islam? What sort of debates emerged from the propping up of the Mbogo/ Kakungulu elitism as the representatives of a hitherto invisible Muslim community? How did counter-elites such as religious theologians contest the power for Muslim representation? How did various Muslim masses challenge the containerizing policies of the colonial state and its elitism to establish alternative centres of Muslim representation? And how did the colonial and elite authorities, in turn, react to such multiple centres of Muslim representation that thereby elevated Islam from its political oblivion? These questions are reflected in the internal debates that arose from within the native Muslim community regarding a few issues: partaking of state privileges (e.g. poll tax exemptions), the Juma-Zukuuli schism (see the following section), the influence of Ganda Muslims outside Buganda and the management of native Muslim land. The attempts to resolve these issues highlighted both the internal politics among the native Muslim community and the attitude of the colonial government over Muslims' affairs: where state stability was threatened, state action was prompt; where not, indifference prevailed.

---

[130] Other Muslim students such as Yusuf Kironde Lule were forced to convert to Christianity as a condition of continuing at Buddo. At Mwiri, in Busoga, privilege played a crucial role to prevent Muslim students from converting to Christianity in mission schools. Students like Abu Mayanja and Anas Kinyiri maintained their Islamic identity in Mwiri because of royal support; others were either converted or chased out, as one revealed. FGD, Iganga, 3 November 2016.

Propping up elites like Mbogo and Kakungulu as the representatives of Islam had allowed the government to marginalize Muslim masses and thereby suppress Muslim autonomy. Its intention was to cultivate a particular ritualistic form of Islam (as opposed to the political) to deny Muslim masses resources of opposing power: the state 'produced new technologies of power, new discourses of resistance, and new hierarchies of knowledge',[131] which worked in the following ways. Under the official bifurcation of society, the native Muslim became a subject of the native authority such that Sharia was governed under customary law. The respective Muslim leaders of the community concerned governed such Muslim 'private' issues as marriage and divorce, death and inheritance. This was so because the Muslims appealed to Mbogo to insist on a separate legal arrangement to govern Muslim social life, especially the right to polygamy.[132] However, the very circumscription of Islam to the ritualistic and the marginalization of Muslim affairs produced the opposite effects: it centralized Islam in the state and brought it to the fore of policy dialogue. As Muslim practices were pushed to the private domain like masjids, new elites emerged to defend the masses against interventions from both the state and opposing elites. The native administration created committees to deal with native Muslim issues on a daily basis using a system of communication based on letter writing, which promised action, although many times not forthcoming; other times noting reference or awaiting feedback from the central authority. Since the power of the Chief Secretary superseded the native administration, the colonial state reserved its right, reason and circumstance to either interfere or not in native Muslim affairs. This back-and-forth movement frustrated the native Muslims and placed them in a position of surrender and humbleness whereby access to many entitlements depended on the mercy of the two administrations. As the state consolidated the power of some Muslim elites to represent the masses, some forces emerged to breed new elites. As a consequence, the nature of opposition to elite power and to the state also changed.[133]

---

[131] Hussin, *The Politics of Islamic Law,* pp. 38–9.
[132] It is this understanding that the Domestic Relations Bill, proposed in 2003 but never passed, would attempt to nullify by describing Muslim polygamy as 'unjust'. See Kiyimba, Abasi (2012), 'The Domestic Relations Bill and Inter-Religious Conflict in Uganda: A Muslim Reading of Personal Law and Religious Pluralism in a Postcolonial Society' in Smith, James H. and Hackett, Rosalind I.J. (Eds) (2012), *Displacing the State: Religion and Conflict in Neoliberal Africa,* University of Notre Dame: Notre Dame, pp. 240–80.
[133] Hussin, *The Politics of Islamic Law,* p. 34.

102   ISLAM IN UGANDA

When the state brought Nuhu Mbogo to settle at Kampala (later at Kibuli) it had created a power vacuum in Butambala, which meant that his successor, Prince Badru Kakungulu would inherit this vacuum. Pressure came from Twaibu Magatto the Ssaza Chief of Butambala who felt that the Muslims in that district needed daily leadership. Magatto got support from Abdallah Ssekimwanyi (a religious scholar) to challenge Kakungulu's leadership of the native Muslims. When in 1922, a theological question emerged as to whether the Jumuah (Friday congregation) could be said alongside the daily *Dhuhur* (afternoon Salat) the native Muslim community was split into two. One side believed that Jumuah was said without Dhuhur on Friday, the other arguing that both could be said on Friday. The 'Jumuah Only' group became the Juma sect while the Jumuah and Dhuhur practitioners became Juma-Zukuuli ('Zukuuli' being the Luganda phonetic equivalent of Dhuhur). Initially, their practices involved giving sermons challenging the other group's knowledge regarding the issue. However, with time, open hostilities emerged that 'threatened' order and stability and they were forced in 1924 to agree to await a government mediator. These contestations that engulfed the Muslim public over the theological debates on Dhuhur Salat in Jumuah revealed the determination of new actors to replace old elites in representing Muslim masses. The emerging issues were framed around the discourse of Islamic theology but, regardless of the outcomes, the politics generated reveals that the matter went beyond theology to representation. Theological differences need not transform into political communities and cause conflict but they actually did, owing to the context of limited exertion in Islamic knowledge among Muslims at the time. As a result, the Juma-Zukuuli impasse was about 'who spoke for Muslims' and 'for Islamic law', and who could 'interpret and change it, and along what lines'.[134]

Twaibu Magatto, Hajji Abudalla Ssekimwanyi, Sabitu Kityo, Abudala Kuwala, Masudi Kisasa, Kalifani Mubalaka, Abudalazake Jambe, Ali Banadawa and Muhamadi Kironde, witnessed by Sir Apollo Kaggwa, Katikkiro, signed a 'secession of hostilities' agreement. The signatories agreed to 'live in peace' and to immediately cease all hostilities towards each other regarding the 'theological interpretations' of Islam while awaiting the decision of the 'khadi' procured by the 'Colonial Government' to decide on the matter. Masudi Kisasa signed on behalf of Prince Badru Kakungulu.[135] Upon procurement, the khadi advised that the Jumuah and

---

[134]   Ibid., p. 32.
[135]   Agreement between Juma and Zukuuli Muslim factions, 10 November 1924, Kampala, See also Kasozi, *The Life of Prince Badru Kakungulu Wasajja.*

MUSLIM COMMUNITIES IN THE COLONIAL ERA 103

Dhuhur issue was a theological matter whose resolution native Muslims were not ready for due to their limited Islamic knowledge; each camp would continue practising what they believed right. In 'procuring' a khadi to advise on Muslim disputes of an Islamic nature, the state had cultivated a new 'vision of Islam that was more patriarchal and state-centered',[136] one that confirmed the state's role as the arbiter of Muslim issues. Critically, the khadi's advice reflected the need to maintain the ideological status quo by arguing against the practice of potentially destabilizing doctrines. In facilitating interpretations of Islam that maintained its order and logic, the colonial state ensured a careful balance between overarching logics and the resources required to maintain its systems of local authority. Gradually, this became unsustainable as further hostilities revealed elite suppression of individual Muslim autonomy. As a consequence, rival institutions claiming to represent the Muslim masses emerged when 'reformers' differed on the trajectory of the reform agenda. These used multiple spaces such as masjids (*darasa* and *khutba*) and other ceremonies (marriage and burial) as sites to perform persuasive discourses that would win over Muslim alliances.

The 'trouble' emerged from one Ali Sherif Ali bin Mohamed, a Muslim in the settler category, who claimed to be interested in teaching the 'proper' Islamic practices including Jumuah. His teachings caused dissension among native Muslims, leading to fights over masjids. Opposing sects began to oust each other from Jumuah and a Mu'alim from one sect could not lead the Jumuah Salat of another camp. Ali Sherif's entry caused some destabilized native Muslims – led by Kakungulu – to seek the assistance, again, of the colonial government on an issue that was 'likely to cause trouble' since it had caused some masjids, both near (Bombo, north of Kampala) and far (Arua, north-west Uganda) to close.[137] These feuds threatened Kakungulu's leadership of the Muslim community in Buganda and beyond; his entourage intended to seek colonial assistance to settle intra-Muslim disputes. The Chief Secretary learned that the Ssaza Chief of Butambala, Musa Ssebalu and his Sheikh Abdallah Ssekimwanyi supported Ali Sherif. He requested the Governor to look into the matter by enforcing the original decision of the khadi and ridiculed Ali Sherif whom he called a heretic taking advantage of 'local Moslems' from whom he solicited 'alms' to survive.[138]

---

[136] Hussin, *The Politics of Islamic Law,* p. 55.
[137] Johnston Davies c/o Baganda Muslims to Chief Secretary, 9 April 1930.
[138] Chief Secretary to Treasurer, 29 June 1933.

The Chief Secretary felt that Ssebalu's and Ssekimwanyi's support for Ali Sherif (heretic or not) was a 'religious matter' in which it was 'not possible for the Government to interfere' as long as the 'adherents' kept within the laws of the country. He noted that although the khadi had 'furnished the government and the disputants' with an opinion regarding the doctrinal issues involved between certain sections of the 'native Muslims', it was beyond 'the intention of Government to enforce' any opinion 'connected with religion'. He advised that the matter be referred to the Provincial Commissioner (Buganda) who would 'endeavour' to 'adjust' the differences by 'discussion and advice'. He also reiterated that if this course had been taken 'without success' then there was no further action for the Government to undertake.[139]

The Buganda Provincial Commissioner replied to Kakungulu regretting inaction since it was not a matter that concerned 'the Government'; Ali Sherif was a visitor on 'his own account' without 'power' to make 'orders' of any nature. He denounced Ali Sherif's possible connection with Government as some Muslims had insinuated while reminding Kakungulu that Ali Sherif was entitled to 'his own opinions' regarding Jumuah and Dhuhuri, ones that none were called to abide by unless they wished so.[140] Inaction was defended by the fact that the Ali Sherif matter had not become a serious 'threat' to the leadership of Kakungulu as to require the direct intervention of the Government. Provincial administrations that represented native authority insulated the central authority by directing grievances to particular offices that dealt with malcontent. So, then as it were, the state agents continued to remind each other of the relevance of the legal divide reflected in the 'approved' policy of indirect rule through native governments wherein they had a 'strong defence' against the insidious effects of anti-British propaganda. Although British colonial law enabled ambitions of political opportunities to 'intelligent' and 'aspiring' natives, which was a positive effect of its governance, it was necessary to prepare for the negative reception in form of symptoms of perceived injustice and oppression. Such protests had to be 'directed' against the Native Government failing which the 'lawful remedy' was in the hands of the aggrieved.[141] The issues surrounding the management of native Muslim land destabilized the Muslim community and enabled new

[139] Chief Secretary's reply to Johnston Davies, 5 May 1930.
[140] Provincial Commissioner (Buganda) to Prince Badru Kakungulu, 22 January 1930.
[141] Gowers to Secretary of State for Colonies, 30 March 1927, CO 536/145/17, pp. 3–4.

centres of Muslim organization to emerge. Since the Agreement did not allocate private land to Muslims as a group, Badru Kakungulu had used his influence among the native authority to request for land, which was to be distributed to the native Muslims as 'public land' and not for their individual benefit as was given to Nuhu Mbogo. The Governor approved ten square miles that were to be distributed equally to the various provinces. As seen above, lay Muslims could subsist on land through other forms of identity such as ethnic and kinship ties to either Muslim or landed non-Muslims.

To accentuate their 'public' character, these ten square miles were described as Designated Mosque Sites and were to be handed over to particular Muslim leaders in particular parts of the country. Three obstacles prevailed against the proper allocation of these lands. First, the native Muslims failed to prepare the cost of transferring the title; and when they found the finances, they were frustrated by the work schedule of the officers of the native Buganda government. Second, the religious schisms that began with the Juma-Zukuuli split divided native Muslims such that the allocating committees had to decide which sheikhs belonged to either group so as to enable equitable distribution.[142] Three, disputes arose from the dynamics of distributing the Designated Mosque Sites. It has been relayed that when land was distributed, the Muslim leaders that received custodianship over them lacked plans and other resources to develop the land. As a result, they would invite some relatives to settle on it and, over time, would preserve about one acre of land for a masjid. Except in some areas such as Kalungu in Masaka where Muslim institutions actually benefited from the allocations, other lands were taken over by relatives of the custodians.[143]

As the recognized head of the Sunni Muslims in Buganda, Badru Kakungulu used his position to 'protect' members of the Juma-Zukuuli sect. One event highlighted this internal feud. In a letter to the Governor, Abdallah Ssekimwanyi reported the matter regarding Muslims chased from a masjid in Bugembe, near Jinja. The explanation was that the masjid belonged to Kakungulu who had succeeded Mbogo; the prevailing thinking at the time was that Muslim land belonged to Mbogo. When the Muslims pleaded their ownership over the land, the District Commissioner declined to hear their case. They proceeded to the Provincial Commissioner, who in turn, directed the District Commissioner at Mengo to hear the case. The latter granted the aggrieved

---

[142] Buganda Government, African Muslim Committee, 1930–1952.
[143] Interview with AK, Makerere, 24 July 2017.

party letters that granted access to the masjids. However, upon return, the District Commissioner of Jinja and the Provincial Commissioner, Eastern, refused and confiscated the workbooks in the masjid, with the excuse that those who prayed Juma 'only' had no masjids. Ssekimwanyi informed the Governor that the District and Provincial Commissioners of Jinja and Mengo, Eastern and Buganda respectively, were informed of his predicament. He was also aware that power lay with the authorities of the relevant areas that shared in the same spirit of rule as elsewhere. He quickly reminded the Governor of the weakness of his faction, vis-à-vis the state. Using language of deep respect and humility, Ssekimwanyi appealed to the Governor to intervene and make restitution to the group of the masjids that they themselves built.[144]

The outcome of the investigation into the dismissal of some Muslims from the masjids emphasized the need to securitize society by granting the mosque spaces to the larger number of Muslims. The politics of majority control began to infiltrate social-political governance of society. Since the Kakungulu-led faction had the largest following, the District Commissioners allowed them these spaces; reminded the Ssekimwanyi-led Juma sect to build their own masjids in spaces granted by the native administration,[145] and for Ssekimwanyi and other Ganda Muslims to stop meddling in Muslim affairs outside Buganda. Since some of the disputes in Busoga arose from 'tribal' concerns whereby the Basoga Muslims wanted 'tribesmen' as sheikhs, whereas certain Baganda 'Muslims' wished to maintain domination outside Buganda.[146] Similar events regarding the dismissal from masjids and their takeover by opposite camps took place in the Western Province.[147] The interference of the Baganda Muslims in spaces outside Buganda was considered a serious matter that invoked the ire of the Chief Secretary. Through the Provincial Commissioner, Buganda, the Secretary queried the grounds upon which Ssekimwanyi, a Ganda Muslim, petitioned the Governor to claim representation of interests for natives outside Buganda.[148] Although the disputes continued, as when sheikhs identifying with one sect could not lead the Salat of a

[144] Ssekimwanyi to Governor, 4 July 1931.
[145] Provincial Commissioner Eastern Province to Chief Secretary, July 1931; Provincial Commissioner Western Province to Chief Secretary, 29 July 1931.
[146] Eastern Province to Chief Secretary.
[147] Provincial Commissioner, Western Province to Chief Secretary, 29 July 1931.
[148] Sandford to Provincial Commissioner Buganda, 15 August 1931.

congregation belonging to another[149], or when Badru Kakungulu was derided for failing to decide one case following the Sharia[150], this was acceptable because he had consolidated the boundaries of the milieu within which the Muslims practised a version of Islam guarded by elites. The actions of counter-elites like Ssekimwanyi were considered anathema to colonial stability since they destabilized the existing representation of Muslims.

Colonial governance and opportunities for Muslims' advancement

While it is correct that colonial governance limited the public role of Islam and Muslims to their elite representative, and the bulk of the masses were pushed to the private domain, it consequently built up multiple Muslim alliances set apart from the official state. Since the intentions of the colonial state had been to govern over a 'de-fanaticized' version of Islam – understood as Muslims' acceptance to live under what they believed to be 'Christian power' – the tactics of administrative governance described above reflect success in that regard.

Although intra-Muslim conflicts broke out over masjids and other spaces, not every Muslim was busy fighting. Others turned their inferior situation into opportunity. When Mbogo was separated from the Butambala group and brought to Kampala, Twaibu Magatto (a Muslim chief of Butambala) took advantage of the leadership vacuum in the Muslim group in Butambala to position himself as the elite Muslim representative in that area. Seeing Muslim youth uneducated and possessing no schools for his brethren, he approached the colonial authorities to look into the matter of Muslims' unemployment. He argued that Muslims were ready to take on jobs as cooks, butchers, drivers and others, except washing lavatories, which they refused especially since pork eaters visited them.[151] Twaibu Magatto's request opened the way for a new group of Muslim workers in the colonial state. The status of their work would later become a question for some Muslim leaders who would forever ponder: 'Muslims were integrated in the colonial economy, yes, but as who?'[152] According to the circumstances of the time however Magatto's intervention enabled Muslims to find work to improve themselves and their families. Working in these 'low' positions allowed Muslims

[149] Buwate Masjid Secretary to Mualim Juma Kisule, 15 September 1937.
[150] Majlis Ulama to Kakungulu, 23 January 1938.
[151] Interview with AK, Makerere 24 July 2017.
[152] Interview with HS, Mbale, 1 December 2016.

to organize themselves into groups that benefited from business networks. They therefore came to supply goods, drive buses, lorries and taxis including owning shops and small abattoirs. Asian Muslim business owners also assisted their native Muslim brethren.[153] Muslims thus took advantage of their inferior political status by accepting jobs others considered low, which however proved important since they came to have a role in public affairs. Regardless of how meagre this improvement seemed, these Muslims could not be ignored. They came to dominate public transport and the movement of colonial produce. Although they indirectly serviced the colonial economy, they would later benefit from these undertakings to found successive business ventures.[154]

The Maulid festivals also became avenues to channel Muslims' political issues. As an Islamic festival, the Maulid refers to celebrations of the birthday of the Prophet Muhammad (PBUH). The first Maulid in Uganda was celebrated in 1918, before the death of Nuhu Mbogo. Since then it came to feature prominently on the social calendar of Muslims in Uganda; it was organized in either the home of a prominent person or in the gardens of a masjid. During the celebrations, many people were invited to speak about Islam, and to feast after. It was very popular since non-Muslims were also invited. Within the atmosphere of the colonial moment, Maulids provided Muslims with a forum to meet and discuss Muslim issues and to share experiences; business networks were also negotiated. Maulids also provided an opportunity for non-Muslims to learn about Islam. Many cases are cited where people converted to Islam at Maulids.[155] The Agenda of the function depended on the intention of the organizer: in the colonial moment, they helped to garner Muslims' social cohesion when many felt the system was against Islam; in the post-colonial moment, Maulids came to serve a different purpose when they became spaces to hammer out 'government policy'.[156] In the moment when Muslims felt to be at the lower end of the social-political scales, they came to channel their energies inwards, amid the various challenges. Maulids became so popular that even the theological Muslim schisms that began in 1922 did not dent their performance. Different Muslim factions could organize their own Maulids, which also created an aura of

---

[153] Kiyimba, 'The Muslim Community in Uganda through One Hundred and Forty Years', pp. 91–2.

[154] Interview with Hajji K, Iganga 3 November 2016.

[155] Interview with AK, Makerere, 24 July 2017.

[156] Kiyimba, 'The Muslim Community in Uganda through One Hundred and Forty Years', pp. 91–2.

competition over who was the best organizer to attract large crowds. Regardless of the disunities, all Muslims took to the Maulid celebration as an opportunity to express their religion and to propagate it. With the support of other factors, the Maulid became a tool for the spread of Islam in Uganda during the colonial moment.

Conclusion

A few observations can be discerned. This chapter has supported one of the major arguments made in the book, which is that colonial governance of Islam and Muslims allowed a set of practices in social-political relations to develop that over time crystallized and became accepted by successive regimes as the normal conduct of relations between Muslims and non-Muslim powers. Colonial governance of Islam and Muslims was borrowed from earlier colonial experiences. Its export to later colonial projects like Uganda allowed for a set of strategies and tactics that could be applied with minimal alterations.

The management of Islam and Muslims however varied according to the stage of the colonial system. In the first twenty years, the colonial state faced instability and uncertainties in managing the native population and for the sake of Uganda, authority and influence was held by the most powerful religious denominations. This is why Anglican adherents, like Katikkiro Apollo Kaggwa of Buganda, used their influence to sway colonial agents like Captain Lugard in reorganizing the state. As the colonial state stabilized in the later years, colonial administration allowed a more certain system of surveillance directed towards Islam and Muslims. In both stages of colonial governance, the state propped up some elites to represent Muslim masses while excluding other opposing elites, which also suppressed the capacity of Muslim masses to express autonomous political consciousness opposed to what they believed to be Christian dominance.

To maintain Mbogo/Kakungulu elitism, the state used its apparatus to prevent counter-elites from emerging. As has been noted above, this schema of colonial governance followed the official template of the official bifurcated system, which was in reality a multifurcation. Muslims from settler groups enjoyed varying degrees of autonomy in comparison to the native Muslims. Although elite representatives linked the masses to the state, this was difficult to sustain because multiple Muslim alliances emerged, and they had separate leaders. Gradually, the troubles over Muslim practices revealed new Muslim elites such as Ssekimwanyi's and similar factions for whom Kakungulu's monopolization of leadership posed an obstacle to personal progress and general Muslim development. Lugard's securitizing legacy had denied Muslims access to fertile counties like Buddu, which diminished their economic output. Such limitations in economic means hampered the expansion of counter-elite organizations. Having received personal land and state gratuities, Mbogo and Kakungulu had resources to contribute to community projects that would 'earn' them respect.[157] This however only confirmed that each Muslim elite was custodian of a particular Muslim alliance – in a now multifurcated Uganda. Other alliances also discovered ways to participate in the state in their 'invisible' capacities as cooks, drivers, butchers, janitors and businessmen. With the support of networks obtained at such important social gatherings as Maulids, Muslims turned their loss of political power into an opportunity to become significant players in the state. In the next chapter, we see how the dynamics of independence demonstrate the rise of Muslims' political significance in the state.

[157] Such as when the Aga Khan supported the construction of Kibuli Unity Masjid and helped to found the African Muslim Community at Wandegeya. These activities increased the honour and status of Badru Kakungulu as the representative of Muslim masses in Uganda: he was identified with progress. See NanoWisdoms Archive of Imamat Speeches, Interviews and Writings, 'Wandegeya Mosque Opening Ceremony' by the Agha Khan, Thursday 17 September 1959, pp. 1ff, available from www.nanowisdoms.org/nwblog/4593 (last accessed 17 February 2022).

CHAPTER 4

Milton Obote Founds his Muslim Alliance

This chapter focuses on the post-colonial articulation of the Muslim question, by which I mean the Muslims' relationship to the post-colonial state. It argues that the status of Islam and Muslims was related to another emerging conundrum after independence, which had to do with the status of the diverse social identities after the end of colonialism. What I refer to as the nationality question emerged when post-colonial leaders such as Milton Obote envisioned a new type of state project divorced from the social classifications of the colonial era. In trying to stamp out tribalism and ethnic parochialism, Obote imagined that citizenship would be based on Ugandan identity whereby other markers such as tribe and ethnicity would have minimal influence over the political trajectory of the state. The chapter shows that the role of Islam and Muslims under Obote's government became limited to maintaining a balance between Obote's national quests and the recalcitrant Buganda establishment. As the legacy of colonial animation of difference (indirect rule) reinforced the dominance of particular ethnic groups, especially the Baganda, whose demand for self-government (federation/secession) obstructed his attempt to construct the national political project, for various reasons Obote appealed to the Muslims as a way to surmount the Buganda obstacle.

First, the Islamic identity, like Catholicism, transcended race and nationality. Unlike the Catholics however, the Muslims had no political party and were not a threat to the Uganda People's Congress (UPC). Obote intended to deploy the Muslims as an alternative centre of power to challenge the recalcitrance of the Mengo establishment and thus provide legitimacy to his government within Buganda. This would, in turn, confirm his legitimacy over the whole country; whoever governed Buganda reigned over Uganda. (His choice of Muslim Ganda leaders revealed the importance of urban Buganda, from which power radiated to the rural.).

112 ISLAM IN UGANDA

Second, Obote perceived Muslims as important allies in a symbiotic relationship. Since the legacy of colonial governance of Islam and Muslims had circumscribed and relegated Islamic practices to the private domain, delimiting their political field pushed their politics to masjids and other micro sites. The Muslims thus had nothing to lose and much to gain from escaping historical political oblivion. As with Lugard's territorial balancing, Obote offered Muslims a better political position within the state and they obliged.

Third, Obote did not fashion the trajectory of the intra-Muslim debate, rather, he realized and directed it, anticipating its outcomes and channelling it to his chosen interests. Colonial governance had propped up Mbogo and Kakungulu as Muslim elites to represent Muslim masses. Even when counter-elites emerged to challenge elite dominance, the tactics of the colonial state had operated to push emerging Muslim issues to their private spaces in the domain of native customary institutions, immensely suppressing Muslim autonomy. As Muslim politics receded to micro spaces, the dominant religious denominations (Protestants and Catholics) used the national political platform to advance their groups' interests. The move towards independence generated a debate that rejected political pluralism and its co-optation or attempted destruction of local polities and cultures into an abstract Ugandan identity.[1] The nationalizing project became constructed atop religious and ethnic undercurrents that fused to influence the national political project, so that preparations for self-government favoured Protestants and Catholics over the Muslims. Obote's early distaste for ethnic parochialism influenced his choice to work with the Muslims.

Fourth, related to the above, Obote perceived the Muslims to be in a weaker position vis-à-vis the Christian groups since their political inexperience confirmed their importance as allies without political ambitions. Again, Obote did not create this situation; colonial statecraft had championed Muslim elite parochialism and alienated the political potential of the Muslim masses. With the looming negotiations for independence, the Christian groups participated in countrywide campaigns over who would receive the reins of power. Unable (and inexperienced) to formulate and respond to the nationality question with a well-articulated alternative of their own, majority Muslim groups continued with their loyalty to Kakungulu, in a rather 'distasteful form of elite chauvinism'.[2] The conclusion of independence negotiations confirmed Muslims as a political

---

[1] For the Indian Muslim experience, see Devji, 'The Idea of a Muslim Community', pp. 118–21.

[2] Ibid., p. 120.

minority and imposed upon them all the 'disempowerment of such a status'.[3] Within this Muslim minority Obote knew there existed a counter-elite force that clamoured to escape from the shackles of historical suppression to establish alternative centres of power. As they anticipated their new role in the state, he looked to these suppressed Muslim elites as the base from which to launch his attack on Ganda royal power. As the state cultivated a role for particular elite Muslim groups within its political schema, it also cultivated an interventionist role for itself within society when it relegated other elite Muslim groups to political limbo. As new Muslim elites emerged to replace the old, the private spaces of Muslim micro-politics (in masjids) became sites of Muslim conflict. The attempt of the state-supported elites to unleash violence on opposing elites transformed masjids from being micro sites to macro spaces of public importance in the national arena. Its implication was reflected in a question that subsequent governments would ask: 'where are my Muslims located?.[4]

This chapter is organized into three sections. The first section discusses the dual character of the nationality problem. On the one hand, the nationality problem concerned the integration of diverse ethnic groups within Uganda as a political unit. On the other, it concerned the attempt by unifying politicians like Obote to deconstruct Buganda's exceptionalism towards reconstructing a broader national political project. The section therefore revisits the debates on how the nationality question was articulated. The second section shows the attempts of the anti-colonial revolt to appeal to particular Muslim groups for particular purposes, which may have worked to influence the grant of independence. The third section discusses how Obote founded his Muslim association to appeal to Muslims in response to the problem of governing Buganda.

The nationality question

The nationality question arose during the era of negotiating with the British for self-government. Substantively, it contained debates about how to include diverse nationalities into the unifying political framework. It thus contained issues of belonging and exclusion within a unified Uganda, the terms of inclusion, the status of those considered alien, and the unifying ideology of the nationalization process. As the debate ensued, its

---

3   Ibid., p. 121.
4   This question is identified with President Yoweri Museveni who on numerous occasions wondered: 'there are Muslims for Iran, Libya and Saudi Arabia; where are my Muslims?' Jamil Mukulu recording, 2012.

parameters focused on the African and non-African. The other side of the nationality question also included the intention to defeat Buganda's exceptionalism. The colonial amalgamation of territorial units to form political structures meant that the state had preceded the unifying national ideology, which impacted on the identity of the nascent political community. In this way, the nationalist politician had two structural models to choose from: the pre-colonial and the colonial. The pre-colonial model followed from the nationalist's perception of the Uganda community that colonial administrative governance had transformed it. To escape the shadow of colonial governance required a rigorous process: creating a national vision (ideology), forming national organizations (political parties) and mobilizing local support for the national project (construction of unity). The critical stage of this process was how to construct a nationalizing ideology that would appeal to diverse local difference. Since indirect rule had ensured that the pre-colonial model co-existed with the colonial state, the challenge of the nationalist politician was how to conceive of pre-colonial structures within the political demands of the present day, and towards unified self-government. Amid pre-colonial political differences, it became a challenge to arrive at a unifying ideological compromise. Consider the settled Buganda idea of nationality on the eve of the colonial encounter, for instance. The basic unit of social organization in Buganda was the clan, headed by an *omutaka* who governed the *obutaka* (ancestral lands), which he held in trust on behalf of the clan members, who could also inhabit other territories outside the *butaka*.

While ties of kinship bound members of one clan together, geographical space was bridged by a metaphysical belief in *lubaale* (spirit intercession) that enabled wellbeing and united sparsely located clan members.[5] Yet the Buganda clan was inclusive, it was not closed. Ganda assimilation processes allowed newcomers to become Baganda and also enter the clan system through a gradual process. Etymologically, the verb *okusenga* (to inhabit) described a process whereby newcomers entered a particular location and the inhabiting subject became *omusenze*. The *musenze* therefore asked (or begged) for land to settle, and when a portion of land was granted this marked a mutual obligation relating to social relations around land. The new settler was obliged to undertake some duties as a form of gratitude towards the landowner. Over time, the *musenze* could marry into an already settled family and transform themselves into first

---

[5] Kodesh, Neil (2010), *Beyond the Royal Gaze: Clanship and Public Healing in Buganda,* University of Virginia Press: London, pp. 69–73.

MILTON OBOTE FOUNDS HIS MUSLIM ALLIANCE   **115**

comers. Gradually, after generations, families who had entered a community as newcomers through *kusenga* relations could consolidate the land-holding status of their descendants through marriage alliances and *obusika* (inheritance).[6] This cycle became complete when the *musenze* could also grant *kusenga* relations to newcomers. To commit to a particular community, *omusenze* would acquire a Ganda clan name and its totem, learn the clan anthem and even perform *okulanya* (pledge allegiance) to the *mutaka* and later to the Kabaka at special ceremonies. This act signified two consequences: one, the individual had become a *subject* of the political authorities in Buganda; second, the individual had *renounced* their previous home and had decided to identify with Buganda as their new home.

This integration of outsiders within the Ganda society enabled a system of fluid relations to the centre of power. To consolidate oneself, the *musenze* would gradually come to pledge their allegiance to the various centres of power and become acculturated fully into the Ganda society. This process bred categories of Baganda: *omuganda wawu* (proto, first inhabitant), *nnansangwa/kasangwaawo* (earliest comer), *kaawokadda* (early comer) and *omusenze* (newcomer). Generations of time marked the difference between these categories. Although the political power of the *bataka* was negated during the colonial period, this social system of assimilation remained in Buganda and was applied to integrate many immigrants such as the Banyarwanda, Jaluo, Bahima and Bagisu,[7] among others. Even individual Asians considered themselves integral members of Uganda society since it was their 'only home'.[8] Now, with British colonialism having reconstructed the Ganda political model and cast it as the unifying system of countrywide colonial government, national unity would be difficult amid real group dominance, as the ensuing debates revealed.

The report on the inquiries of the Uganda Constitutional Committee revealed a debate on the perceptions surrounding the nationality question and its possible resolution. It demonstrated the attitudes of various constituencies regarding multiple questions: What did citizenship of Uganda mean? Which category of people would partake of it? Where would

---

[6]   See also Schoenbrun, David Lee (1998), *A Green Place, A Good Place: Agrarian Change, Gender, and Social Identity in the Great Lakes Region to the 15th Century,* Fountain: Kampala, p. 183–4; Hanson, Holly E. (2003), *Landed Obligation: The Practice of Power in Buganda,* Heinemann: Portsmouth.

[7]   Banywaranda emigrated from Ruanda-Urundi; Jaluo came from the northern parts of Uganda; Bahima from Western Uganda and the Bagisu from Eastern Uganda.

[8]   Joshi, Ravi, 'This is Our Only Home', *Uganda Argus,* 18 February 1959.

they reside? What were the terms and conditions of such residence? Was political participation in the 'new' Uganda based on race or other considerations? How was the very aspect of difference perceived? If race was a marker of political difference, under what ingredients would those considered alien be integrated within the national platform so as to 'belong'? As the following debates reveal, being 'Ugandan' (identity) connoted two aspects: first, it was an 'imposition' from those who had power. Second, it was also a subjective 'assertion' from those who desired to belong.[9] It was not enough for power to *regard* one as belonging to the national identity; the concerned individuals were also required to *pronounce* themselves as ready to be subject to the political authorities.

From the outset, it was unclear whether citizenship in the new Uganda would be predicated upon fixed terms of residence, racial categorizations or through displays of social-political-economic subservience to the established regional and central authorities. A debate began between 'Black Africanists' – those who wished to see Uganda as an 'African' country, understood as only for 'black' people – non-racists who perceived racial harmony as the basis of progress for all, and the Ganda secessionists who believed in special negotiations for political constituencies like Buganda. All three groups considered themselves as 'nationalist'. The first group, the Black Africanists believed that non-Africans (this category was considered to include the non-black people) could not participate in political activities such as electing representatives or being nominated for the same until they had been granted citizenship. Sendikwanawa, a member of the Democratic Party, shared the belief of the Kyabazinga (king) of Busoga, William Nadiope, that non-Africans could be nominated by the Governor to participate in the Legislative Council until independence leadership defined other means to political participation.[10]

The chairperson of the committee, Mr Wild, wondered why the non-African population were differentiated from the Banyarwanda who also seemed to fall in the similar category of non-citizens. Sendikwanawa denied that the Banyarwanda fit the category of non-citizens. He argued that since they (Banyarwanda) had settled, lived and paid taxes in Buganda for some time, they were 'automatically' *regarded* as Baganda. This did not convince Wild because it pointed to racial difference as predetermining political difference since non-Africans had also settled, lived and paid

---

[9] For a corollary, see Mamdani, Mahmood (2010), S*aviors and Survivors: Darfur, Politics and the War on Terror*, CODESRIA: Dakar, p. 118, chapter 3 ('Writing race into history').

[10] *Constitutional Committee Papers on Governance*, 1959–1960, No. 4, p. 3

taxes for some time in Buganda, but would be *considered* as non-citizens. The challenges arose from the confusion of political difference with racial traits. Sendikwanawa argued that the reason for considering non-Africans as non-citizens was because the people concerned had not proceeded to pronounce themselves as Kabaka's *subjects* unlike the Banyarwanda who had settled, lived, paid taxes and also *accepted* to become subjects of the Kabaka. Sendikwanawa's intervention revealed the Ganda experience of assimilation as a double-sided phenomenon; it was not enough that one was *allowed* to settle in Buganda. It was also critical that the individual *pronounced* their acceptance to belong, and was confirmed in such processes as *okulanya* whereby the newcomer performed chants of allegiance to various political authorities, from the clan hierarchies to the Kabaka. For the non-Africans, maintaining their identity within Buganda had not been the problem, rather their unwillingness to *pronounce* themselves as Kabaka's subjects. When Wild pressed Sendikwanawa to explain what would be the status of non-Africans who accepted to become Kabaka's subjects, the latter's response implied that he preferred acceptance for non-Africans, rather than them becoming subjects.[11]

Why did Sendikwanawa paint the native as a single category yet there were sub-groups within it? As highlighted above, *basenze*, such as the Banyarwanda, were not at a similar stage of *kusenga*, their differences were marked by the length of time of one's residence. This mode of assimilation was most popular in Buganda as opposed to the other areas. Why would this debate privilege the Ganda experience and occlude others? As Obote wondered, how would residence be considered for provinces such as West Nile (north-west Uganda) that did not have a kabaka/king? Sendikwanawa's response was that residence in any location was predicated on obedience to the relevant political authority.[12] To this, Ingham pressed: 'If an Asian becomes the subject of the Protectorate Government, is he not in the same position towards the Protectorate Government as a Munyarwanda is towards the Kabaka's Government in this area?'[13] 'Not really', Sendikwanawa noted, 'because the Protectorate Government' is 'a foreign power', so it could not be similar to subjectivity under the Kabaka's government.[14] The key question for the debate came to 'where does one consider home'? Sendikwanawa argued in this way because he felt 'non-Africans' like Asians and Europeans still

[11] Ibid., p. 4.
[12] Ibid., p. 5.
[13] Ibid.
[14] Ibid.

considered themselves as belonging to their 'mother country'. Since they had not *pronounced* themselves as belonging to Buganda, they still had 'homes' to return to unlike the Baganda and the Banyarwanda who *considered* themselves and had come to be *regarded* as permanently 'native' to their locations.[15]

Sendikwanawa's interventions did not seem to settle the fusion of political with racial difference. As Cuthbert Obwangor (member of the Uganda Legislative Council for Teso District) questioned the cause of the 'fear' that the former intended to deny voting rights to individuals because of their racial traits,[16] it came down to Sendikwanawa's conviction that Uganda was going to be 'primarily an African state'.[17] What did this mean? Did this imply that there would be 'second-class' citizenship? Sendikwanawa was speaking to the experiences that had privileged the settler vis-à-vis the native. In the new Uganda, he imagined that the privilege of settler individuals basing on their racial traits and its implication on social-economic benefits would be dismantled. Settler privilege was the biggest issue. As an Asian representative, Mr C.K. Patel (one of the two members of the Uganda Legislative Council representing the Asian community) wondered how this 'Africanization' would operate to integrate non-Africans (Asians) into Ugandan citizenship.[18] One ex official of the Wild Committee, Leonard Mugwanya, argued that political representation was not a racial matter. It was far more important to build a Uganda 'where race disappears' and all people identified with the country would live in harmony and work towards its progress.[19] In the context of the legacy of colonially animated difference, how was this to actually work? How was the national politician to escape from the limiting category of 'tribe' towards constructing a new national political imagination that would not only accommodate difference in diversity but also cater for the internal differentiations within particular ethnic groups? To transcend these categories and construct a national image, one had to dispense with the Buganda specialness constructed during the colonial moment. It was a huge impediment to resolving the nationality question.

[15] Ibid., pp. 3–15.
[16] Ibid., p. 10.
[17] Ibid.
[18] Ibid., p. 13.
[19] Ibid., p. 3.

Buganda 'exceptionalism'

What did Ugandan nationality question presuppose? What were its contradictions and tensions? What did it reveal and suppress? The nationality question in Uganda presupposed the unification of the different nationalities that had been territorialized under colonial rule. Regarding its location, it was situated alongside the colonial animation of difference much more identified with the British reification of Buganda as a special polity. As the nationalist politicians demonstrated their commitment to the unification of an ethnically diverse country, the nationality question identified Buganda political power as the enemy to the nationalist project, which had to be suppressed at all costs. Why was nationalist discourse in Uganda juxtaposed to Buganda's specialness? Phares Mutibwa has argued that the 'special' place of Buganda was amplified in the colonial moment when the colonial state elevated Ganda political structures to national importance, which made the Baganda 'arrogant' and 'proud' in their approach to the political problems.[20] Yet, the special tag is true for all Uganda because 'each territorial unit had been divided and run as if it were an independent entity and this naturally fostered the growth of excessive and exclusive concern with parochial matters'.[21] This polarization of society also had religious implications.[22] The early establishment of educational centres in Buganda gave it an edge over other areas, and was coupled to the Ganda ideology that resolved around the need to preserve one's own cultural and political integrity while seeking to retain the advantages to be gained from contact with the foreign.[23] In many ways, the Baganda considered themselves an open society that had welcomed and integrated new ideas, a value that the British used to political advantage.[24]

The idea of Buganda as an 'open' society operated along a number of levels. Whereas social inclusion of *basenze* into the Ganda social

---

[20] Mutibwa, Phares (1992), *Uganda Since Independence: A Story of Unfulfilled Hopes,* Fountain: Kampala, p. 11. See also Low, D.A. (1971), *Buganda in Modern History,* Weidenfeld & Nicolson: London, pp. 227–32.

[21] Karugire, S.R. (1980), *A Political History of Uganda,* Heinemann: Nairobi, pp. 145, 148–9.

[22] Mudoola, Dan M. (1992), *Interest Groups and Institution Building Processes in Uganda: 1962–1971,* Makerere Institute of Social Research: Kampala, p. 10.

[23] Low, *Buganda in Modern History*, p. 230.

[24] Mukasa, Ham (1998 [1904]), *Uganda's Katikkiro in England,* Manchester University Press: Manchester; see also Low, D.A. (2009), *Fabrication of Empire: The British and the Uganda Kingdoms, 1890–1902,* Cambridge University Press: Cambridge, pp. 320–32.

120   ISLAM IN UGANDA

fabric continued, access to political privilege was delimited by the entry of 'group' interests, especially after 1900, in the various political offices. Special groups like Kabaka Yekka began to dictate the political trajectory of events in Buganda by excluding those considered threats to their interests. The 1900 Buganda Agreement had *intensified* the transformation of Buganda's political spaces from the *bataka* (decentralized) to the Kabaka and *bakungu* chiefs at Mengo (centralized). Its economic and political power was also reinforced by the support of the colonial state.[25] The politics regarding the internal administration of Mengo and Buganda set a precedent that affected the nationality question.

Within Mengo, top officials made up the Lukiiko[26] and had a right to vote on the bills to be approved. They appointed chiefs at the lower levels; no power delimited their terms of office. The Lukiiko members' behaviour was akin to the Luganda proverb '*Enkima tesala gwa kibira*' (the monkey does not arbitrate a case regarding the forest); they would not approve important legislations that would undermine their social-economic-political privileges. Few families however gained power after the religious wars of 1888 when the British intervened to cause a Protestant ascendancy in Buganda and formed the group possessing 'real' power at Mengo. Their victory was legally enshrined in the 1900 Agreement.[27] It was the members from these families that constituted Kabaka Yekka as a vehicle of the Mengo establishment to protect its control over Buganda.[28] When the nationality question emerged to challenge parochial interests in Uganda, Kabaka Yekka leaders rode on kabakaship (what Kasozi calls a hydra)[29] to appeal to Buganda and protect their interests. This 'specialness' of the Buganda political leadership dramatized the decolonizing moment within Uganda to the chagrin of Milton Obote and Joseph Kiwanuka, leaders of the Uganda National Congress, which later became the Uganda People's Congress.

In 1953, Kabaka Muteesa II was 'deported' to Britain for his refusal to cooperate with the British Government regarding the rumour of East African Federation, Independence (separation of Buganda from the rest),

---

25   Kasozi, A.B.K. (2013), *Bitter Bread of Exile: The Financial Troubles of Sir Edward Muteesa II during his last exile,* Progressive Publishing House: Kampala, p. 18.

26   Lukiiko refers to 'Assembly' (i.e., here, the Buganda Parliament). It comes from the verb *okukiika*, which means to 'represent' a group in a large meeting.

27   Kasozi, *Bitter Bread of Exile,* p. 19.

28   Ibid.

29   Ibid.

and transfer of Buganda affairs to the Foreign Office.[30] The whole matter was about Buganda's negotiation for a special status in the grant of independence. A three-month deliberation at the Namirembe Conference renewed British-Buganda bonds of government. Kabaka Muteesa's kabaka-ship became ceremonial, and ministries were created for Buganda with permanent secretaries. This 1955 Agreement referenced the 1900 and 1894 Agreements in Buganda and other native ordinances in Uganda. Upon his return in 1955, Muteesa received a hero's welcome.[31] Towards the London negotiations to grant independence, Buganda officialdom had continued to push for federal status but when the Kabaka and his envoys failed in that quest,[32] the Lukiiko nonetheless voted for secession and set up a nine-man committee to draft a petition to the Queen of its complete independence.[33] Britain informed Buganda that the secession was illegal since the existing Buganda Agreements (1894, 1900, 1955) alongside other ordinances) could only be 'varied by mutual consent'.[34] When the independence negotiations were finalized, the constitution still provided a federal status for Buganda in comparison to the other areas. In the end, Obote's Uganda People's Congress (UPC) and the Kabaka Yekka (king only) (KY) parties negotiated to form a government. Kenneth Ingham has shown how Obote's attempt to forge national unity recast politics into the divide-and-rule practices of the colonial era.[35] The UPC-KY alliance faltered[36] when, in 1966, Obote attacked

---

30 Secretary of State for colonies (1953), *Uganda Protectorate: Withdrawal of Recognition from Kabaka Mutesa II of Buganda,* HM Stationery: London, p. 6–13.

31 Ingham, Kenneth (1962), *A History of East Africa,* Longmans: London, p. 418.

32 'Deadlock in London over Buganda's Sovereignty', *Uganda Argus,* 22 September 1960.

33 'Lukiiko votes in favour of secession', *Uganda Argus,* 24 September 1960.

34 'Buganda cannot break treaty: Council told decision rests with U.K. 27 September 1960.

35 Ingham, Kenneth (1994), *Obote: A Political Biography,* Routledge: London, pp. 43–146.

36 Kabaka Muteesa II (1967), explained the expedient character of the UPC-KY alliance in his *Desecration of my Kingdom,* Constable: London, p. 160, stating thus:

> An alliance between Buganda and U.P.C was suggested, with innumerable promises of respect for our position after independence. He [Obote] would step down, and I should choose whoever I wished to be Prime Minister. Though I did not particularly like him, for he is not a particularly likeable man, I agreed to the alliance without misgivings.

122 ISLAM IN UGANDA

the Lubiri (Kabaka's Palace).[37] The main justification for the attack was that Buganda was suffering from 'KY disease' and KY itself was suffering from 'ethnocentrism'.[38] To Obote, this KY disease was the obstacle to national unity and had to be extirpated at all costs. In this quest, he appealed to the Muslims.

Muslims in the anti-colonial revolt

Obote would appeal to the Muslim identity to further his political interests. Why and how the Muslim became important as Uganda drew towards independence had to do both with the conditions of the Muslims and the Christian groups (Catholics and Protestants). Towards the end of the Second World War, another *bataka* movement had emerged in Buganda. Unlike the first movement of the 1920s, the second movement emerged around 1941 and some of its intentions were to agitate for the Africanization of both political power and the economy. Led by Joshua Kaate and some prominent *bataka*, they argued that since the intention of the Second World War had been to defeat a resurgent Nazi Germany, the British should follow up the end of the war by granting independence to the native *ethnic* groups, akin to the defeat of Nazi domination.[39] By 1949, Joshua Kaate and other *bataka* were imprisoned, but the agitation for self-rule did not dissipate.

He understood our fears for the position of Buganda; we shared his hopes for a united, prosperous and free Uganda. Kintu was alone in opposing this new friendship. Obote had said that he meant to crush the Baganda, and Kintu would not forgive or trust him. We waved it aside as an impetuous remark made to please crowds. Now we thought him reformed, the obvious and best ally against Kiwanuka and the hated D.P. ... Obote assured us that all the details would be ironed out later in discussions between the relevant Minister of the Lukiiko and of the National Assembly. We could count on him. 'Trust me,' he said and smiled reassuringly. With only faint misgivings, we did.

[37] 'New Law may restrict K.Y. movements' *Uganda Argus*, 10 January 1966; 'Katikiro's motion on Penal Bill' *Uganda Argus,* 20 January 1966; Gingo G.W. (nd), *Pulaani Y'Obote Gyeyakola Okusanyalaza Uganda*, Nakivubo; Karugire, *A Political History of Uganda,* p. 179; Kabwegyere, Tarsis B. (1995), *The Politics of State Formation and Destruction in Uganda*, Fountain: Kampala, p. 209–11.

[38] 'Dr. Obote hits at opposition to Penal Bill', *Uganda Argus*, 27 January 1966.

[39] Interview with FGE, Kampala, 12 August 2017.

A new underground movement (officially named Katwe People's Council) emerged, riding on Joshua Kaate's persona to continue agitating for self-rule, this time using militant means. It was led by Christian apostates such as Paulo Muwanga and Paul Ssennendo – these two initially became Catholic, then Protestant, and later shed both Christian identities, referring to themselves as 'Communists'.[40] In 1952, this movement replicated the activities of the Kenya Land and Freedom Army (Mau Mau) rebellion in Kenya and proceeded with clandestine military training in the middle of a large forest situated between Gayaza and Namugongo.[41] Although led by non-Muslims, its arms-bearing unit was restricted to a group of Muslims and 'Abadahemuka' (the trusted ones),[42] who had been recruited from Rwandese immigrants by John Kale (shortened from Karyekyezi, his Rwandese name) to buttress its militancy. These two groups were chosen because, unlike them, the non-Muslim Ganda such as the Protestants were close to state power and could easily be infiltrated. The Catholics on the other hand had an elaborate system of organization that included networks of political radicalism and activism by organizations such as the Old Boys Associations and the Catholic Teachers Associations that worked as a 'covert intelligence network overseeing parishioners practices'.[43] Fearful of such Catholic activism, the colonial state had also established an elaborate spy network to respond to Catholic radicalism. The leaders of the movement were also concerned that the Catholics could betray the rebellion when they went for confessions. This could not be said of the Muslim group and the Abadahemuka. They were allowed to have guns and one Hajji Ausi Ruzinda was an expert in making bombs (improvised explosives). The movement proceeded to threaten the colonial state, which branded it a 'Communist threat' believing that their guns were imported from the Soviet Union.

In January 1954, they raided a government armoury at the Cadet Corps of Kisubi Mission College and stole guns.[44] The movement's leadership threatened the then looming celebrations to mark sixty years of British

---

40 Ibid.
41 Ibid.
42 Kirundi, from the verb *guhemuka*, which means: to betray, not keep one's word, to dishonour. 'Abadahemuka' is the opposite. Discussion with Haydee Bangerezako, Makerere 14 July 2017.
43 Summers, Carol (2009), 'Catholic Action and Ugandan Radicalism: Political Activism in Buganda, 1930–1950', *Journal of Religion in Africa*, Vol. 39, Fasc. 1, pp. 60–90, pp. 67–84.
44 'Fire Arms Stolen from Kisubi Armoury', *Uganda Herald*, 26 January 1954.

colonial rule in Uganda, and the murder of a white settler disrupted Queen Elizabeth's visiting schedule. The colonial state eventually infiltrated the movement and went about appeasing its leadership by appointing its members as ministers and administrators in the 1955 local government reforms. Hajji Kassim Male was appointed a Minister of Education in the Kabaka's government in Mengo. As the state appeased its leadership, the movement began to disperse. Its leadership believed that it influenced the 1955 reforms and the January 1960 declaration by Harold Macmillan in which he stated that Britain would begin negotiating for internal self-government for the colonies.[45] British fears of the spread of Communism in Africa may however have been a preponderant factor in the early commitment to grant internal self-rule.[46]

This contribution of the Muslims to the anti-colonial revolt was later broadened by their alliance with the UPC. As Uganda drew towards self-government, the Christian religious groups jostled for who would inherit the reigns of state power. The Catholics consisted of the largest population by religious identity in Uganda and used their Catholic activism to assert themselves. The Protestants were however unwilling to relinquish their control over the state and when the Catholics founded DP in 1954 as a political party to rally them against the Protestants, the latter responded by defeating Matayo Mugwanya's attempt to become Buganda's Katikkiro in 1956.[47] Within this religiously inspired struggle for political power, the Muslims became important again and they formally joined the Protestants.

Abasi Kiyimba has identified three factors that influenced the Muslims' political alliance with the Protestants. First, the most recent and bitterest of the religious wars in Buganda at the dawn of the century had involved the Muslims against the Catholics. The latter had won that war and the former never forgot their defeat. Second, unlike the Protestants, who would allow Muslims into their schools (although they sometimes required conversion), Catholics detested the Muslims and would strictly require that they either convert or strictly follow the Christian rites. Third, the Muslims had been in political limbo for a long time and desired a new entry point. Since the Protestants were fewer

---

[45] Macmillan, Harold, 'Wind of Change' Speech to both Houses of Parliament, South Africa, 3 February 1960.

[46] Interview with FGE, Kampala, 12 August 2017.

[47] Kiyimba, Abasi (1990), 'The Muslim Community in Uganda through One Hundred and Forty Years: The Trials and Tribulations of a Muslim Minority', *Journal of African Religion and Philosophy,* Vol. 1, No. 2', pp. 98–9.

they needed the Muslims more than did the Catholics.[48] When therefore Kassim Male became minister of Education in Kabaka's government he was followed by other Muslims such as Abu Mayanja and Ntege-Lubwama. It was these Muslims who joined the Protestants to form the leadership of the Kabaka Yekka party. Outside Buganda, Muslims in various parts of the country joined the Protestant-leaning UPC. Prominent Muslim elites like Shaban Nkutu and Ali Balunywa in Busoga, Abasi Balinda in Ankole, Ausi Rwakaikara in Bunyoro and Badru Wegulo in Bukedi became key figures in the UPC, and its leadership recognized the need to appeal to the Muslims as a community. Milton Obote wound up founding the National Association for the Advancement of Muslims (NAAM) to achieve his political interests.

Obote and his Muslim organization

How did the nationality question influence the Muslim question in Uganda? I contend in this section that the capacity of the Islamic identity to transcend nationality was Obote's response to Buganda's exceptionalism. Since the Islamic identity transcended race and nationality, Obote used it as an alternative centre of power to challenge the recalcitrance of the Mengo establishment and thus provide legitimacy to his government within Buganda. Although this was also true of the Catholic identity, the Catholics had a political party, the DP, which was not limited to Buganda and thus posed a challenge to Obote's UPC. The Muslims however had no party to challenge Obote and could easily be integrated within it. As Obote perceived Muslims as important allies in a symbiotic relationship, they also saw an opportunity to gain in escaping historical political oblivion. As he realized the trajectory of the intra-Muslim debate, directed it, anticipated its outcomes and channelled it to his chosen interests, Obote took advantage of existing splits among Muslim elites in their counter-claims to represent Muslim masses. Owing to their political inexperience, Muslims could be trusted as allies without political ambitions. He took advantage of the desire of Muslim elites to establish alternative centres of power so as to escape Kakungulu's dominance.

Generally, this was Obote's response to the challenge of governing Buganda after the events of 1966. To govern the country, he needed the backing of the group that inhabited the central part of the country – the Baganda. Since the UPC-KY alliance was obsolete, Obote had to court

[48] Ibid.

the various Ganda groups organized under particular associations to increase the number of his Ganda composition within the UPC.[49] His personalization of power had a social implication; it spread to the groups and eradicated institutional democracy. Before independence, the Muslim leadership in Uganda had split between various factions. Majority Muslims still believed that Kakungulu was the leader of the Muslim community in Uganda. Unlike the early colonial moment when the question of Muslim representation bothered the colonial state, the Muslim community had gradually become revealed, as when the state chose Mbogo/Kakungulu as Muslim representatives (internal wrangles had also enabled self-revelation). Here, Obote's challenge moved from 'who represented the Muslims' to 'which Muslim group shall accept to work with the state'. In other words, 'who were "Obote's Muslims"?'

Due to the split of the UPC-KY alliance, Kakungulu, as a Ganda royal, would not work with the UPC government. His loyalty to the Kabaka meant that UPC was denied the backing of such a large Muslim following that Kakungulu represented. Obote was not deterred: he proceeded to found his own association to 'advance' the Muslim cause in Uganda, and named it National Association for the Advancement of Muslims (NAAM), under the leadership of his cousin, Adoko Nekyon, who allegedly converted to Islam for the purpose of its leadership. What were Obote's intentions in intruding into the Muslims' space? Since the Muslim identity transcended nationalism, Obote used it to anchor the legitimacy of his regime within Buganda. Although NAAM appealed to the Muslims in Uganda, it was a distraction whose real object was to split Ganda Muslim loyalty towards Prince Badru Kakungulu's Uganda Muslim Community (UMC – founded 1947) and create an alternate large Ganda following under the patronage of the state. The events that proceeded the founding of NAAM revealed this fact as the target was the social base of Ganda political power; violence was both a means and a consequence.

The debate as to whether NAAM was born of the UPC leadership is not settled. Sheikh Abdul Obeid Kamulegeya, who was the Vice President of NAAM, said that the idea for its founding was conceived in Mecca, Saudi

---

[49]   Gingo, *Pulaani Y'Obote Gyeyakola Okusanyalaza Uganda*, p. 2, citing Obote's intimation that he had important Mengo ministers under his control: 'Within the Kabaka's government, I only trust Mr. Mayanja [Nkangi] and Mr. F. Walugembe because they tell me the secrets from the Kabaka's government. I shall appoint them in key positions of my government since they secretly hide their support towards my government yet they are inside the Kabaka's government. With their support, Mengo is in my palm'.

Arabia. At a Muslim conference in 1965, the World Muslim League had sent travel tickets to the leaders of Muslims in Uganda to attend the World Conference on Muslim Development and Solidarity. Kamulegeya was designated the leader of the Ugandan delegation at the conference, which resolved that all Muslim participants were to set up national offices of the Muslim World League in their countries. Upon return home, Kamulegeya relayed the object of Muslim unity, development and global linkages. At various ceremonies to unpack the deliberations of the Meccan conference, Kamulegeya was postured as having political ambitions to unseat the leadership of Kakungulu as head of the Muslims in Uganda.[50] Kamulegeya's leadership over the Uganda branch of the World Muslim League was equated by state functionaries and some Muslim associations to leadership of all Muslims in the country. Baganda Muslim leaders connived with the leaders in Mengo (the seat of Buganda government) to deny Kamulegeya land for opening up the office. When Adoko Nekyon and Shaban Nkutu (ministers in Obote's government) heard of this, they welcomed Kamulegeya, who left Kibuli to become the Vice President of NAAM.

Before the founding of NAAM in 1965, Muslim leaders, especially Kakungulu, had been active participants in the political scene albeit overshadowed by Anglican and Catholic dominance.[51] Prior to the UPC-KY alliance, Kakungulu had used his leadership of the Muslim community to secure government support for Muslims outside Buganda. The end of the alliance meant that Muslim support of Obote's government had to be channelled through other agents. Why NAAM was founded has been credited to Obote's personalization of power; on why he targeted Muslims, Kasozi has noted their organizational weakness in comparison to the Christian groups.[52] But the impetus behind the formation of NAAM was the desire of non-Baganda Muslims to create institutional as opposed to personal frameworks of improving Muslims in Uganda. As a consequence, this affected Kakungulu whose loyalty to Buganda had been perceived as making Muslim leadership in Uganda hereditary.

Internally, Muslims had challenged Kakungulu's leadership for various reasons. Owing to his non-Islamic education at Kings College Buddo, Kakungulu was perceived by a section of the Muslim sheikhs as fomenting the secularization of Muslims especially when the state grafted secular

---

[50] Sheikh Abdul Obeid Kamulegeya, interview August 2016.

[51] Kasozi, A.B.K. (1996),*The Life of Prince Badru Kakungulu Wasajja and the Development of a Forward-Looking Muslim Community in Uganda, 1907–1991,* Progressive: Kampala, pp. 86–97, 128–48.

[52] Ibid., pp. 152–8.

studies into the Muslim schools. The sheikhs believed that such education would dilute Islam and lead their children to hell and that it had cultivated a 'modernized' Muslim subject: the sheikhs detested the 'arrogance' of the Muslim youth attending secular schools. As the accounting leader of the Muslims, Kakungulu was responsible for this 'decay' in the Muslim society. Some sheikhs attacked the Muslim schools teaching secular studies, vandalized them and sometimes beat the students.[53]

To strengthen its leadership base, in opposition to Kakungulu's group, NAAM 'elected' Sheikh Swaibu Ssemakula to become Mufti of Uganda and emphasized that he was the spiritual leader of all Muslims in Uganda.[54] A house of sheikhs, hastily appointed by Sheikh Ssemakula, elected him as Mufti at the Busoga Muslim headquarters at Bugembe, Jinja, inside a school building whose doors and windows were allegedly bolted. After the election, a resolution was passed unanimously declaring that all Muslims of Uganda recognize Sheikh Ssemakula as their only leader and Sheikh Mivule deputy leader. Various sheikhs crossed from the Kakungulu group and went over to NAAM. Kasozi identified this crossover with the poor economic status of many sheikhs who looked to NAAM as an opportunity for employment.[55]

But how could Obote support the election of a Muganda as Mufti within NAAM yet his intention was to challenge Ganda dominance of the Uganda political landscape? The response is that Obote was not opposed to the Baganda as a nationality but to the political leadership at Mengo. Therefore, making a Ganda *mukopi* (commoner) the head of NAAM was to challenge the royal status of Prince Badru Kakungulu as head of the UMC and the political patronage that his leadership enjoyed from Mengo.

When NAAM was formed, both the UMC and the African Muslim Community recognized a new enemy and shelved their wrangles,[56] uniting under the leadership of Prince Badru Kakungulu. They responded to Ssemakula's election as Mufti by denying that he represented all Muslims in Uganda since NAAM was the only Mulsim association sitting at Jinja during his election.[57] In a public exchange during one parliamentary debate, Abu Mayanja asked Shaban Nkutu on the question regarding Muslim

---

[53] FGD, Nakalama (Busoga), 5 November 2016.
[54] 'Muslims Elect Uganda Leader', *Uganda Argus*, 3 April 1967, p. 2.
[55] Kasozi, *The Life of Prince Badru Kakungulu Wasajja,* p. 157.
[56] The UMC had previously broken into two splinter groups: Jamaat-et-Islam, led by Sheikh Ssemakula and Juma & Zukuuli led by Sheikh Abudalami Mivule. It was these two who had been integrated into NAAM.
[57] FGD, Nakalama (Busoga), 5 November 2016.

leadership in the country. When Obote actually responded to the question, it demonstrated his interest in the Muslim matter. Mayanja's question arose from Nkutu's public remarks regarding the Government's recognition of Sheikh Ssemakula as Mufti and as the head of all Muslims in Uganda; that non-supporters of NAAM were disloyal to the state. Obote's response was that since Ssemakula had been elected as Mufti, the Government had to accord him honour in the name of Muslims in Uganda. Obote sidestepped the question on 'disloyal' groups noting that he had little time to respond to media rumours; although it was public knowledge that Ssemakula was elected with the backing of Obote.[58]

Once Obote propped up NAAM as the Muslim association that his government favoured, violence erupted among the Muslims belonging to the opposite camps. The rivalry between NAAM and Kakungulu's group was reflected at various events such as the Eid celebrations in January 1967. Kakungulu called for the Eid prayers on 12 January while Mufti Ssemakula called for the celebrations on 13, saying the moon had not been sighted.[59] Since NAAM did not own masjids, it began to violently confiscate those that belonged to the opposing Muslim associations in various locations across the country. A spate of violence erupted in Bugerere (Eastern Buganda) where two Muslim groups fought over a masjid and many were injured; Masaka (southern Buganda) where houses were burned; Busoga (Eastern Uganda), where Muslim groups claimed that NAAM followers violently took over their masjids, Ankole (Western Uganda) where the police intervened in a Muslim wrangle and killed supporters of the UMC. When the police intervened, it did so to protect the interests of NAAM.[60]

After these violent events, Mufti Ssemakula visited Obote who thanked him for his devotion to the advancement of the Muslim cause, and reminded him that the government was informed about another Muslim faction (Kakungulu's group) that was using the Islamic religion as a means to political advancement. And that the government had not intervened to arrest them due to the respect it accorded masjids as places of worship.[61] The death of Muslims in Ankole prompted a written response from the chairperson of the Uganda Muslim Students Association, Isa K.K. Lukwago,

---

[58] Ibid.
[59] The sighting of a new moon marks the beginning of a new month within the Islamic calendar, and thus the end of the fasting period and beginning of Eid.
[60] Kiyimba, 'The Muslim Community in Uganda through One Hundred and Forty Years', p. 100.
[61] *Uganda Argus*, 1 October 1968.

130   ISLAM IN UGANDA

who noted that NAAM's attempt to impose itself onto the Muslims as the only credible Muslim entity in Uganda spoke to ulterior motives beyond the Muslim cause. Lukwago added that the Mufti's visit to Obote was perceived as a victory lap in which he congratulated himself after killing pro-Kakungulu Muslims.[62] The tensions continued until Obote decided to arrest the leader of the opposing faction. In October 1970, Kakungulu was arrested and imprisoned until Idi Amin's coup in 1971.

A debate ensued as to the importance of NAAM, its benefits and costs. Sheikh Anas Kaliisa has argued that NAAM has to be understood as Obote's political project with a residual benefit for the Muslims. For Obote, NAAM was an opportunity to regain lost ground in Buganda, which he achieved when he sidelined Ganda royal power (represented by Kakungulu) in preference for Ssemakula and Kamulegeya. For the Muslims, NAAM reflected the foundational moment of establishing 'impersonal' structures that would enable institutional democracy outside the shadow of important personalities; the integration of NAAM members into the government structures also benefited many Muslim activities to the country; the NAAM constitution was the founding text of the future Uganda Muslim Supreme Council.[63] Others have argued that the violence that NAAM exhibited cannot be justified by residual benefits: 'we lost many loved ones when Obote's violence came to our villages; masjids were desecrated. How can we explain this loss? Don't tell us we got a public image when Obote brought us to the limelight. He used us for himself.'[64]

Conclusion

A few observations emerge from this chapter. As we have seen in the previous chapter, colonial governance of Islam and Muslims had eventually stabilized and established settled practices that turned Muslims into a political minority. The colonial state had instituted a bifurcated system of governance that consequently multifurcated society. As Islam and Muslim practices were relegated to the private realm, their political potential became appended to whichever of the non-Muslim parties could look to Muslims as important mediators in Uganda's political trajectory. This is what Milton Obote witnessed as Prime Minister at independence.

[62]   Lukwago to Sheikh Swaibu Ssemakula, 2 October 1968.
[63]   Kaliisa, Anas Abdunoor (1994), 'Leadership Crisis Among Muslims of Uganda (1850–1993)', Masters Dissertation, Kampala: Makerere University, p. 184.
[64]   FGD, Mbarara, 1 August 2016.

Facing a recalcitrant Ganda nationalism that desired for special status in the new unified Uganda, Obote looked for ways to push through his state project without at the same time alienating the Baganda whom he considered important players in the national political climate. Failing to trust alternative political players, Obote looked to Islam and Muslims for various benefits as a way to improve his social-political standing among the Baganda. As Muslims needed limelight from the political limbo they had been driven into since late 1890s, Obote was just eager to oblige. Yet, as an agent, Obote was also working in a larger historical structure. In founding NAAM, he was merely using his political power and influence to establish counter-elites to Mbogo's and Kakungulu's leadership of Islam and Muslims. Like these men, Obote's Muslim elites were buoyed by political power. The violence that engulfed the Muslim community at this time spoke of the state's desire to control, manage and direct Muslim social-political leaning towards Obote's government.

Obote's political tinkering with Islam and Muslims presented a challenging dilemma. While on the one hand it brought some sections of Muslims to the fore of mediating national politics, it at the same time marginalized significant sections of Muslims that suffered the brunt of state-orchestrated violence either because they sought to connect with Kakungulu's group, with other groups, or to remain autonomous. Obote followed up the legacy of the colonial state by supporting one group of Muslim elites while denigrating those opposed to his state project and in doing this, he created an atmosphere of intra-Muslim violence orchestrated by the state. Further, by allowing masjids and other sites of Muslim social power to become spaces of intra-Muslim violence, Obote redirected Islam and Muslims from the private realm where they had been languishing into the public arena. In this way, Muslim politicking, organization and conflict began to permeate national political discourse. Yet these strategies and tactics of statecraft did not originate with the Muslim groups; they were merely willing participants in Obote's desire to contain Buganda's recalcitrance. Muslims benefits were residual to Obote's unifying state project. Obote's founding of NAAM as his Muslim alliance shows that various leaders cultivated a role for Islam and Muslims when they encountered challenges in trying to construct their state projects. As the next chapter shows, Idi Amin conceived of state patronage of all Muslim groups as the best way to overcome the historical subjugation of Islam and Muslims. This of course had important implications for the future of Islam in Uganda.

CHAPTER 5

Idi Amin Attempts to Islamize the State

This chapter situates Amin and his relationship with the Muslim community within his quest for political legitimacy following the military coup. It argues that his articulation of the role Islam and Muslims would play in the state was closely related to the resolution of the nationality question as a basis of initial political support. It demonstrates that Amin courted Islamic ideology and Muslims for two major reasons: to gain political support after the international backlash following the Asian expulsion, and to end their historical marginalization in Uganda. Succinctly, his solution to the nationality problem brought a Western political backlash that forced him to court the Arabs/Muslims.

At home, Amin sought out Muslim unity for political support. Although Muslims reaped the political benefits of his regime, the biggest economic share went to his own ethnic group. This state patronage destabilized the historical balance of power both internally within the Muslim factions and externally with the Christian groups. Upon Amin's overthrow, sections of the Muslim population were targeted because of the anger, fear and hatred for the violence orchestrated under his regime. Muslims therefore became scapegoats for those misdeeds and suffered political retribution orchestrated by those who considered themselves victims of Amin's dictatorship.

This chapter describes the dynamics of Amin's attempt to right what he perceived as two historical wrongs in the country. First, Amin desired to settle the nationality question, perceived as the Asian problem; his solution was to expel Asian groups. Having come to power through a military coup, Amin rode on popular demand for the Africanization of the economy to expel Asians as a means to political legitimacy. Second, Amin perceived it his duty to right what he understood as historical Muslim marginalization in Uganda. As the Asian expulsion however revealed international political implications that challenged his government, Amin decided to court the Arab/Muslim states to provide international support to his regime. Internally, Amin appealed to Muslims' political support, which he could only acquire by attempting to unite them. For in their divided condition, they would not assist his political quest.[1]

The founding of the Uganda Muslim Supreme Council (UMSC, of which more below) and state patronage demonstrate Amin's attempt to draw Muslims close to political power, which destabilized the historical distribution of political influence in Uganda at two levels. First, within the Muslim community, the diverse Muslim alliances continued to subsist under the UMSC. Amin's centralization of Muslim leadership led to internal elite dominance when the schisms of the Obote I era re-emerged. The history of internal Muslim organization with both the National Association for the Advancement of Muslims (NAAM) and the Uganda Muslim Community (UMC) challenged Amin's attempt to end Muslim factionalism. Since NAAM members like Obeid Kamulegeya had political experience acquired from the Obote era, and since the Kakungulu-led UMC had felt the brunt of NAAM-directed conflicts, Amin's centralization merely revealed the deep-seated political wrangles and power rivalry between Kakungulu's Kibuli and the latent NAAM agents in the UMSC. The unifying leadership of the UMSC reproduced the very structure of Muslim power that it had intended to heal thereby revealing the contradictory nature of Amin's attempt to centralize Muslim leadership. As internal wrangles resurfaced, Amin took over its leadership and announced himself the patron of Muslims in Uganda, with immense implications for Muslim autonomy.

Second, Muslim state patronage destabilized the historical distribution of power between Muslims and Christian groups in Uganda. As Chapters 3 and 4 demonstrated, the political role of Muslims had been secondary to the Christian groups. Although Obote's founding of NAAM had brought Muslims closer to political power, it was never envisaged that they would inherit the state. And although he had a nationalistic outlook, Amin's later patronage of Muslims was interpreted as an attempt to Islamize the country. The wave of violence that engulfed his regime, especially targeting non-Muslim personalities, was interpreted as religiously inspired, inviting a fear of Islam and the targeting of Muslims as the backers of the Amin regime.

The chapter is organized in three sections. The first focuses on the first phase of Amin's government, what I call reorganization. I use this section to argue and demonstrate how Amin postulated a nationalistic image by

---

[1]   Kiyimba, 'The Muslim Community in Uganda through One Hundred and Forty Years', p. 101.

attempting to resolve what he perceived as deep-seated historical problems. It demonstrates how Amin's Asian expulsion projected him as a nationalist leader as a basis to acquire political legitimacy following the coup, with implications for his international image. The second section of this chapter focuses on the second phase of Amin's government, what I call consolidation. I argue here that Amin appealed to the Islamic identity and the Muslims to support his political project following the international backlash over his Asian expulsion, as he courted Arab/Muslim countries for economic and political support. His centralization of diverse Muslim alliances in Uganda under the UMSC as an institution maintained by state patronage reflects his desire to unify the Muslim constituency as the basis for political support. The section also demonstrates that Amin's Muslim patronage favoured particular groups as opposed to others; it allowed a particular group of Muslims to benefit from state privileges in multiple ways. As those close to power received material progress, those distant from it received residual benefits and status of protection; satisfied in the fact that they lived under Muslim leadership.[2] The third section discusses how the end of Amin's regime invited a wave of violence directed at Muslims but orchestrated by political victims of the Amin regime. It concludes by emphasizing the institutional legacy of the UMSC as an organ for Muslim unity and how successive regimes like Obote II (1980–85) and Okello Lutwa (1985–86) used its structures to appoint Muslim leaders favourable to their political interests.

Reorganizing the country: the Asian expulsion

After the military coup of 25 January 1971, Idi Amin became President of Uganda. It was the first time in post-colonial Uganda that an individual who also identified as a Muslim had held such a powerful position. Soldiers of the Uganda Army ousted Apollo Milton Obote while he was attending a Commonwealth Heads of Government meeting in Singapore, and announced Idi Amin as President of Uganda. Part of his reorganization of the country was to resolve two historical problems: the Asian challenge and Muslim marginalization in Uganda. Regarding the first wrong, Amin believed that the 'Africanization' (understood as on behalf of 'Black' people) of the economy would reduce economic exploitation

---

[2] The mutation of the Islamic greeting would reveal this. The response to the Muslim greeting 'Asaalam Alaykum' (peace be upon you) changed from 'Walaykum salaam' (and peace to you too), to 'Afuga Musiramu' (the president is Muslim). Personal communication from a Muslim elder, Kampala, 2016.

of 'Ugandans' and therefore decided to expel the groups he deemed responsible: the Asians and their British benefactors. Although considered nationalistic, the Asian expulsion was actually Amin's strategy of riding on popular mood to acquire political legitimacy following the coup. The resolution of the second historical problem would be more difficult than the first, as I shall show in the second section.

In a series of public pronouncements, Idi Amin argued that individuals of Asian origin were a threat to the social-economic independence of Uganda. The communications he used to address the nation highlight his thinking regarding the Asian challenge. According to Idi Amin, the Asians' vices were their domination of the economy at the expense of the 'indigenous' Uganda African and their failure to integrate themselves into the 'Ugandan' identity by maintaining their Asian identity.[3]

First, Amin identified the vice of economic domination with 'crimes' of 'economic sabotage' and other malpractices such as exploiting indigenous Ugandans while corrupting state officials. Amin reasoned that to achieve economic independence, the Asians could not be allowed to be dominating, controlling or monopolizing the business of the 'nation'.[4] He believed it his duty to safeguard the 'welfare' of all 'Ugandans' by wresting economic dominance from the hands of 'Asian foreigners' and giving it to the 'nationals of this country'. We can see from the outset that Amin articulated a vision of the nation-state project markedly different from Obote's. Whereas Obote's state project was about unifying the nation, which constituted all people resident within the state, including multiple races, for Amin, the nation was black. This articulation can be seen as a matter of statecraft and political pragmatism for Amin following the military coup. For, as indicated below, not all those considered 'foreigners' were actually to be chased away by the set of proclamations he made, showing that the claim to be a black nation worked as a pragmatic tactic to earn popular public support after the coup.

Second, Amin chastised the Asians for maintaining a closed identity. He presented Asian identity as a pathological category to convince the 'indigenous' Ugandans of the need to extirpate a 'problem'. Amin argued that the Asians' 'closed' identity influenced their refusal to integrate

---

[3]   'Message to the Nation by his Excellence General Idi Amin Dada, On British Citizens of Asian Origin and Citizens of India, Pakistan and Bangladesh living in Uganda', during the weekend of 12 and 13 August 1972, pp. 1–7 (hereinafter, Amin, Message to the nation). *Uganda Gazette*, Government Printer, Entebbe.

[4]   Ibid.

with 'Ugandan Africans'. It 'perturbed' his government that many of the 'Asians' had 'refused to identify' with, and to have faith in Uganda, a country that had 'nursed' them and from which they had 'amassed' resources.[5] Amin knew that Obote's government had offered Asians citizenship but the majority had turned it down; that those who accepted did so 'half-heartedly' – meaning that they maintained dual citizenship with other countries. It would seem that Amin perceived citizenship as a mutually exclusive phenomenon; the Asians were required to denounce claims of residence to other locations and commit to Uganda as 'home'. As the nationality debate in the previous chapter demonstrated, 'Ugandans' were disturbed by the idea that some 'settlers' had other 'homes' to which they could return.[6] It would seem that the Asians were living in fear of the politics of their 'new location' such that the very possibility of expulsion influenced the reluctance to 'belong' to Uganda, and to maintain dual citizenship as an exit strategy.

Then he turned his sights onto the British for two issues. First, when Amin decided to expel Asians, the British had launched what he interpreted as a 'global hate campaign' directed at a 'small developing country desperately struggling to take control' of its 'national wealth previously pillaged by foreigners'.[7] Second, the British were responsible for constructing the historical colonial policies from which the 'Asian problem' emerged. Amin believed that the British were 'too well grounded in political history to have been unaware of the ultimate results of these policies', which enforced economic expediency whose overall effect was 'political dynamite'.[8] With the highlight of Asian and British historical injustices, Amin denied any racial bias in his decision and galvanized all 'Ugandans' to 'salvage' the nation.[9] The only exceptions to the expulsion were employees of government and its other bodies. Professionals in various sectors of industry and in international organizations were also exempted.[10] Amin proceeded to nationalize some British firms and properties amid British 'threats' such as cutting off foreign assistance.[11] Amin convened a conference to realize his beliefs. Training programmes were to induct people

[5] Ibid., p. 4.
[6] See section in Chapter 4, 'The nationality question'.
[7] President Idi Amin Dada, 'Midnight Address to the Nation', 17 December 1972. *Uganda Gazette*, Government Printer, Entebbe.
[8] Ibid., pp. 24–5.
[9] Ibid., pp. 5–6.
[10] Ibid., pp. 1–2.
[11] Ibid.

into how to manage businesses.[12]Government reorganized the administration of the country beyond the 'haphazard' and 'irrational' administrative units of the colonial era to enable 'effective' administration at the grass roots and encourage 'local initiative'.[13] Social-political spaces such as infrastructure,[14] social relations[15] and social time[16] were also transformed.

How truly nationalistic was the Asian expulsion, or was it a ploy for political legitimacy? It should be noted from the outset that some of the Asians Amin expelled were Muslims, which may have bothered Amin but it did not deter his policy because he had interpreted the nationality question in racist terms. To Amin, the nation was 'black' and any other racial category was considered alien. Amin's action would cast him alongside the 'Black Africanist' side of the debate on the nationality question.[17] A few voices however reveal the intention of the Asian expulsion, which endeared Amin to the people. Some have considered it the most popular action ever taken by a Uganda leader.[18] Ali Mazrui termed it an assertion of power.[19] When I raised the matter of the Asian expulsion in a discussion with elders who experienced the Amin regime, they unanimously agreed that Amin's decision was very popular among 'Black Ugandans' because they hoped it would realize the Africanization of the economy regardless of its intentions:

[12] President Idi Amin Dada, speech on the occasion of the conference of representatives of the people on the transfer of economy into the hands of Ugandans, 29 August 1972, Kampala International Conference Centre, *Uganda Gazette*, Government Printer, Entebbe.

[13] Amin, Conference speech, pp. 14–15.

[14] Amin changed the titles of various streets and roads identified with 'English' names and renamed them after African nationalists and famous 'Third World' revolutionaries, so as to shake off 'signs of imperialism'. Prince Charles Drive in Kololo, Kampala, was for instance, renamed '25th January Avenue' to signify the date when the Second Republic of Uganda was born (the military coup of 25 January 1971).

[15] Kampala Club was renamed 'Government Club'. Section 162 (1) (ee) of the Penal Code Act (Amendment), 6 June 1972, banned miniskirts and other clothing so as to make Ugandan fashion more African in outlook.

[16] Bars and nightclubs received new time schedules.

[17] See section in Chapter 4, 'The nationality question'.

[18] FGD, Iganga, 3 November 2016.

[19] Mazrui, Ali (1980), 'Between Development and Decay: Anarchy, Tyranny and Progress under Amin', *Third World Quarterly*, Vol. 2, No. 1, pp. 44–58, p. 53.

ISLAM IN UGANDA

> The expulsion promised some sort of real emancipation after all the promises of independence. You should know the Asians worked as middlemen and there was little chance for the black person to advance economically. But Amin pronounced radical changes and we got excited. Many of us benefited little from the expulsion. But his message gave us hope that we could have a chance also.[20]

Others have argued that we need to judge Amin's intentions in the context of his professional background and more specifically in the nature of his acquisition of power:

> First of all, Amin was a soldier and he took power through a military coup. As a professional soldier, he had less contact with people. But after the coup, he was required to look for a popular base. Expelling what many people considered economic challenges would give him a political base. Second, as a soldier, he was trained in fighting wars. Does it surprise us that he called the expulsion and the nationalization of companies as economic wars? So you see the make-up of the man and his actions wanted to excite the nation so as to gain popular support for his regime.[21]

These views reveal that Amin realized the prevailing public mood and took advantage of it. Although his coup was a popular act, he knew that it was not durable unless followed up by successive popular displays of change. He therefore identified a popular issue and decided to wage 'war' on it. Its resolution culminated in the Asian expulsion, which won Amin more popularity and designated him as the 'people's president'. Such piecemeal responses would not however undergird a durable political order especially when international opposition to the Asian expulsion threatened the economic security of his government.

At the international level, the Asian expulsion set in motion a series of political blowbacks that disrupted Amin's government. As foreign governments such as India, Israel, United States and Britain, denigrated Amin's decision, his relations with Western powers became difficult. Britain cut off its foreign aid, India promised repercussions and the United States closed its embassy in Kampala. Israel also closed its diplomatic and military ties to Uganda.[22] To offset these challenges, Amin appealed to the Arab Muslims. Internally, he needed a durable political base to undergird his regime. Although his coup had ridden on the unpopularity surrounding

---

[20] FGD, Iganga, 3 November 2016.
[21] Interview with AK, 24 July 2017.
[22] *Uganda Argus*, 24 and 31 March 1972.

Obote's government, such support was not durable and Amin therefore needed to reposition himself.[23] As a Muslim, he appealed to his religious constituency for durable support.

Amin and the Muslims: the phase of consolidation

How Amin appealed to the Islamic identity and the Muslims to support his political project in response to the political criticism over his Asian expulsion formed the core of the Muslim question of the time. Briefly, it was about leadership and representation. Sub-questions surrounding the public role of Islam in the state, why and how Amin sought to centralize Muslim leadership in the country at the expense of decentralized Muslim religious autonomy constituted the broader Muslim question. I argue in this section that Amin appealed to Islam as an ideology to support his quest for durable political legitimacy. Islam here came to play a role akin to the Sudanic state of the Sultanate of Dar Fur and later under Muteesa I in pre-colonial Buganda.[24] His appeal to the Arab/Muslim countries provided many benefits to government, which also happened to support Islam and Muslims. Internally, Amin's centralization of diverse Muslim alliances under one umbrella body enabled a unified Muslim constituency as the social base of his political power. However, this had adverse effects such as reproducing the internal power rivalries of the competing Muslim factions. Amin's Muslim patronage favoured particular groups as opposed to others; it allowed a particular group of Muslims to benefit from state privileges in multiple ways.

Debates on the historical role of Idi Amin in the Muslim community coalesce around a central question as to whether he truly had Islam and Muslims at heart or he 'used' both to achieve his ends. Some have wondered whether Amin achieved a Muslim revolution in Uganda. Other scholars have argued that we need to situate Amin in the camp of men like Obote who 'used' and 'interfered' in Muslim spaces for their own political agendas.[25] Kasumba has refuted the claim that Idi Amin was a 'Muslim hero' who came to 'salvage' Muslims. He believes that Amin's politics

---

23 Kiyimba, 'The Muslim Community in Uganda through One Hundred and Forty Years', pp. 101.

24 Mamdani, Mahmood (2010), *Saviors and Survivors: Darfur, Politics and the War on Terror*, CODESRIA: Dakar, chapter 2, p. 53.

25 Kasumba, Yusuf (2015) 'Attempts at a Rejuvenation of Muslim Identity in Uganda: The Era of Idi Amin (1971–1979)', *Danubius*, No. XXXIII, pp. 379–408.

did little to champion the Muslim cause; although some evidence points to the Muslim community as the largest beneficiary of Amin's regime, this was a residual consequence of the political atmosphere of the time.[26] What Kasumba implies is that, even as a leader that identified with Islam and the Muslims, Amin failed to conceive of a systematic plan to undertake a social-political revolution by elevating Muslim society from its 'marginal' position in the country. Amin's contributions to the Muslim community were in other words cosmetic and not far-reaching.[27]

Another scholar has argued that Amin did not 'use' Islam and Muslims but his regime must be situated in his multiple identities: Amin perceived himself a nationalist, Muslim and an ethnic person, any of which must have influenced his political choices. More particularly, Amin was acting in a complex political environment that militated against any Muslim revolution however much he may have desired it. Therefore, '[s]cholars like Kasumba who fail to understand Amin's unique place in Uganda's history' unfairly chastise him.[28] This scholarship argues that Idi Amin should not be read as a revolutionary figure because he was confronting forces beyond his possibility to extirpate. Having inherited a country largely influenced by the historical trajectory of Christian power, it would be difficult for any individual, however monumentally his power extended, to reverse such a long historical trajectory.[29] One Muslim leader has argued that his contribution to the

> Muslim community was not residual, he was after all a Muslim and he wanted his co-religionists to advance as well as the Christian groups. But was it a revolution? I doubt it. Did he wish to advance Islam and Muslims? Yes. But how can we also explain his stance against fellow Muslims like Moses Ali, Obeid Kamulegeya and Mustafa Idris? At particular moments, Amin saw these Muslims as a threat to his interests. So we need to look beyond Islam as identity and focus on its role in national politics, it's a political matter.[30]

According to these latter views, Amin was the president of a country who also happened to be Muslim. His nationalistic appeal may have stood out but 'it was just part of his personal make up, as a military man, he considered discipline important in the success of any plan. We must also pay

[26] Ibid., p. 380.
[27] Ibid., p. 385.
[28] Interview with AK, Makerere University, 24 July 2017.
[29] Ibid.
[30] Interview with Chief Khadi, Masaka, 13 August 2017.

attention to the fact that some of Amin's Muslim contributions were reactions to particular circumstances as opposed to carefully thought-out plans that systematized intended actions'.[31]

In the wake of the international reaction to the Asian expulsion, Amin undertook various foreign visits to Arab/Muslim states, which ensured various benefits. Some of these visits may have been out of pomp but they turned out beneficial to the Ugandan community and some special benefits went to the Muslim community.[32] A few cases highlight this. He went for a tour of the Arab/Muslim world and visited nine countries in June 1962. Libya and Saudi Arabia provided the largest amount of economic aid to Uganda. In Libya, he signed the Tripoli Communiqué with Muammar Gaddafi, which assured Amin international support. On 21 February 1972, a Libyan diplomatic contingent arrived in Uganda to discuss the promotion of cooperation between both countries. Although Islamic schools and masjids would be built, other areas such as trade, economic and technical assistance to the Air Force and the Uganda Army, featured prominently.[33] Having secured these commitments for cooperation, Amin terminated his relations with Israel.[34]

Amin went to Mecca and visited King Faisal who reciprocated by visiting Uganda in November 1972. Faisal praised Amin's anti-Israel approach and promised economic and other assistance towards Islam in Uganda. Gaddafi also visited Uganda in 1973. In 1974, Uganda was admitted as a member of the Organisation of Islamic Cooperation (OIC) and it officially became a Muslim state. Amin lobbied the OIC to found an English-speaking Islamic University to be built in Uganda and he would later use his influence while in exile to realize this request.[35] Although these foreign visits enabled Amin to gain resources that compensated for the loss of Western grants, they also enabled him to acquire resources that would improve the Muslim condition in Uganda. Although Muslims became involved in the close working of the state, this did not proceed from an established plan of action; Amin undertook no serious investigation into the Muslims' condition as a prelude to its uplift, he made simple inquiries that he used as the basis of his actions. A few cases highlight this.

[31] Interview with AK, Makerere University, 24 July 2017.
[32] Ibid.
[33] *Uganda Argus*, 28 February 1972.
[34] *Uganda Argus*, 24 and 31 March 1972.
[35] Professor Abasi Kiyimba, Ramadan Facilitation workshop, Kibuli, 28 May 2017.

142   ISLAM IN UGANDA

When Amin went for the annual pilgrimage in Mecca, the Ugandan press corps escorted him to cover the rites. Upon reaching Jeddah, Amin reminded the non-Muslims that they were not invited near the Kaaba and therefore summoned the 'Muslim' press officers to follow him. Amin was shocked when he saw only one Muslim journalist follow him to the Kaaba. He was distraught upon learning that non-Muslims dominated the presidential press corps. When he returned to Kampala he asked Abu Mayanja to identify Muslims that could be employed in government and the civil service, Mayanja responded that there was few of his calibre.[36] Amin's impact on Muslims' advanced education was influenced by the Jeddah incident but intensified by another in Kalungu, Masaka. He had gone to visit a Muslim-registered school only to learn that the head teacher was a non-Muslim. When he inquired as to how a Muslim institution could be led by a non-Muslim, he was informed that there were no Muslims at the requisite level to head the school. He thus ordered the head teacher to vacate his position and for a Muslim to take over. A lower grade teacher took over as head teacher, which begun the popular saying '*buli mbuzi ku nkondo yaayo*' (let every goat be tethered to its pole), which meant that head teachers were to concentrate on heading institutions of their religious denominations.[37]

When he learned that there were no Muslim teachers to instruct Muslim students in Islamic studies, Amin ordered that a group of Islamic-oriented teachers be sent to the Uganda Poytechnic Kyambogo, in Kampala, for a four-month teacher-training course in Islamic studies. These were also tasked with developing comprehensive Islamic syllabi for both Ordinary and Advanced Levels, which have never been reviewed to date.[38] These incidents convinced Amin that Muslims' education in Uganda was still low and he established a Muslim scholarship desk in State House to solicit for advanced education from established universities in the Arab and Muslim world. He made it his duty to request for educational facilities for Ugandan Muslim students whenever he took foreign trips. Saudi Arabia, Pakistan, Libya, Iraq, Egypt, Sudan and other countries responded with many scholarships. These students however returned after Amin's ouster in 1979, but they proceeded to influence Muslim affairs in Uganda.[39] Although touted as a Muslim educational project, the Islamic University built in 1988 in Mbale (Eastern Uganda) was also an outcome of unintended causes. According

---

[36]   Interview with AK, Makerere University, 24 July 2017.
[37]   Interview with Chief Khadi, Masaka, 13 August 2017.
[38]   Interview with AK, Makerere University, 24 July 2017.
[39]   Ibid.

to one scholar, Amin went to Lahore under the 'pomp and glamour' of attending an international conference, but returned with a university.[40] In 1974, Amin went to Lahore, Pakistan, to attend the conference of the OIC countries. His visit caused discomfort in non-Muslim circles in Uganda; some scholars designated him a religious stranger.[41] His actions however enabled Uganda to host an Islamic University and gain admission to the membership of the OIC since it contained a Muslim population; and OIC membership allowed Uganda to easily access development finance from the Islamic Development Bank. This last benefit explains why successive non-Muslim regimes declined to de-register Uganda from OIC membership. Amin achieved this because Uganda had a Muslim population that could be identified to benefit from these opportunities.[42]

To consolidate his regime, Amin founded the UMSC and he became its patron. Its founding reflected Amin's attempt to centralize Muslim leadership in Uganda. It would serve particular purposes. As an institution, the UMSC would coordinate Muslim activities and account for the benefits of Amin's foreign visits. The unification of Muslim factions guaranteed Amin a united social base that would provide durable political support for his regime, demonstrating that the doctrinal disagreements of Muslims were minute, and a united Muslim body could accommodate them.[43] Amin founded a department of religious affairs in the President's Office, which he used to check on the religious situation in the country. This department was akin to an intelligence-gathering unit that informed the President about the internal schisms among Muslim groups. To resolve Muslim factionalism, Amin sent religious denominations, including the Christian groups, to a conference in Kabale (south-west Uganda) to identify ways of ending religious discords. Fearing that one Muslim faction would favour its own interests, the first Muslims' meeting was chaired by a Protestant.[44] The deliberations at Kabale indicated that Buganda region had received a large share of resources directed at Islam to the detriment of other regions. To improve this situation, an administrative institution was imagined, headed by a secretariat, to govern Islam and Muslim affairs. Other reforms included the reform of education and the

---

[40] FGD, Mbale, 1 December 2016.

[41] See particularly Mazrui, Ali A. (1977), 'Religious Strangers in Uganda: From Emin Pasha to Amin Dada', *African Affairs,* Vol. 76, No. 302, pp. 21–8.

[42] Kiyimba, 'The Muslim Community in Uganda through One Hundred and Forty Years', p. 102.

[43] Ibid., pp. 96–7.

[44] Kasozi, *The Life of Prince Badru Kakungulu Wasajja,* pp. 188–9.

democratic election of religious leaders.[45] On 1 June 1972, Amin inaugurated the Uganda Muslim Supreme Council (UMSC) as an institution to advance the affairs of all Muslims in Uganda. He bequeathed resources of the departing Asian community to the UMSC,[46] which became the richest landlord in the country bar the Kabaka.

Was Uganda considered a Muslim state just because the OIC had admitted it in its ranks? Iza Hussin has argued that the Islamic character of a state can neither be based on the content of its laws nor the state's willingness to enforce them. The assumption that the laws of the 'Quran and the laws of the state would be nearly as equivalent as modern man can manage' is a powerful demand that centralizes the role of the state in defining, containing and delivering Islam.[47] The assumptions however overlook the fact that there are multiple interpretations of Islam and also various expressions of being Muslim. Just as there is the Islamic law of the Sharia, a matter for the Khadi court to decide, there is also the 'Islamic law of the community, passed down from' one's grandmother. The Sharia that the state applies may be different from the one that 'men and women call upon to critique' its actions. The 'Islamic law', however and by whomever it is invoked therefore seems to carry the 'shades of all these meanings and the grey areas between them'.[48] Following Hussin, I believe the Islamic character of Amin's regime can be seen in the assertions of the minority Muslims who claimed belonging to 'Muslim' leadership regardless of the fact that non-Muslims formed the majority of the population.

The actual life of the UMSC revealed challenges that demonstrate the difficulty of Amin's attempt to centralize Muslim leadership, which also reflect the strong commitments of the various elite leaders to maintain control of their separate Muslim bodies. Since many Muslim leaders feared Amin's military machine, they chose silence over manifest display of opposition. State patronage over Islam and the Muslims therefore failed to extinguish the diverse Muslim alliances and their representative factions as internal elite dominance reproduced the schisms of the Obote era. State patronage also favoured particular groups as opposed to others. Amin's ethnic kinsmen significantly benefited from state privileges in multiple ways. As they received material progress, others received residual benefits. Let me highlight some of these challenges.

---

[45]   *Minutes of the Kabale Religious Conference,* May 1972.
[46]   Amin to Captain Noah Muhammad, 27 September 1973.
[47]   Hussin, *The Politics of Islamic Law,* p. 4.
[48]   Ibid., p. 6.

Amin's centralization of Muslim leadership faced obstacles from the vested interests of particular factions, many of whom would have preferred decentralized structures in which each of the old factions were allowed a degree of independence.[49] Centralization had some difficulties. First, the UMSC was conceived as a political entity, founded by a political command of the President. By implication, micro and macro politics were to taint its life during Amin's and successive regimes.[50] The UMSC structure allowed three Muslim delegates from each district, who would combine with delegates from other districts to constitute its General Assembly. The elected delegates were however still divided along their previous factions. When a chief khadi was conceived, it was considered prudent to also found the position of deputy chief khadi so as to allow honour and status to a defeated constituency, whose losing member would become deputy khadi. When Amin saw that Abdul Razzaq Matovu was to become Chief Khadi, he allegedly told the electoral body to appoint Sheikh Ali Kkulumba as his deputy so as to balance up the leadership and reduce the possible fall out.[51] The state thus continued to play a balancing role to offset political discontent.

Second, the political life of the UMSC exhibited political novices against experienced Muslim politicians. Using its experiences gained in the Obote era, NAAM leadership came to dominate Muslim politics to the detriment of Muslim leaders from the Kibuli-based UMC. Political party affiliation also interfered here, where Shaban Nkutu and Obeid Kamulegeya, UPC-NAAM stalwarts, used their connections in the army and other offices to influence Muslim policy.[52] Prince Badru Kakungulu refused to participate in the activities that founded the UMSC. Although it was Idi Amin who released him from Obote's imprisonment, and it was Amin who also returned the remains of the deceased Kabaka Muteesa II from Britain, Kakungulu's status as a member of the Buganda royal family had created rumours that many Ganda Muslims looked up to him as the one to restore Buganda power at Mengo.[53] He remained at his residence in Kibuli but did not openly oppose Idi Amin. To dissolve the bickering among factions, Amin donated Kampala Hill (present-day Old

---

[49]   Kaliisa, Anas Abdunoor (1994), 'Leadership Crisis Among Muslims of Uganda (1850–1993)', Masters Dissertation, Kampala: Makerere University, p. 199.

[50]   FGD, Mbale, 1 December 2016.

[51]   Kasozi, *The Life of Prince Badru Kakungulu Wasajja*, pp. 188–9.

[52]   Ibid., p. 189–90.

[53]   Ibid., pp. 190–92.

146   ISLAM IN UGANDA

Kampala) to build what he considered neutral headquarters that would not be identified with existing factions – added to the properties the UMSC received from the expelled Asian Muslim associations such as the Jammat Ismailia Association, the Sunni Association, Daudi Bohora and others.[54]

Third, Amin made dictatorial decisions regarding Islamic and Muslim issues without the UMSC leadership structures. On one occasion, for instance, he declared that Eid el-Fitri (celebrations after fasting) would be celebrated on 18 November and that disobedience would be punished severely, thereby overruling the Islamic tradition of sighting the new moon before Eid. When Muslims declined to attend his Eid celebrations, Amin interpreted that Ganda Muslims, especially Kakungulu, had caused the mass Muslim rebellion.[55] It has been argued however that the internal leadership challenges of administering the UMSC *invited* Amin to interfere with its activities. The UMSC leadership experienced conflict over the roles of its key political officers especially the Chief Khadi and the Deputy Chief Khadi. The centralization of Muslim leadership had suppressed private Muslim organizations that looked at the UMSC as the threat to their livelihood, and they used this as an opportunity to cause dissension.[56]

Fearing that a Muslim leader would taint the report, Amin instituted an inquiry into the discords at the UMSC, in 1975, headed by a Christian military chaplain. Amin followed the report from the inquiry by dismissing the Chief Khadi, Abdul Razzaq Matovu, and his deputies, and appointed Sheikh Yusuf Sulaiman Matovu as a replacement. He too was dismissed before he could settle in office. Soon Amin threatened that he would ask 'Christians' to run the affairs of the Muslims if they failed to avoid discord. He followed through with his threat when he appointed a Colonel Mondo, a non-Muslim, to chair an inquiry into the operation of the UMSC especially the mosque building committee that then Brigadier Moses Ali chaired. Upon the completion of the inquiry, a non-Muslim official from the ministry of finance had to counter-sign all UMSC cheques. Thus between 1975 and April 1979, UMSC was an entity in name, but it was run by the head of state who made major leadership decisions.[57] Neither did the Council meet at the various levels of management, and district khadis were directly appointed from the headquarters. In this environment of control, social, political and financial accountability

---

[54]   Report of the Executive Committee of the Uganda Muslim Supreme Council, 18 December 1972, Minute 33/72.
[55]   Kasozi, *The Life of Prince Badru Kakungulu Wasajja,* p. 192.
[56]   Ibid., p. 195.
[57]   Ibid., pp. 195–7.

became difficult; criticisms became difficult to mount as the authority of the head of state could not be questioned. It was on this last point that Kakungulu founded 'the Kibuli Club' as an informal club of educated and business elites in which the members clandestinely discussed Islamic and Muslims' issues.[58]

The institutional legacy of UMSC

The impact of Amin's regime on Uganda's political scene cannot be underestimated. His military approach to social-political-economic issues meant that he was many times dubbed a military dictator. The results of his nevertheless pragmatic approach to governance were far-reaching. Amin's rule allowed a broader role for Islam and Muslims in the state and accorded them a new status hitherto unimagined, when Muslims became among the most powerful people in Uganda who enjoyed state privileges.[59] The onset of the 1979 war however pushed Islam and Muslims to the defensive. The anti-Amin fighting force coined the phrase 'fighting Aminism' as a justification to commit crimes against Muslims in various parts of the country.[60] The charge was that Muslims had supported and benefited from Amin's regime. A.B.K. Kasozi argues however that not every Muslim benefited equally from Amin's regime. Many Muslims from West Nile and Nubians who shared Amin's ethnic identity were close beneficiaries of state privilege and properties, particularly those in the army. These were opposed to southerners who also suffered under Amin's regime, in some ways.[61] The violence targeting Islamic spaces and Muslims was much felt in Ankole and Masaka in the south-west where the exiles returning from Tanzania, mainly supporters of Obote, ordered the massacre of Muslims due to both their Islamic identity and as non-UPC supporters.[62] The return of Obote to political power after the elections in December 1980 recast UPC-leaning Muslim elites as the dominant players in the UMSC.

Amin has been blamed for setting an example that successive governments followed to interfere in the activities of the UMSC. Yusuf Kasumba has argued that regardless of Amin's intentions, his interference reduced UMSC to a state organ to serve his political interests, something that later

---

[58] Ibid., p. 202.

[59] Mazrui, 'Between Development and Decay', p. 52.

[60] Kiyimba, Abasi (2012), 'A Detailed Account of the 1979 Massacre of Muslims in Western Uganda', *The Campus Journal*, 31 July.

[61] Kasozi, *The Life of Prince Badru Kakungulu Wasajja*, p. 198.

[62] FGD, Mbarara, 3 August 2016.

regimes adopted.[63] Discussions with Muslim elders in Busoga revealed that they share Kasumba's views. These elders argued that when Amin placed Muslims very close to his power, it meant that he feared them. This was a signal to future holders of political power that they should also keep the Muslim factions very close to power: after all, 'if their own [Amin] feared them, we should be more concerned'.[64] In response to these claims, it is important to remember that the intrusion of power into sacred spaces – Kasumba's 'interference' – has a history that predates Amin. What should be emphasized are the intentions that political power seeks when it intrudes into religious spaces. Amin was not the first leader to accommodate Muslims under his regime; the colonial state set the example that Obote imitated for political interests. Although Amin's advancement of Muslims supported his political legitimacy, his intrusion into the UMSC also served benevolent motives.

Unlike the colonial authorities and Obote, Amin was actually a Muslim who desired to advance his religion. Unfortunately, he was also the head of state. When he fused these two obligations, the UMSC wore a political garb and it was identified more with the decisions of its benefactor. Intervention must therefore be situated within a social-political-personal context that seeks to understand the intentions that drive the actor. Amin's intervention was also induced by the failure of the leaders to identify proper working relationships, which invited him to resolve internal discords. The fact that the UMSC survived its founder implies that he intended it as a lifelong project to unite Muslims. The problem was never with the institution but rather with the agency of particular actors.

This analysis therefore situates intrusion in a tripartite relationship: the social-political context of the time, the intentions of intrusive power, and the invitation from particular forms of conduct. Basing on the level of anti-Muslim anxieties that preceded Amin's ousting, one would imagine that the liberators wanted to extirpate all signs of 'Aminism' including his institutions. The UMSC survived Amin's overthrow as an institution because its structure was harmless. It only mattered which individuals presided over it. Successive leaders ensured that 'friendly' Muslim elites led the UMSC and its representative control over multiple Muslim alliances. Political intrusion in Muslim spaces continued when Obote II (1980–85) rekindled his alliance with former NAAM elites. Okello Lutwa (President 1985–86) also cultivated his Muslim leadership in opposition to UPC-NAAM.

---

[63] Kasumba, 'Attempts at a rejuvenation of Muslim Identity in Uganda', p. 402.
[64] FGD, Iganga, 3 November 2016.

The return of Obote to Uganda's political scene however highlighted a particular issue that had implications on the Muslim question: the role of non-Muslim elites who combine with Muslim elites to influence the trajectory of Muslim affairs. When Sheikh Abdu Obeid Kamulegeya vied with Sheikh Kassim Mulumba for the leadership of the UMSC, their disagreements invited mediation from Mubarak Qasamallah from the World Muslim League in 1981. In what became the Qasamallah Unity Accord, Kassim Mulumba was to become Mufti (Chief Khadi, as it were) and Kamulegeya to deputize. The Unity Accord was however difficult to implement because Kamulegeya – albeit lacking popular support – had the support of the 'secular' elite in the UPC Obote II government that went back to the NAAM era under Obote I. The Muslim elites in Kamulegeya's camp included UPC stalwarts like Abu Mayanja, Sulayman Kiggundu, Issa Lukwago and others, who had experience of the national political arena and seemed determined to galvanize UPC support for their candidate. Mulumba's side, on the contrary, had sheikhs inexperienced in the political negotiations and manipulations that ensued. Within this particular juncture, the UMSC came to mirror the political realities of its founding moment.[65] The Chief Khadi-elect became isolated and surrounded by hostile individuals that made work difficult, if not impossible. President Obote began to by-pass Mulumba to deal with his friend Kamulegeya. In 1983 Mulumba resigned and Kamulegeya became Chief Khadi. Unexpectedly, Mulumba succumbed to 'popular demand' and rescinded his resignation to re-assert claims to his former office. Non-Muslim UPC elites galvanized all state support to defeat Mulumba's claims by deploying security agencies to disperse his mammoth crowds from masjids in Kampala. Relocated to Lubaga road, Mulumba's supporters lost morale.[66]

Non-Muslim elites however also supported Mulumba's claim to UMSC leadership. Paulo Muwanga, Obote's Vice President, also used his state resources to support Mulumba, allegedly owing to a social friendship.[67] Violent clashes would erupt when police officers from Obote's office came to disperse a Maulid festival to which Paulo Muwanga had also given police protection. The policemen from the higher office usually determined the outcome. Kamulegeya however used state support to undertake a country-wide eviction of Mulumba's supporters from masjids and Muslim district

[65] Interview with Hajji HS, Mbale, 1 December 2016.
[66] Kiyimba, 'The Muslim Community in Uganda through One Hundred and Forty Years', p. 105.
[67] The two first met in Cairo when Sheikh Mulumba was studying in Egypt and Muwanga was Uganda's Ambassador to Egypt, during the Obote I regime.

150 ISLAM IN UGANDA

offices. The use of brutal force reminded many of the days of the first republic when NAAM deployed its agents to confiscate masjids. Invited to a Muslim workshop in July 1984, Obote informed Kamulegeya that he should ignore Mulumba's claims to UMSC leadership, which symbolized his intention to use all means to support him. When the military coup of July 1985 ousted Obote and brought Tito Okello Lutwa to power, non-Muslim elites were instrumental in chasing Kamulegeya out of the UMSC and installing Mulumba as Chief Khadi. His first official act was to lead prayers at Lutwa's swearing-in ceremony.[68]

Conclusion

In concluding this chapter, several key points arise. Idi Amin appealed to a prevailing national mood to popularize his regime following the military coup. His resolution of the first historical problem (the Asians' expulsion) however brought international challenges to his government. He therefore appealed to his Muslim constituency both nationally and internationally to gain the social base for his political legitimacy. His patronage of Muslims was short of a revolution because historical forces substantially maintained the social power of Christian groups in Uganda.

Amin's largest contribution to Islam and Muslims can be seen in three major ways. First, the founding of the UMSC enabled state patronage that actually advanced Islam and Muslims in the country regardless of its challenges. Second, Amin brought Muslims close to political power and therefore provoked anti-Muslim anxieties from Christian groups that interpreted this as an attempt to Islamize the state. Third, Amin's 'students' – those that benefited from state scholarships – returned after his ouster to become some of the key players in the Islamic reform movement. The re-emergence of intra-Muslim squabbles during the Obote II and Lutwa governments, which were intensified by the protagonists' relationship with non-Muslim elites in the state, bred an intra-Muslim debate on the role of non-Muslim leaders in Muslim affairs. This debate was anchored in a reformist discourse led by students from the Arab world who had benefited from state scholarships. Tired of the leadership of 'old' sheikhs, this youthful Muslim alliance desired a new role for Islam within a majorly non-Muslim society and a limited role for the state within Islam and Muslims. The debates of this reformist discourse form the subject of the next chapter.

---

[68] Kiyimba, 'The Muslim Community in Uganda through One Hundred and Forty Years', p. 105; Kasozi, *The Life of Prince Badru Kakungulu Wasajja*, pp. 225–37.

CHAPTER 6

Islamic Reform and Intra-Muslim Violence

This chapter discusses the nature and character of the Islamic reform movement in Uganda under the National Resistance Movement (NRM) regime. It contends that the violent attitude of the Islamic reform movement bred a language of radical expressions of Islam internal to the general Muslim public. It considers that the intra-Muslim debate within the Tabligh/Salafiyya movement informed multiple social-political imaginations when various splits in elite Muslim leaderships perceived and sought to cultivate a role of reformist Islam within the Uganda state. As one side argued that Muslim youth were an important fulcrum in reforming the state to found a *dawla* Islamiya (Islamic state) another argued that Muslims were safe within the majorly non-Muslim state. The paralysis within this debate bred a wave of intra-Muslim violence that culminated in conflict around masjids as sites of Muslim power. These instances of Muslim violence and the consequent Allied Democratic Forces (ADF) rebellion invited intervention from the state to counter the Tabligh threat using its military and political machinery.

The chapter demonstrates that Islamic reform was a product of three important moments that reinforced each other. First, the role of Idi Amin in attempting to construct a single unified Islamic centre under state patronage had met with momentary success when Amin's patronage welded Muslims under a single force, which convinced many Muslims of the opportunities of Muslim unity. The nascent reformist debate therefore spoke to ways of transcending historical marginalization by consolidating the gains of Muslim unity. As reformers took a nostalgic view of the Salaf, they imagined a new role for Islam within a majorly non-Muslim society. How to overcome this Muslim minority status came to dominate the reformist debate.

Second, returning Muslim students of Islamic studies that had gone abroad to Libya (Tripoli), Saudi Arabia (Jeddah, Madina), Pakistan

(Lahore), Sudan (Khartoum) and Misr (Al-Azhar), became agents of local reform in connection with the various structures and spheres where they studied. (Returning students took after their Alma Mater, e.g. those from Madina designated themselves Ba nna Madina.) Many of these returning students became Islamic preachers in urban masjids or took up teaching positions in Islamic schools. The urban concentration of the reform centres meant that Muslim representation was still bedevilled by its historical burdens of the colonial and Obote eras. As these urban-based preachers went to rural spaces to purify 'traditional' practices by enforcing a 'correct' form of Islam, religious propagation (*dawah*) shifted from *nasiha* (advice) to *naqd* (critique) thereby breeding resistance from the very public it targeted. Two major consequences resulted from this: (i) the Tabligh movement split into various factions that sought to assert discursive coherence over other groups. It was these splits that bred the ADF rebellion; (ii) the fragmentation of reformist debate also fragmented already existing Muslim alliances into many internal factions, which reflected the contradictions embedded in the quest for Muslim unity. When the agents of Islamic reform attached themselves to the Kibuli and Old Kampala centres of Muslim leadership in Uganda, other Muslims began to articulate Islam differently by organizing their practices around other centres such as universities, business clubs and other political associations to express their disappointment with the 'traditional' centres of Muslim leadership and their monopoly over Islamic organization. So, the question of 'who are the Muslims?' and 'where are they located?' cannot be answered by simply pointing to the popular sites of Muslim identity, but rather through acknowledging the diverse, multiple and contradictory ways in which all those who claim to belong to Islam articulate themselves.

Third, the intra-Muslim debates bred a wave of violence that cultivated a *special* role for the state within the Muslim organizations. This occurred on two fronts: (i) The hostile character of the *dawah* movement bred a Muslim backlash that in turn bred a new language of Muslim radicalism. A category of Tabligh were marked as 'radical' and 'uncompromising' characters – meaning that radicalism among Muslims was also born within the moment of reform. (ii) The emergence of Muslim groups that sought to use violence to reform the state also invited the state to intervene in Muslim politics using violent counter strategies, with consequences for the various Muslim individuals and the general Muslim community.

This chapter is divided into three sections that focus on the various issues that emerged within various moments of reform. The first discusses the need, nature and character of reformist Islam within Uganda. It argues that the violence of the intra-Muslim reform agenda bred a language of Muslim

ISLAMIC REFORM AND INTRA-MUSLIM VIOLENCE   153

radicalism which also founded the first excuse for state infiltration of the Muslim social-political spaces. The second section discusses the internal debate regarding the reform agenda among the Muslim groups. It argues that the internal debate bred splits within the reform movement, which also had three consequences. (i) It enabled a reformist movement that was 'friendly' to NRM political power. (ii) It bred diverse Muslim factions tired of Muslim elite hegemony and ones that desired to cultivate more autonomous individual expressions of Islam that included joining national political platforms, either independently or in conjunction with others, Muslims or non-Muslims. Such groups were composed of male and female Muslim politicians, university graduates, business people and social-cultural icons. (iii) It constructed another reformist faction hostile and opposed to NRM political power. The third section of this chapter discusses the end of the ADF rebellion and its implication for Muslim relations within the state in Uganda. As these sections demonstrate, the question of Muslims' expression of Islam and the response of the state to those articulations formed the core of the Muslim puzzle under the NRM regime.

The Tabliq/Salafiyya and Islamic reform in Uganda

The debate on reformist Islam in Uganda has coalesced around a set of questions: How (under what conditions) did the Islamic reform movement emerge and what interpretation of Islam did it articulate? What was its role and how did it understand it? In what ways was it connected to the historical global Islamic reformist movements? Who were its agents? What was the character of its *dawah* (propagation of Islamic principles)? Which Muslim public did it target and how did they receive the reformist message? What was its connection to both existing Muslim leadership and non-Muslim power? I hope to respond to these questions in this section. Etymologically, Tabligh means calling people to the right way or delivering the true message. In Muslim history, Tabligh is identified with the first usage by the Prophet Muhammad (PBUH) in his last sermon in the farewell pilgrimage in 632 C.E. when he asked his audience: 'have I delivered the message? Oh Allah be my witness.'[1] As a movement for Islamic propagation (*dawah*), the Tabligh began as an offshoot of the Tabligh *jamat* from northern India,[2] whose ideas were exported to Uganda

---

[1]   See https://hadithoftheday.com/the-last-sermon (accessed 30 May 2019).

[2]   See e.g. Mumtaz, Ahmad (1995), 'Tabligh Jamat', in John L. Esposito (Ed.), *The Oxford Encyclopedia of the Modern Islamic World,* 4, Oxford University Press: New York, pp. 165–9; Marloes, Janson (2005), 'Roaming about

in the 1960s. Although the group was named Tabligh, Salafiya was its core ideology. Used to connote the ways and manners of the pious predecessors (*As-Salaf as-Salih*), Salafism emerged as a centralizing ideology to replace the theological schisms reflected in the Juma-Zukuuli conflicts of the previous decades.

Salafism denotes interpretations of Islam that claim to have originated in the beliefs and practices of the early generations of Muslims.[3] Henri Lauzière identifies two strands in the debate over Salafism – the 'modernist' and the 'purist'. The former is used in reference to Muslim reformers such as Jamal al-Din al-Afghani, Muhammad Abduh and Rashid Rida who 'sought to reconcile Islam with the social, political and intellectual ideals of the Enlightenment' by advocating for a balanced approach to a comprehensive transformation of Muslim societies in ways that did not denigrate the 'strength and relevance of Islam in the modern era'.[4] Lauzière locates the 'purist' strand of Salafism in the attempt of self-proclaimed Salafists to 'purify' the religion of Islam from all innovations, deviations and external influences.[5] He locates the transformation from the modernist to the purist versions of Salafism and he gives critical agency to successive Muslim reformers in the Hijaz. As Salafist doctrine begun to morph in the early twentieth century, purist Salafis begun to define its parameters; one such definition came from Muhammad Munir al-Dimashqi who conceptualized the theological bounds of Salafism as the belief in the descriptive attributes of Allah as He describes Himself and as the Prophet Muhammad (PBUH) described Him, that is 'by affirming divine attributes in their plain sense, without alteration, metaphorical interpretation, denial and anthropomorphism and, above all, without modality'.[6]

Other Muslim reformers like 'Allal al-Farsi linked Salafism to 'the promotion of reason … the fight against stagnancy … and, most importantly, the overall renaissance and uplifting of Muslim society in modern times through an enlightenment of thought'.[7] Lauzière is convinced that the different conceptions of Salafism emerged within the context of specific social-political circumstances that shaped the imaginations of the Muslim

---

for God's Sake: The Upsurge of Tabligh Jamat in the Gambia', *Journal of Religion in Africa,* vol. 35, No. 4, pp. 450–81.

[3] Lauzière, Henri (2016), *The Making of Salafism: Islamic Reform in the Twentieth Century,* Columbia University Press: New York.

[4] Lauzière, *The Making of Salafism*, pp. 4–5.

[5] Lauzière, *The Making of Salafism*, p. 6.

[6] Lauzière, *The Making of Salafism,* pp. 97–8.

[7] Lauzière, *The Making of Salafism*, p 100.

reformers; such forces as late colonialism and nationalism indubitably shaped the logic, rationale and the responses of Muslim activists.[8] Terje Østebø has argued that approaches to Salafism must attempt to understand the context of the place where Salafism claims its origins and the forces that condition the arrival of Salafism in its new location such that we historicize the trans-boundary interactions as well as the agency of the reformers.[9] The experiences described in this chapter reveal that a purist strand of Salafism prevailed over the modern variant.

The conditions that necessitated the Islamic reform agenda among Muslims in Uganda were multiple and had to do with the history of Islam in the country. Although the Muslim spirit had rejuvenated during the colonial era, there was 'poor practice' of Islamic principles; a theological reform of the Muslim society was considered as the fundamental step. The reformers believed that the first generation of Muslims in Uganda had not perfected the unicity of Allah (*Tawhid*) and it was considered normal for a Muslim to proceed to prayer and supplication (Salat) while wearing *nsiriba/yirizi* (amulets) believed to protect against evil spirits. Many Muslim families dabbled in *shirk* (polytheism) while publicly displaying commitment to *Tawhid*.[10] Regarding fundamental Islamic practices like *sawm* (fasting) many Bazeyi (elderly, old guard Muslims) could perform fasting but while committing *shirk*.[11] They considered the consumption of alcohol, the eating of pork and other prohibited cuisine as the only haraam (forbidden) Islamic practices. With such a description of Islamic practice, it would seem that it was not Islam that needed to be reformed but rather the Islamization of Uganda society through *dawah*.

The agents of reformist Islam in Uganda were initially individuals – Sheikhs Kailan, Hakawaat and Abdul Razzaq Matovu were prominent agents of the first attempt. Due to the daunting task, an organization was imagined in preference to individual sheikhs since it would lighten the burden of reaching distant areas. A group of sheikhs met at Bilal Islamic Institute, in Wakiso District, and discussed how best to revive Islamic belief and practices among Muslims.[12] Many of the sheikhs in this group

---

[8] Ibid.

[9] Østebø, Terje (2011), 'Local Reformers and the Search for Change: The Emergence of Salafism in Bale, Ethiopia', *Africa: Journal of the International African Institute*, Vol. 81, No. 4, pp. 628–48, p. 629.

[10] FGD, Kisenyi, 10 July 2016; Umar Swidiq Ndawula, *khutba* at Masjid Noor, William Street, Kampala, August 2015.

[11] Ndawula, ibid.

[12] The sheikhs included: Muhammad Kizito Zziwa, Juma Kayiwa, Muhammad

were former students of Sheikh Abdul Rahman Hakawaat, a Syrian who preached the teachings of Muhammad bin Abdul Wahhab.[13] Abdul Rahman Hakawaat taught at the Bwaise Masjid near Kampala and used his sessions to denounce acts of *bida* (innovation) among the Muslims: especially festivals celebrating Maulid (the Prophet Muhammad's birthday, PBUH), observing *lumbe* (last funeral rights), *dua* (congregational supplication) and *talqiin* (burial supplication). Other acts of *bida* included all cultural practices that were considered anathema to Islamic principles, such as consuming meat considered halaal, but which cultural beliefs forbade such as where totemic. Ganda culture also forbade a man from marrying a woman of the same clan. Practices regarding dietary restrictions to women such as forbidding chicken, fish and mutton were also declared un-Islamic for they were akin to forbidding what Allah had allowed.[14]

The major teachings of the Tabligh included the following 'obligatory' practices: growing a beard; trimming the trousers to somewhere above the ankle; strict observance of Muslim code of dress for both men and women; *talqiin* is haraam; prayer (Salat) in accordance with the teachings of Ibn Hanbal as opposed to the 'Ugandan Muslims' who 'belong' to 'Shafii' school of legal thought; 'Maulid' is forbidden; one congregational Salat in every Masji;, shoes may not be removed for *janaza* (burial Salat); 'taking pictures is haraam', 'shaking hands with a woman is haraam' and possessing a *miswak* (wooden toothbrush) was encouraged. Thus, in the name of reform, the Tabligh challenged many of the cultural practices of the Muslims in Uganda and used the Nakasero Masjid as the space to challenge the Bazeyi whom they perceived as the vanguard of the 'old' beliefs. Just how 'un-Islamic' were the prohibitions is however a matter for both legal jurisprudence and the character of propagating *dawah* to a fitting audience. Also, to whom were the gates of *ijtihad* (exertion) closed? The fact that 'Islamic' knowledge had not permeated the Muslim public in Uganda at that time meant that a category of Ugandan *fuqaha* (experts in *fiqh*) became the guardians of *dawah* and taught, at their level of understanding, the nominal Muslims. In this context, *ijtihad* was closed to those considered lacking in knowledge.

    Kizza, Abdul Wahhab Ssemakula, Isa Yiga, Hajji Musa Mivule and Abubaker Musoke.

[13]   Muhammad, Ibn Abdul Wahhab (1998), *Kitab-at-Tawheed Explained*, IIPH: Riyadh.

[14]   'Ekika Ekiganda n'ekika nga bwe kitegeerwa mu Busiramu' (The Ganda clans and ethnic identity in Islam), *Vicegerent*, Vol. 1, No. 10, November 1987, p. 13.

Since the above Ugandan teachings sought to resonate with the global Salafist movements, we must – in order to help us understand how new groups of local actors sustained their *dawah* to increase group membership and widen networks among local followers – understand the structural changes that linked local spaces with such articulations.[15] This means that various reform phases outside Uganda had enabled processes of change that allowed multiple, transposable and intersection among structures, thereby revealing their fluid and heterogeneous nature. The consequence is that actors are understood both collectively and individually (as when group *feeling* informed the continuity of particular individual *acceptance* of some practices), as possessing both 'transformative and reflective capacities to maneuver within complex structures whilst accommodating currents of change'.[16] This demonstrates that Salafism as a reform ideology was susceptible to internal debates thereby revealing how the agents of Salafism in Uganda 'prepared, elaborated, maintained and resisted'[17] the reform agenda. The complex process of Islamic reform did not therefore play out in the dialectics between two equally homogenous groups of reformers (Tabligh youth) and traditionalists (Bazeyi), but it entailed compound negotiations in which a diversified body of actors with preferred views were deeply involved in the accommodation, appropriation and localization of Salafism.[18] This nonetheless means that the complex moment of Islamic reform must consider the political context of the state structure within which the reform agenda is expressed as opposed to focusing on the Islamic reform movement in its local-global linkages, especially localities of interaction that 'move beyond the Islamic universe'.[19]

Internal splits in the Tabliq

Nakasero Masjid is situated on Entebbe road adjacent to the Kampala customs depot (commonly known as Goods Shed) as one moves towards the Clock Tower junction to join Queensway. It had belonged to an Asian Muslim group but was handed over to the UMSC when President Idi Amin expelled the Asian community. When – during the Obote II government – the

[15]   Østebø, 'Local Reformers and the Search for Change', p. 629.
[16]   Ibid., p. 631.
[17]   Ibid.
[18]   Ibid.
[19]   Bezabeh, Samson (2014), 'Review of Terje A. Østebø, *Localising Salafism: Religious Change among Oromo Muslims in Bale, Ethiopia*', *Contemporary Islam* Vol. 8, No. 2, pp. 181–3.

158   ISLAM IN UGANDA

leader of the Muslim youth (Muhammad Yunus Kamoga) was given an office at the UMSC headquarters, he used it to influence a new wave of *khutba* from young sheikhs, recent graduates from the Islamic institutions in Pakistani, Sudan and Misr and the Muslim Arab world. The main topics regarded critiques directed at the practices of the Bazeyi that were equated to *bida;* the Bazeyi also participated in these lectures with counter-critiques. Although the youth had been accommodated at the UMSC as a means to consolidate Obeid Kamulegeya's control of the Muslim institutions in the country, their confrontational *khutba* were perceived as a threat to the leadership of the Bazeyi, and the youth were relocated to Nakasero Masjid. Those that harboured reformist rhetoric also relocated to Nakasero, including Muhammad Kizito Zziwa. Rashid Rida has stated that the renewal of Muslim practices need not segregate between the young and old. He noted that, as a process, renewing was a law of 'social association' integral to nature but 'counterweighted by the preservation' of the old practices. Within this process, there was no place for opposition between the new and the old ways provided that each understood its place without 'neglect or excess'. To Rashid Rida, the Islamic reform entailed 'renewing its guidance', clarifying the certitude of its truth while refuting *bida* and the 'extremism' of its followers. Consequently, both the new and the old would have their place and it would be a matter of 'ignorance to prefer one over the other in absolute terms'.[20] How did Islamic reformers in Uganda adhere to Rida's position?

The act by which Sheikh Muhammad Zziwa Kizito took over the leadership of Nakasero and established the Tabligh in that Masjid has been derided and it would later reveal the nature of the schism that came to exist among the members. It totally compromised new Islamic knowledge from co-existing with 'old' Ganda religious systems. The character of this *dawah* was interpreted as radical. According to Yusuf Qaradawi, religious extremism takes four basic forms. First, bigotry and intolerance, which make a person obstinately devoted to his own opinions and prejudices, as well as rigidity, which deprives one of clear vision regarding the interests of others, the purposes of Sharia or context of place and time. Second, the perpetual commitment to excessiveness in practices. Third, the 'out-of-time and out-of-place religious excessiveness and overburdening of others', for instance when 'applying Islamic principles to people in non-Muslim countries or to people who have only recently converted to Islam,

---

[20]   Cf. Kurzman, Charles (Ed.) (2002), *Modernist Islam 1840–1940: A Sourcebook,* Oxford University Press: Oxford, p. 81.

as well as to newly committed Muslims'. Fourth, 'harshness', 'crudeness' or 'roughness' in treating and approaching people during *dawah*.[21]

Zziwa was a Muganda Economics graduate from Pakistan. Together with colleagues, he had founded *darasa* (teaching sessions) in masjids and other spaces to preach against *bida*. He had founded the Society for Preaching Islam, Denouncement of Innovation, Qadianism and Atheism (SPIDIQA) to realize his objective of eradicating *bida* among Muslims, beginning in Buganda. Abul A'la Maududi Qadian's expositions influenced Zziwa.[22] Many Muslim individuals spoken to during this research agree that, whereas the reform of Muslim society was necessary, the character of the *dawah* articulated by some early reformers was inappropriate. Many Muslims who witnessed those events said Zziwa and his group had a confrontational attitude. During one Salat session led by one Mzeyi sheikh within Nakasero Masjid, Zziwa went outside the Masjid windows and shouted to the Muslims *jamat* (congregation) inside to stop the Salat because the Mzeyi Imam was leading wrongly. The *jamat* left the Salat and Zziwa established himself as the Amir of the Tabligh Community. His leadership witnessed controversial fatwas (Islamic religious rulings) such as pronouncing *takfir* (Islamic apostasy) for Muslims whom he felt did not display Tabligh practices. Attending a *lumbe* was analogous to falling into a pit latrine. The youthful audience of these 'fatwas' always obliged with laughter. Many of his *khutba* (sermons) ridiculed Muslim authority for failing to preach the 'correct Islamic way'. Zziwa's confrontational *khutba* incensed the wider Muslim public and he was accused of transgressing the limits of moderation in *dawah*. When he began to ridicule and abuse the learned scholars of *fiqh* (Islamic jurisprudence), many under the Tabligh felt that Zziwa had exceeded his limits. He was dismissed and replaced with Muhammad Yunus Kamoga as Amir (leader) of the Tabligh, deputized by Jamil Mukulu. Other prominent sheikhs included: Idris Lwaazi, Muhammad Kiggundu, Sulaiman Kakeeto, Abdallah Kalanzi, Hassan Kirya, Murtada Bukenya and Abdul Karim Ssentamu.[23] Zziwa's exit marked the first split within the Tabligh.

Under Muhammad Kamoga as Amir, the Tabligh reorganized and streamlined structures of leadership by founding a national network. Leadership became hierarchical with the office of the Amir reproduced at the district, county and village levels. The Tabligh membership consisted

---

[21] Qaradawi, Yusuf (1987), *Islamic Awakening: Between Rejection and Extremism,* American Trust: Virginia, p. 4.

[22] Maududi, Abul A'la (nd), *The Qadian Problem,* PVT: Lahore.

[23] FGD, Nakasero, 2 July 2016.

of both unemployed Muslim youth and those in part-time employment who could spare time after their jobs to listen to various *khutba*. Many young sheikhs, especially returning graduates of the foreign universities, were allowed platform at Nakasero to speak about 'social injustices' done against Muslims especially in Uganda's recent history, including such events as the 1979 Muslim massacres in southern Buganda and Ankole. They wondered what the UMSC leadership could do in response to what Abasi Kiyimba's fresh investigations in Ankole had concluded was the responsibility of the highest office in the NRM government.[24] When the *khutba* spoke about perceived Christian injustices against Muslims in Uganda, the Tabligh audience was charged, filled with resentment and hatred directed against two centres of power. The immediate was the UMSC whose leadership had 'failed even to conceive of a willed' plan to improve the Muslim condition, with many of its leadership defined as 'stooges' of the state. Yoweri Museveni's government was identified as the other centre of power that was 'determined to keep Muslims in their historical place as third-rate' citizens. Both challenges were inextricably linked, and how the Tabligh leadership attempted to overcome both determined its trajectory. I return to this in the next section.

During Kamoga's restructuring, many organs were formed within the Tabligh, beginning at Nakasero and radiating to other areas. Women's groups became established (*amirat*s – female Muslim leaders – operated parallel to the amirs). An internal body (morality force/unit/organ), to enjoin good and forbid evil, was established. Its dual directive was to enforce law and order, internally within the group, and to defend it against enemies from without. Internally, the morality organ enforced such rules as dress code, punctuality for Salat and *darasa* and general hygiene. The Tabligh male member had to grow his beard and shorten his trousers. Shaving the beard would attract designations like 'orange face' or '*hajati*'[25] and likened to 'baby dolls'. Similarly, a Tabligh male who failed to shorten his trousers would be likened to a 'Hajati' since Muslim women are allowed to wear longer attire reaching to the feet. When males with longer trousers approached the Salat in *jamat*, sometimes the trousers would be forcefully cut off and reduced to the Tabligh standard size or if it

---

[24] Kiyimba, Abasi (1989), *Is the 1979 Muslim Blood Bath in Bushenyi History?* Kampala.

[25] Although the word 'Hajati' designates a Muslim woman who has completed the rights of Hajj (pilgrimage) in Mecca, it is loosely used in Uganda to refer to any woman who regularly wears the full-body garb.

were the Imam leading the Salat with longer trousers, the followers would boycott it.[26]

For the male Muslim Tabligh, it was compulsory to attend the *fajr* (dawn) Salat in *jamat* (congregation) because *darasa* (learning session) usually followed it. Failure to attend both sometimes led to flogging.[27] If some Muslims consistently failed to attend important meetings, their immediate leaders described them as 'lazy' Muslims and not worthy of belonging to the group. It was considered important for the Tabligh community to participate in religious activities, even those that involved longer travel like burial rites. The Tabligh interpretation of the burial rites in Islam differed from those of the Bazeyi. What is called *talqiin* is the recitation of particular mixed phrases to 'initiate' the deceased into their new 'life'. While the *Bazeyi* perceived it as a supplication to Allah to show mercy to the deceased, the Tabligh asked for *daril* (evidence) from authentic Islamic sources to legitimate its practice, without which they would perform silence at the burial. On one occasion, the Tabligh arrived at the mourning site to inter a prominent Muslim in Mbarara, only to realize there was a military convoy that the deceased's family had prepared to challenge their intentions of a performed silence (all mourners at the graveyard were expected to fall in with their practices). When the commander of the military officers told the head of the Tabligh delegation to desist from their 'usual' mourning practices, he was told to consider his commands carefully for the Tabligh 'desired death more than the military commander and his officers desired life'. The interment ceremony proceeded in silence.

Externally, it was in preparation for such potential confrontations with 'outside' forces that the morality organ discharged its other directive of protecting the Tabligh from 'enemies'. Members were prepared for any violent (physical) confrontation if any outside authority became an obstacle to their perception of *dawah*. Training in Taekwondo and wrestling became general practices for particular Tabligh units in various secret locations. They had also benefited from the military training that the state operated through the 'mchaka-mchaka' programme.[28] These

---

[26] One respondent sheikh reminded how he went to give a *darasa* at the Islamic institute in Bugembe, Jinja, and his would-be students said '*tufunye ssenyiga mussomero*' (a big influenza has attacked our institution), referring to the 'dilution' of Tabligh doctrine reflected in the longer trousers that the sheikh wore.

[27] FGD, Wandegeya, 4 July 2016.

[28] Mchaka-mchaka began in the 1990s as a state project to instill basic military skills among the youthful population.

'militant units' were thus conceived as integral to the reformation and were deployed to protect Tabligh interests. The radical rhetoric revealed itself in the violent clashes among opposing groups in the attempt to control various masjids. In Kampala, Masjid Noor along William Street became a battle scene when the Tabligh chased out the Bazeyi and established another stronghold in Kampala after Nakasero. Other clashes occurred in Kyazanga (Lwengo, formerly Masaka District), Mbale and Mbarara in the early 1990s. Ultimately, the violent turn of the Tabligh *dawah* culminated with the 1991 invasion of the UMSC headquarters to oust the Bazeyi, which also operated as the excuse for state infiltration of the Tabligh. Unlike the character of the first split, which focused on intra-Muslim politics, the second split was conditioned by the debate surrounding the nature of Tabligh relations with state power.

The second split within the Tabligh occurred in 1996 although its prelude is credited to the events of 1987–89 and February 1991. (The section below, 'The ADF and "political Islam"', provides a lengthy discussion of this split.) At the beginning of 1991, there was a court ruling to decide the rightful office bearers of the UMSC. The judgement had declared that Saad Luwemba was the Mufti of the Muslims in Uganda as opposed to Rajab Kakooza. The offices of the UMSC were housed in the property that had belonged to the Aga Khan, the head of the Ismaili Muslim community, which had been transferred to the UMSC during President Idi Amin's decree. The economic restructuring policies of the NRM government gave an open-door return policy to the Uganda Asian community dispersed in different parts of the globe. If the state had returned the property to its owner, the UMSC had to vacate. The challenge was that the sitting tenant was unwilling to leave. In this stalemate, the state desired a compromising sheikh as Mufti to ease its task. Saad Luwemba was propped up in opposition to Rajab Kakooza. A few days before the court ruling, President Yoweri Museveni visited Iran accompanied by Saad Luwemba. The Tabligh interpreted this as state support for Luwemba, Mufti in waiting. They felt that the new Mufti was a 'stooge' of the state, something they detested. Having set up camp in Masjid Noor, William Street, the leaders marched to attack, and laid siege to the UMSC headquarters. It took the intervention of the state, which resulted in the deaths of four police officers and the arrests of 432 Tabligh members, before hostilities ceased. The internal leadership of the group was disrupted. During the siege the Tabligh leadership was torn between continuing the physical confrontation and retreat. The Amir, Muhammad Yunus Kamoga favoured a negotiated retreat to consider the whole situation and plan anew. The deputy Amir, Jamil Mukulu – with a large constituency – favoured a

ISLAMIC REFORM AND INTRA-MUSLIM VIOLENCE   **163**

continuation of the hostilities until 'victory'. As the state police and military gained the upper hand, the Amir escaped and was exiled to Kenya only to return in 2009.[29] His deputy insisted that the Amir had committed a heinous crime of escaping from battle. All along, Jamil Mukulu had considered the siege a jihad (Muslim holy war) and since its rules forbade retreat from war, Muhammad Kamoga was designated a 'traitor'. When Mukulu was imprisoned with a large group of Tabligh youth, he continued to call for jihad against the 'kaafir' (infidel) regime of President Yoweri Museveni.

State infiltration of the Tabligh was blamed on the lax leadership character of the new Amir. The events surrounding the siege on the UMSC headquarters occurred when Sheikh Sulaiman Kakeeto was finishing his studies abroad. As the arrests of Mukulu and the exile of Kamoga created a leadership vacuum, the other Tabligh sheikhs escaped arrest and were not willing to fill this vacuum. Further, the state desired that a 'friendly' leadership take over the Masjid due to its location on Entebbe road, one of the most important transport arteries in Kampala city. Thus, the Mufti, Saad Luwemba, took over the Masjid and handed it to the leadership of Kakeeto. To demonstrate success over the Tabligh, the Bazeyi returned to Nakasero and 'jubilated' by performing *burda* (an evening activity to send supplications to the Prophet Muhammad, PBUH), a practice anathema to Tabligh belief. Sheikh Sulaiman Kakeeto had established himself as a moderate character and he became the Imam of the Nakasero Masjid. His 'diplomatic' approach endeared him to the Luwemba leadership and he was chosen to become the Tabligh Amir, deputized by Sheikh Kalanzi. The new Tabligh leadership at Nakasero mutated into a non-confrontational group, and denounced violence while compromising with the Bazeyi at the UMSC. They embarked on Muslim projects and built masjids, schools and other *waqf* (Muslim endowments) at various locations in the country.

The focus on *dawah* activities around the country attracted new members into the Tabligh especially considering its changed character. Trouble

---

[29]   Available documents reveal that Sheikh Muhammad Kamoga joined with Sheikh Muhammad Kiggundu in 1992 to found a rebel movement (Uganda National Freedom Movement/Army – UNFM/A) that operated in the West Nile region of north-west Uganda and reached into Sudan (now South Sudan). How Kamoga changed from renouncing violence during the siege at UMSC headquarters has not been established, given that the founding documents of the UNFM/A designate him as 'Chief Advisor/Founder'. The causes for their rebellion ranged from 'freedom of worship' to Muslim marginalization and 'sectarianism' in President Yoweri Museveni's government.

re-erupted upon the release of the former Tabligh sheikhs. Some of the released clerics accepted the new situation they found at Nakasero while others in Jamil Mukulu's constituency felt that '*tutandikira wetwaakoma*' (let us continue from where we stopped). The Kakeeto leadership refused to accommodate what it considered radical convictions. As Mukulu exited Nakasero, Kakeeto's leadership suffered from the infiltration of the state. Weekly convoys of the Tabligh to attend *darasa* in various parts of the country were a sight that signified their organizational capacity and binding beliefs system. When President Museveni witnessed this, he wondered who led this large group and how he managed these different individuals. The President cautioned Kakeeto that a 'leader has to travel with protection' (guns) and also 'travel well' (private car) – and provided the necessary facilitation. Once Kakeeto accepted these state enticements, many interpreted that he had been 'bought'. When a wave of arrests targeting Tabligh leadership and youths began, finger pointing focused on Kakeeto. Later information revealed that Kakeeto's consorting with the state was responsible for the mass incarceration of Tabligh members whom the state deemed a 'danger to national security'.[30]

Another split became inevitable. Among others, Sheikhs Idris Lwaazi (who allegedly later died under state torture in Katojo prison in Western Uganda), Abdul Karim Ssentamu, Hassan Kirya, Abdul Hakim Ssekimpi Tamusuza (the first two were assassinated, the last passed away in Kibuli hospital under 'mysterious' circumstances), all left Nakasero Masjid and established a new base at Market Street in Kampala. Before moving to the new location, some thought the best alternative was to evict Kakeeto and his group. The opposing faction came to Makerere University Masjid and hid a training unit in the women's wing inside the masjid where they clandestinely instructed themselves in Taekwondo and other forms of offensive physical confrontations. The objective was to proceed to attack Nakasero and evict Kakeeto. The ensuing clash spilt blood, and state police was called to quell the 'attack'. Further police investigations revealed that the 'invading force' had marched from Makerere University Masjid; deeper intelligence discovered they had trained inside that Masjid. The Masjid Imam was arrested to explain how a Tabligh faction came to hide inside his 'office'. As he pleaded his innocence and ignorance of Tabligh activities, he was remanded for two weeks.[31] As the eviction of Kakeeto came

---

[30]   The then Brigadier Henry Tumukunde told *Mambo Bado,* a Luganda talk show on CBS Radio that they received intelligence from Kakeeto regarding whom to arrest.

[31]   FGD, Makerere University, 6 July 2016.

to be protected by the intervention of state police, the new faction settled for Market Street.

According to many respondents, the 1996 split among the Tabligh has to be situated within the political context of the presidential elections of that year.[32] It would be difficult to imagine a

> group of prominent sheikhs breaking away from the main faction unless there was a serious challenge to their understanding of the *dawah*. If they said Kakeeto mismanaged Tabligh finances, surely they could find solutions for financial accountability. But there was a bigger issue that caused their exit. It has to do with NRM politics.[33]

The year 1996 marked the first general and presidential election since 1986 when the NRM government came to power. A group of Muslims founded a political party – JEEMA[34] – and fronted Muhammad Kibirige as its presidential candidate. The objective of JEEMA was not to win the national presidency on the Muslim ticket. According to some of the founders, JEEMA was conceived to restore Muslims' belief in their political potential as nationals of Uganda. Since the 1979 war had tarnished the Muslims' image, it was believed that a political platform would support this revitalization. To succeed, the project needed the support of 'all Muslims' in important positions of leadership. Individuals like Hussein Kyanjo, Imam Kasozi and other prominent Muslims canvassed for the support of JEEMA. At Nakasero, Kakeeto's NRM leanings disturbed the JEEMA leadership. He was seen as a sellout who had betrayed the 'Muslim' cause.

The Tabligh splinter group at Market Street denounced its relation with Kakeeto and proceeded to found its own organization, Jamiat Dawah Salafiyya (hereafter 'Salafiyya'), headed by Abdul Karim Ssekimpi (since deceased). This group continued to spread *dawah* imbued with political nuances when it stressed Muslim marginalization and accused the state of 'meddling' with Muslim conflicts by propping up the 'corrupt' administration of Saad Luwemba at the UMSC. When in 1997 a series of bombs exploded in various localities in Kampala, most especially in the Nakulabye suburb, the government took advantage of the prevailing animosity between Kakeeto and the Salafiyya to accuse the latter of causing 'insecurity' in Kampala. Another wave of state arrests directed at the Salafiyya ensued. Like before, fingers pointed to Kakeeto's group

---

[32] FGD, Wandegeya, 8 July 2016.

[33] Ibid.

[34] 'JEEMA' stood for 'Justice, Education, Economic revitalization, Morality and African unity'.

for 'betraying' Muslims and selling their 'secrets' to the state. The state of fear within the Tabligh and Salafiyya groups subsided in 2000 when the clerics and the state reached an agreement for the denunciation of violence. This amnesty also included members of the ADF and the Uganda National Freedom Movement/Army (UNFM/A), notably Sheikh Major Muhammad Kiggundu (assassinated on 26 November 2016) and Sheikh Muhammad Yunus Kamoga. The amnesty concluded in Nairobi in 2000 was conditioned on the state fulfilment of particular promises including: provision of security to returnees, especially the officers; provision of welfare; election of the Mufti of Uganda, among others.[35]

How did the Muslim public respond to acts of manifest violence? Muhammad Abduh had emphasized that the attempt to reform the social fabric of Muslim groups had to consider their traditions and customs so as to design sanctions befitting their situation. If the leaders failed to design sanctions comprehensible and discernible to its subjects, those sanctions would 'harm' the people. Thus, the sanctions that governed a 'vile' and 'base' society differed from those that governed a 'compliant' and 'noble' one. While the former were harsh and severe in punishment, the latter were equitable and light in punishment.[36] The attempt to exhort Muslims to abide by *Tawhid* took a confrontational character and ended up alienating the very society it intended to reform. When some Muslim youth were violently accosted for not shortening trousers or debased for shaving beards, ridiculed and flogged for not attending important communal activities, they came to hate their leaders and stayed away from the masjids. A backlash occurred within the Muslim public and debates ensued in small circles of Muslim families and Bazeyi masjids about '*ekizibu kya aba Tabligh*' (the Tabligh challenge). These debates bred recalcitrant grammars that critiqued the approach of the Tabligh in matters of Islam. Many Muslim families stopped sending their children to study Islam from 'problematic' sheikhs rumoured to belong to the Tabligh. Muslims consciously spread rumours to inform each other of which sheikhs could be 'safe' to deal with in Islamic issues. Ultimately, the language of '*nnalukalala*' (uncompromising, radical) emerged to designate Tabligh behaviour. Many

---

[35] *Agreement of the Nairobi Peace Talks between the Uganda Government and the UNFM/A,* May 2000.

[36] Muhammad, 'Abduh (1881), 'Ikhtilaf al-qawanin bi-ikhtilaf ahwal al-umam' (Laws Should Change in Accordance with the Conditions of Nations)', in Muhammad 'Imara (Ed.), *Al-A 'Mal al-kamila* (The Complete Works), Mu'assasat al- 'Arabiyya li al Dirasat wa al-Nashr: Lebanon, 1972, pp. 309–15.

families would not marry their daughters to Tabligh (actual, rumoured or potential). Tabligh would marry internally and the grammar of Muslim social binaries widened further.[37] Those flogged for delaying Salat queried the *eeman* (faith) of their tormentors. This backlash reflected hatred and deep resentment against Tabligh teachings. With reason, many questioned the hastiness of the *dawah* and a few knowledgeable Muslims queried the Tabligh concerning the haste. Did not the Prophet 'teach kindly even to his worst enemies? Give us time to understand the message to which you call us and if we consider it, then maybe we shall change.'[38]

The situation worsened when confrontational *dawah* met resistance. Due to the character of the reform agent, Islam became the enemy. Thus in the reform of faith, Tabligh had alienated its social base and violated the basic principle of Islamic *dawah*, moderation; in the defence of Islam, Tabligh had attempted to police the *nafsi* (soul) of individual Muslims and misunderstood the bounds of their duty. The backlash of Muslim masses against Tabligh *dawah* enabled new Muslim publics to emerge. Multiple centres of Muslim organization emerged beyond the traditional power centres at Kibuli and Old Kampala and the other urban spaces. Many Muslim professional doctors, graduates, public servants, politicians, women parliamentarians, councillors and businessmen have cultivated other spaces to express their Muslim identity in ways that do not claim to identify with Muslim leadership in the country. The multiple categories of Muslims perceived the politics of national Muslim leadership as a disgrace to the basic message of Islam – understood as *dawah* through exemplary morals.[39]

This mass exodus of Muslims from elite organizations was itself historically influenced by elite power when on the eve of national elections in 1980 Prince Badru Kakungulu advised Muslims to seek alternative ways to fashion their lives. A.B.K. Kasozi has quoted him: 'My advice would be that Muslims in this country should fashion their political behaviour in the same style as other people. Each one of us should join whatever party his conscience leads him to but should always keep in mind the interests of the Muslim Community in his political career. We have passed the stage when we should act as, or be seen to act, as a block. Acting as a block in a diversified society could destroy our community if we are caught at the wrong side or if the holders of power are changed. I do not advise the boycotting of elections nor do I advise that we should all get into one party. Each one

---

[37] FGD, August 2015.
[38] FGD, Kisenyi, 6 July 2016.
[39] Interview with Muslim professionals, Mbale, November 2016.

168   ISLAM IN UGANDA

of you should go into a party you feel like ... we must be realistic. We live in Uganda and must behave like other Ugandans'.[40]

The violent events between 1980 and 1990 revealed the importance of Kakungulu's advice. Many individual Muslims began to channel their Muslim identity around national politics, business and social causes, Muslims joined political platforms, the unemployed looked for work in the transport and other industries. If the intra-Muslim politics freed up individual Muslim autonomy while enabling multiple centres of Muslim power to emerge, the ADF rebellion would intensify it.

The ADF and 'political Islam': the other face of the Tabligh

The violent turn of the reform movement has global antecedents. The cause of the Muslim Brotherhood in Egypt has historically been identified with Salafism as an ideology to mobilize masses to reform society and politics.[41] By claiming to return to As-Salaf as-Salih as the standard of Islamic practice, Salafist ideology summoned Islamic doctrine in its entirety as opposed to its circumscribed form, including its political aspect. Haggai Erlich (reviewing Terje A. Østebø, *Localising Salafism*) has argued that classical Islam was 'both a religion and the state. [Prophet] Muhammad (PBUH) did not only preach morality; he also established an enormous Islamic empire for the nation of believers' such that whoever aspired to 'the return of these norms' had to work for the 'proper political system'. 'Politics' however is also a *diversified* term: one 'can work patiently and moderately and for an open, pluralist, and tolerant system', or one can 'work violently for the destruction of all opponents', but 'once one defines oneself' as a Salafi, 'one's identity is political'.[42]

Under what conditions did the reformist debate among the Tabligh divide between *reform as dawah* and *reform as rush to the bush*? How did the attempts to 'localize' Salafism breed multiple debates and varied results? Why and how did the ADF become the faction of choice to

---

[40]   Kasozi, *The Life of Prince Badru Kakungulu Wasajja,* pp. 229–30.

[41]   Qutb, Sayyid (2006), *Ma'alim fi'l-tareeq* (Milestones), Maktabah: Birmingham; Al-Ghazali, Zainab (2006), *Return of the Pharaoh: Memoir in Nasir's Prison,* Leicester: The Islamic Foundation; Qutb, Sayyid (2015 [nd]), *Fi Dhilal Al-Quran* (In the Shade of the Quran) Vol. 1, Markfield: The Islamic Foundation.

[42]   Erlich, Haggai (2015), 'Review of Terje A. Østebø, *Localising Salafism: Religious Change among Oromo Muslims in Bale, Ethiopia,* Brill: Leiden', *Northeast African Studies,* Vol. 15, No. 1, pp. 199–202, p. 201.

lead the anti-NRM Muslim rebellion? Did this demonstrate the actors' personal desire for power such that Salafist ideology was a vehicle for group mobilization? What did Islam and Muslims in Uganda have to do with the rebellion? What environment supported its initial formation and what conditions militated against its success as a movement to capture state power?

The conditions that cast the Tabligh reform debate between *dawah* and political jihad have to do with two developments. First, the need for intra-Muslim reform of religious practices – understood as purifying Islam from the 'shackles of tradition' – had been identified as an important step in reforming national Muslim leadership (to dethrone the Bazeyi and inaugurate the youth). Second, some groups critically considered the reform of the state as a structure that subjected Muslims to social-political-economic marginalization. How to proceed along these two developments would later divide the Tabligh. On one side stood those who believed that as long as the state allowed Muslims religious space to articulate Islam and extend *dawah* to reform the practices of Muslim masses, Islamic reform of the state (Muslim revolution) was not only irrelevant but also impossible. On the other side stood some who believed that the reform of Muslim leadership and Muslim masses had to proceed alongside the reform of the political structure so as to establish a Muslim state (*dawla* Islamiya) governed by Islamic law (Sharia). Although a major division and the attendant splits emerged within a particular moment after the events of 1991 (the invasion of the Supreme Council), it had a brief history in the events of 1987–89 that had united Tabligh leadership.

According to Jamil Mukulu, the Tabligh leadership received a message from Jeddah, Saudi Arabia, in 1987.[43] It concerned a planned meeting in Mombasa, Kenya, which the Tabligh leadership – comprising Yunus Kamoga, Deputy Amir, Jamil Mukulu (in jail since 2015) and Abdul Karim Ssentamu (assassinated in 2012, but considered a top cleric in the Tabligh leadership at the time) – were to attend. The events that followed this meeting demonstrate the context within which the Tabligh leadership united and later divided; ones that reveal the widening schism that intensified violence and invited state intervention. As the trio proceeded to Mombasa and met with their host, Jamil Mukulu was chosen to speak for the Tabligh leadership (Kampala camp) while the host insisted that he represented big interests from Jeddah. The message from Jeddah was that the

---

[43] Jamil Mukulu Recordings, 2012, interviews with former ADF rebels and Sheiks from other break away factions have corroborated the information contained in these recordings.

Tabligh 'should mobilize the Muslim youth and acquire guns to dislodge the Yoweri Museveni government from power'.[44] As the spokesperson for the Kampala camp, Mukulu responded that 'they' were ready to realize this call to arms on condition that they would institute Islamic Sharia after ousting Museveni from power. His two colleagues nodded with approval over this suggestion. Mukulu notes that 'we were convinced that since the messenger represented interests from Jeddah where oil money is located, the war would not fail'.[45] The Jeddah representative however felt that the post-war institution of Sharia should not be considered a condition for starting the war, insisting that a 'shared Muslim identity' was a good basis to begin the war. The host returned to Jeddah and promised to communicate the way forward.[46]

When the Jeddah camp contacted the Kampala camp after some time, his message was as originally stated – that the war should begin on the basis of a shared 'Muslim identity' and not on the condition of instituting Sharia. As Mukulu emphasizes, the Jeddah camp had 'no interest in instituting Sharia in Uganda but desired to have a Muslim government'.[47] Whether the Jeddah camp imagined an Amin-like arrangement where the state protected the Muslims under its patronage is difficult to surmise. Regardless, Jamil Mukulu refused. As the representative of the Kampala camp, he retorted that he and his colleagues were not ready to begin war without the Sharia in mind: 'Allah has commanded us not to judge except by using the Quran and Sunnah'.[48] The trio dismissed the idea of allowing any one to lead just because he had an Islamic name. If the Jeddah camp would not fund the war, Mukulu and his colleagues looked inwardly to themselves to find necessary resources to begin.

The year 1989 marked the third anniversary of the NRM revolution in Uganda. In many ways, stable political structures had not materialized; the northern corridor had not been pacified and in many places the NRM regime was still fighting opponents, while integrating others.[49] Mukulu and his colleagues took advantage of the fragile political structure and began collecting guns. The objective was to 'cause an Islamic revolution in Uganda so as to make Islam the higher power; Islam could not judge

[44] Ibid.
[45] Ibid.
[46] Ibid.
[47] Ibid.
[48] Ibid.
[49] Mamdani, Mahmood (1988), 'Uganda in Transition: Two years of the NRA/ NRM', *Third World Quarterly*, Vol. 10, No. 3, pp. 1155–81.

except if the "gun" propelled it to state power'.[50] In other words, violent warfare was the easiest way for Muslims to capture state power and implement Islamic Sharia. Mukulu was tasked with collecting guns from Gulu, Northern Uganda. The proximity of Gulu town to ongoing conflicts[51] in Uganda and the region made it a proliferation ground for used guns. These were transported to Kampala under 'difficult circumstances since roadblocks and vehicle searches were a common practice'. In Kampala, 'we would divide the guns into bunches and give each to some core leaders to store in different locations'.[52] They made contact with a former FEDEMU[53] soldier who trained 'us on how to assemble guns and ammunition, and to use bombs'.[54] The operation had grown into a sophisticated enterprise that needed recruits; it ceased from being a secret of the top Tabligh leadership. Where and how to train recruits would prove a challenge. Mukulu noted one of the leaders identified a piece of land in Namagoma, along Masaka road where they could undertake 'advanced' military training. The Namagoma area was considered a place to 'train trainers' and they referred other leaders to train.[55]

A salient feature of the Tabligh movement has been its mobilization of Muslim youth. For all the resources that the Tabligh leadership desired but could not get (such as bigger guns and missiles), there was one critical resource that was in plentiful supply: young Muslims. No wonder that the Jeddah camp had confirmed its importance. The Tabligh leadership did not manufacture the 'problem' of Muslim youth; they took advantage of and channelled histories of Muslim frustration with existing political power. The regions of Buganda, Busoga and Eastern Uganda provided a recruiting ground for a potential Tabligh army. Many of the Muslim youth

---

[50] Jamil Mukulu recordings, 2012.
[51] By 1989, with roads that radiated out to Kampala, North Eastern Zaire and Southern Sudan, Gulu had become a regional trade hub, as well as a centre of inter-cultural/religious connections. The Sudanese People's Liberation Movement/Army (SPLM/A) conflict with Sudan was still raging while remnants of rebel forces – such as the Lord's Resistance Army, Uganda National Rescue Front, and other unorganized units allied to individual commanders – were in West Nile.
[52] Jamil Mukulu recordings, 2012.
[53] FEDEMU, the Federal Democratic Movement, was one of the groups that emerged during the anti-Amin struggle to attempt to acquire state power. Together with others, it was later incorporated under the NRM leadership.
[54] Jamil Mukulu recordings, 2012.
[55] Ibid.

in these regions were unemployed; some had become too aged to fit into the grafting school system that required one to study both Islamic and secular subjects.[56] When they finished primary education, they 'dropped out' of school and partook of 'simple' employment: those of the urban areas pushed wheel barrows, fetched water, worked for Asian businesses in town and also taught Islamic studies at nursery and primary schools a few days a week.[57] The Muslim youth in the rural areas worked in small plots to cultivate food and to offer their labour in exchange for food or some more space to cultivate their own food crops.[58] Both the urban and rural Muslim youth had plenty of time after their routine chores, which they used to attend *darasa* in the evenings to listen to different speakers. The conditions of their day-to-day life seemed natural until the Tabligh leadership convinced them otherwise. Like Obote's making of NAAM, this group had nothing to lose but all to gain from a successful revolution.

To reach its recruiting base, the Tabligh leadership used taped audio recordings of *khutba* that were circulated throughout Buganda, Busoga and Eastern Uganda. Jamil Mukulu made the recordings and his words were 'sharp' and 'confrontational', intended to wake up the Muslim 'sleeping giant'. He shaped his discourse with the Muslim youth within the context of historical 'Christian' marginalization of Muslims. His early recordings show that the Christian power were responsible for the Muslim predicament (but his later messages blamed the Muslim as well). Mukulu used the challenges of the daily Muslim routine to pack and deliver his message. Rural areas experienced a deep aversion to Islam. The year 1990 witnessed a continuing Islamophobia in many parts of Uganda; in Busoga masjids were attacked and burned and Muslims were murdered. Mukulu used these atrocities as the examples to showcase what he believed to be 'Christians' aversion to Islam'.[59] This message fell on a fertile audience; and the revolution was underway. How could it proceed?

The control of Muslim leadership in Uganda was under the Bazeyi (old guard), which the Tabligh had identified as an important obstacle to Muslim development in the country. To acquire national legitimacy, they identified

---

[56] Interview with former ADF rebel, Kisenyi, 12 July 2016.

[57] Ibid.

[58] FGDs in Busoga, November 2016.

[59] Ibid. Many respondents spoken to in Busoga in November 2016 disagreed with Mukulu's later decision to wage 'jihad' but all agreed with him that the conditions of the time allowed the Muslim youth in Busoga to receive and accept his message; Mukulu promised them a 'better' life beyond their 'normal'.

the UMSC as the initial target of their revolution. In order to reach their 'prize' they first demonstrated their organizational and mobilizing strength on a smaller site. In 1991, the Tabligh youth were mobilized to lay siege at a masjid in Makindye, Kampala, to dislodge one Mzeyi sheikh who 'dabbled in *bida*'. This incident was immensely symbolic because it confirmed the mobilization skills of the Tabligh, whose importance later events would demonstrate, and also witnessed the use of a Muslim flag with imprinted words of the Islamic creed,[60] which was secretly carried and hoisted whenever the group moved to its target space. The flag signified the desire for a Muslim revolution.[61] After the 'successful' Makindye siege, the next target was to dislodge Mufti Saad Luwemba from Muslim leadership.

According to the 'veterans' of the Tabligh invasion of the UMSC (some later became foot soldiers in the ADF) the Tabligh could not just take over without any support from the Supreme Council. They needed the support of an already existing Muslim leader to 'front' their project. They chose Rajab Kakooza who was locked in a court battle with Saad Luwemba over who was the 'legitimate' Mufti. The Tabligh supported Kakooza because they believed Luwemba was a Shia, and that he was supported by the state. Since the decision of the court in the matter was expected on a Tuesday; the Tabligh moved from Nakasero on a Monday to anticipate the court's decision and established a base at Old Kampala.[62] When the court decision of February 1991 declared Luwemba Mufti, the Tabligh dissented and laid siege on the Supreme Council, hoisted their flag and announced that Nakasero Masjid and Masjid Noor would be locked for the Jumuah; every Tabligh had to turn up at Old Kampala. This announcement mobilized Muslims nationally who came from various parts of Uganda to oust state 'stooges' from the UMSC.[63]

The state mobilized a counter force headed by the military police. This operation proceeded alongside a nation-wide security search for the Tabligh in all Muslim spaces as the Tabligh 'problem' revealed the apparent weakness of the state structure and its susceptibility to another political revolution. They surrounded the Supreme Council during Jumuah and the police fired tear gas in the middle of the *khutba* to disperse the siege. Muslim youth pulled tools of violence such as pangas (machetes),

---

[60] This act imitated the historical Islamic battles when classical Muslims raised banners in war to signify that they were fighting to defend Islam.

[61] FGD with five former ADF Rebels, Makindye (Kampala), 11 July 2016; Jamil Mukulu recordings 2012.

[62] FGD with former ADF Rebel, Kampala, 13 July 2016.

[63] Ibid.

174   ISLAM IN UGANDA

stones, metal bars, clubs and other weapons to counteract police violence. In the scuffle, four police officers died. When a UPDF officer arrived at the scene and asked who had murdered the police officers, one sheikh replied: 'our commandos did it'.[64] The UPDF officer called in the military police who surrounded the whole area. When the police entered the Old Kampala Masjid near the sunset prayer, Jamil Mukulu is said to have asked: 'are we not the ones on the truth?'[65] This question implied that the Tabligh should continue fighting until they either won or were killed. Others disagreed however and advised their brethren to surrender. Buses entered to take the Tabligh convicts to the Central Police Station in Kampala where they arrived under tight security to experience the first round of police torture. Jailed to Luzira prison the next day, Tabligh were released after about three months while Jamil Mukulu was released after over a year.[66]

More than any other event, the arrest and imprisonment of the Tabligh leadership divided the actors on the issue concerning how to proceed with their ambitions. While in prison Jamil Mukulu continued with his plans for a full-scale military rebellion, a different environment informed the relationship of the Tabligh leadership with the state. What happened between the moment of Mukulu's arrest and imprisonment that changed the perspective of his former colleagues? When Mukulu was in prison, other leaders in the Tabligh denounced the proposed military rebellion. Upon release, Mukulu retorted '*Wetwaakoma we tutandikira*' (we begin from where we stopped), and he resuscitated his recruitment plans, while his colleagues maintained that the change in circumstances ruled out all-out war. Although the looming 1996 national elections was a major factor in this second split, an internal debate within the core Tabligh leadership had informed one group that war was not only unnecessary but also impractical. By then, President Museveni's support had consolidated Saad Luwemba as Mufti at the Supreme Council and Luwemba had, in turn, chosen Kakeeto as Tabligh Amir at Nakasero. These events marked state infiltration of the major Tabligh faction.

Jamil Mukulu has stated that when members of his group denounced political jihad they reneged on their promises and became traitors: 'when released from prison, I retuned thinking that Ssentamu was progressing with our plan. But the state had co-opted him and changed his views on jihad. Even Kamoga refused to join me. He ran to Kenya.'[67] Released from

---

[64]   FGD with former ADF Rebels, Makindye (Kampala), 11 July 2016.
[65]   Ibid.
[66]   FGD with former ADF rebels, Wandegeya, 14 July 2016.
[67]   Jamil Mukulu recordings, 2012.

ISLAMIC REFORM AND INTRA-MUSLIM VIOLENCE   **175**

prison, Mukulu was denied space to preach his jihadist' language, and he was 'forced' – like the Tabligh splinter groups that emerged – to establish his own masjid at Mengo near Lubiri ring road, Kampala, 1993–94.

At Mengo, Mukulu courted trouble when his 'moving *darasa*'[68] was seen as revolution in the making. Many youths had continued to listen to his audio recordings and his new base became more popular than Nakasero and other Tabligh spaces. By this time (1993–95), attrocities directed at Muslims had continued in many rural areas. Mukulu built his message on these wrongs and called on the state to intervene. I would like to reproduce a message from his recordings:

> If these atrocities do not stop, we shall speak a different language [violence], we are peaceful where there is peace ... we shall pick up guns ... this is not a threat, its reality. And if one side picks up the guns, even the Talaf [Mukulu's opponents] shall pick up guns, we are capable of making an army. This Tumwine [UPDF officer] was an artist who went to bush and he returned a major general. When we go to police we are not helped, the state wants to make us into opportunists; stop politicizing us, do not make us a fertile ground for recruitment.[69]

The above message called on the state to remember that Muslims were part of Uganda society and that it had a duty to guard against atrocities; it also reminded the state that Muslims were capable of defending their rights through force of arms. Mukulu's second message was directed at the Muslim youth. He reminded them:

> we shall pick up the gun and fight ... the AK47 is just a gun and whoever can pick it up can cause results ... they want money and life; they want life more than we do. We can fight them, we have nothing to lose: if we are killed, we shall go to Jannah, if we win, they shall lose. Do not fear them. Museveni's intention is to erase Islam from this country; we are the youth and we understand all the language unlike the Bazeeyi.[70]

Muslim youth received this message and looked to Mukulu as the leader to deliver them from historical marginalization. As hordes of Tabligh youth rushed to listen to Mukulu's messages, Nakasero and other Tabligh spaces were concerned. Unlike the first split, this second split was not about

---

[68]   These were teaching sessions delivered in Muslims' private residences and at various masjids in rotating weekly patterns.

[69]   'Embeera y'obusalafi' (the state of Salafism), Jamil Mukulu, Recordings, Kampala, 1994.

[70]   Ibid.

losing followers to a new leadership. Rather it concerned a widely held belief that the language of political jihad was 'toxic' and it would lead Muslim youth astray.[71] This was compounded by the fact that Mukulu's message continued to attract followers. While many people shared the belief that the social-political-economic situation favoured other religions more than it did Muslims, political jihad was dismissed as an alternative to the Muslim predicament.

How could Mukulu be persuaded to 'tone' down his message? Mukulu mentions that Ssentamu met him to persuade him to 'forget jihad' and that 'I should follow Islam as he [Ssentamu] interpreted it. He informed me that they as leaders did not want me to proceed with it. This statement meant that he had changed his views on jihad.'[72] Mukulu reminded Ssentamu that his message was more important at the time because Christian powers had invaded the sites of Islamic practice (Old Kampala and Nakasero). He said: 'the invasion of Old Kampala failed because our objective of dislodging Luwemba from Supreme Council failed and even spread to Nakasero where Luwemba gave the Nakasero keys to Kakeeto'.[73] As Mukulu declined to tone down his 'radical' language, his opponents chose a different course. Here, multiple Tabligh leaderships joined to preach against Mukulu's jihad message. As Ssentamu and Kiggundu returned Mukulu's 'guns and ammunitions and bombs', they also spoke against his activities, revealed the 'secrets' they had with Mukulu, and designated him a *khawarij* (heretic).[74] As Madina graduates were chided for cultivating the space in which Mukulu's radical message thrived, they too redirected the anger at Mukulu and his ignorance of Islamic teachings.[75] These new designations marked Mukulu and his faction for exorcism from the Tabligh when Kakeeto and others began beating up Muslim youth in Mukulu's camp so as to prevent them from hearing the jihad message.[76] With his image tarnished, his members were beaten and humiliated. In Masaka, one sheikh made it his duty to prevent Mukulu-allied Tabligh from sprouting, to no avail. Failing to separate Mukulu from his followers, authorities denied him a peaceful atmosphere to construct his Mengo masjid.

[71] FGD with sheikhs and elders, Iganga, 3 November 2016.
[72] Ibid.
[73] Ibid.
[74] Jamil Mukulu recordings, 2012.
[75] Ibid.
[76] FGD with former Tabligh members in Mukulu's Mengo Masjid, Kampala, 19 July 2016.

When pressed on whether Mukulu *continued to think* about jihad at that time in his Mengo space, the former Tabligh members in his camp say that his message spoke about jihad but he was not *ready*. They argue that the violent attacks against Mukulu disorganized his plans to build the masjid in Mengo; Mukulu was pushed into a wall and he decided to begin war, not against Nakasero and Old Kampala, but their benefactors, the state.[77] How do we reconcile the statement that Mukulu was not 'ready' with his own admissions that jihad was conceived during the early 1987–98 era only to be disturbed by his imprisonment? Mukulu has said that political jihad was the objective; the formative moment was ongoing until it was interrupted.[78] As his recordings from the camps in Zaire/DRC) highlight, he was committed to jihad but had not decided the 'opportune' moment to begin attacks. Pushed to the wall and denied operating space, Mukulu recruited the first 265 ADF fighters, who marched to Buseruka, Hoima (Western Uganda) to begin full-scale rebel activities.

The state's response was tailored to different circumstances. In the pre-rebellion moment, the state sought to appease Mukulu and his faction. A string of masjids was constructed in various parts of the country to appease Mukulu's Tabligh faction and to convince them to desist from war. These masjids are spread in many places in Busoga, Buganda, Eastern Uganda; they are identified as 'Museveni's gifts to Mukulu's Tabligh'.[79] The other response of the state to the ADF rebellion was gradual intelligence infiltration, open military engagement and assassination of its top commanders, and political promises directed at some of their commanding officers. This military response was predicated upon the military nature of the threat – and more. The ADF rebellion begun in Buganda, led by Baganda Muslims who recruited fighters from provinces such as Busoga and Eastern Uganda. Since the NRM regime had declared that Buganda (Kampala) was the centre of any regime's legitimacy from which power radiated to the regions, Buganda had to be pacified at all costs. With the emergence of the rebellion, the ADF Tabligh became the political underbelly of the NRM regime in Buganda.

The ADF rebellion began with 265 Muslims (15 were women) in Buseruka, Hoima District, Western Uganda. The idea was to attack police stations and to acquire more guns. The rebellion had begun with sixteen guns, which had been initially kept in private houses.[80] Government forces

---

[77] Ibid.
[78] Jamil Mukulu Recordings, 2012.
[79] Discussions in Busoga, Mbale and Masaka revealed these sites.
[80] Interview with former ADF rebel, Kampala, 19 July 2016. Some respondents disagreed on the exact number of guns.

attacked the ADF camp in Buseruka, arrested some, killed the others, while forty-five remnants ran to Ntoroko landing site and boarded boats to escape to Zaire/DRC. Jamil Mukulu was not part of this camp and those arrested were returned to Mengo and initially imprisoned in Lubiri palace[81] but later transferred to Luzira. They were released after six years in 2000.[82]

Meanwhile, as the ADF Tabligh faction engaged the state in a rebellion geared towards capturing state power, another debate had sprung up within Nakasero. According to the former ADF rebels, Jamil Mukulu's project was received with mixed feelings in the Nakasero camp. While some felt that the Tabligh leadership at Nakasero should denounce Mukulu, others wondered: 'if Mukulu actually succeeds in his rebellion against Museveni, he will establish a government that we shall not participate in, we are his enemies'.[83] This fear influenced Muhammad Kiggundu to found the UNFM/A as a counter force to the ADF struggle against Museveni, and they chose to go to Arua area in north-west Uganda, near Zaire, as the base of their operations. Unfortunately, these met a deadly ambush when Sudanese People's Liberation Movement (SPLM) leader John Garang's fighters mistook them for Lord's Resistance Army rebels and killed many of them. The remnants did not marshal a significant threat to the NRM; some were given amnesty and others were integrated into the UPDF.[84] The UNFM/A was not as popular as the ADF.

The amnesty agreement between the state and all rebel movements was signed at Nairobi in 2000, and allowed the release of all ADF fighters captured at Buseruka. It also allowed ADF a recruiting base from battle-hardened youth who heard that the war still raged, and ran back to Hoima, Bundibugyo, Kasese and Eastern Congo to join their colleagues. When the ADF attacked Kasese, Western Uganda (first in November 1996 and later in August 1998), it mobilized more recruits. Those released under amnesty in 2000 also ran back to support their colleagues because they felt their rebellion was winning some battles.[85] New waves of recruitment continued around the same message: political jihad and Islamic Sharia were the solution to Muslim challenges in Uganda. The objective was to engage the UPDF in battles that would ultimately move to capture state power in Kampala. The group feeling influenced individual choices that, as long as

---

[81] This was before the government handed over these premises to the Kabaka-ship, years after the restitution of the Buganda traditional institution in 1993.

[82] Ibid.

[83] Interview with former UNFM/A rebel, Kampala, 19 July 2016.

[84] Ibid.

[85] FGD with former ADF Rebels, Makindye (Kampala), 11 July 2016.

ISLAMIC REFORM AND INTRA-MUSLIM VIOLENCE **179**

the war waged, one could not abandon the group lest one apostatized.[86] What was the possibility of success? How realistic was the initial decision to wage war in the first place? Does the uncertainty of success explain why Ssentamu and other sheikhs spoke against it? The responses of the former rebels have stated that, within the moment of the 1990s, they had hope for success. According to the circumstances of the time,

> we were convinced and we also believed that we were fighting a good cause. When we actually began the war and encountered government forces in Buseruka, those forty-five who escaped through Ntoroko to Zaire symbolized that we would continue the war and become victorious. When we also attacked government forces in Kasese we got morale and thought that success would eventually come.[87]

The recordings of Jamil Mukulu obtained from his *khutba* and *darasa* in the camp reveal a picture that highlights some responses to the question concerning the feasibility of success. In a series of recordings made in 2012, Mukulu used a special session he calls 'Ffe tuli ku kituufu' (we are the only ones on the truth) to attack the Kampala Tabligh, the state and its agents, and all his opponents. He used the lecture session to explain how his faction is the only one on the 'truth' in contrast to those Tabligh leaders and groups that he left in Kampala. With this claim, he challenges anyone else to bring forth evidence to challenge their (ADF's) monopoly of 'truth'.[88] In the same session, Mukulu proceeds to provide the details of his 'government' and how he had 'succeeded' to establish *dawla* Islamiya in the mountains (rebel camps), away from the '*kaafir*' state in Uganda. He says, 'we are enjoying true Islam here. We do not have CMI [Uganda intelligence organ], we have no churches to abuse Allah that he has a son, we are not living in a *kaafir* state.'[89]

As he advanced his cause vis-à-vis his 'opponents', Mukulu reminded his followers that, since Sharia governed his 'mujahidin' (holy fighters), those intending to join him should first 'purify' their selves from '*shirk*' and '*kufr*' (polytheism and disbelief) and then wear 'garbs of *Tawhid*' [Islamic monotheism] and the Sunnah [and] prepare to practise them truly.'[90] He further warned that the camp as '*madina-t-tawhid*' (city of Islamic monotheism) was not a place to work for the earthly life but for

---

[86]   Ibid.
[87]   Ibid.
[88]   Jamil Mukulu, Recordings, 4 October 2012.
[89]   Ibid.
[90]   Ibid.

180 ISLAM IN UGANDA

the hereafter. Those Muslims who stayed in Uganda the '*dawla kufriya* (*kaafir* state), *nifaqiya* (state of hypocrites), *shrikiya* (state of polytheism)' should remember that they lived in '*nagis*' (dirt) and if they were comfortable under '*kaafir* laws' they were also '*kaafir*'.[91] The implication was that any Muslim who refused to migrate to Mukulu's camp had apostatized, including all Muslim leaders like parliamentarians who made laws in Uganda.[92] I would like to interpret Mukulu's language as a sign of desperation for significance. Frustrated by the increasing desertion of his forces following government counter-insurgence in the Kasese region, Mukulu painted a picture of a successful Islamic revolution in his camp to entice new members to his idea of *dawla* Islamiya. This frustration also bred desperation for new recruits since his fighters had greatly reduced in number.[93] I base this analysis on government counter-insurgence tactics that defeat his statements.

First, Mukulu was at pains to paint a picture of pure Islamic governance devoid of '*kaafir*' influence yet in his very midst state spies operated to inform on his whereabouts. These same spies passed the state information on ADF top commanders who later accepted state advances and abandoned the ADF rebellion.[94] Mukulu called the Uganda experience one of '*dawla nifaqiya*' but hypocrisy operated in his very midst. When his commanders escaped from camp and accepted state lures, they informed on the military operations in the camp, and ADF operations became compromised. When Mukulu's strategy became lost in tactics like urban bomb attacks, the state approached the very ADF bomb experts to inform on their colleagues and used them to eliminate the ADF bomb threat in Kampala.[95]

Second, Mukulu's message in the *darasa* sessions spoke of desperation for new recruits. Many of his soldiers were captured in various places and taken to government offices in Kyanjoka, Kasese, Western Uganda, for amnesty screening. Former rebels were pardoned if they accepted amnesty, but if they participated in the rebellion again, they would face the death penalty or life imprisonment.[96] When granted amnesty, the state representative sent the former rebels to Kaweweeta barracks, Western Uganda, for full military training, after which another screening would proceed at the Chieftaincy of Military Intelligence (CMI) headquarters in

91   Ibid.
92   Ibid.
93   FGD with former ADF rebels, 19 July 2016.
94   Ibid.
95   Interview with former ADF bomb expert, Kampala, 20 July 2016.
96   Ibid.

Kampala to sieve the intelligence officers from the foot soldiers. At CMI, bomb experts and intelligence gatherers were identified as the new UPDF recruits to inform on their 'new enemy', the ADF.[97]

But not all accepted integration in the UPDF; some refused. Their reason was that if the rebellion began as a way to fight the NRM '*kaafir*' army, accepting integration into UPDF and CMI under state payment meant that the rebel had failed and the state won. In other words, the state had succeeded in weakening the Muslim and turned him into its asset. For such a Muslim, this meant continuing serving a '*kaafir*' army and coercing Muslims with state power just for a few shillings in monthly salary.[98] This state of affairs frustrated Mukulu because it confirmed that his project had failed to cultivate a strong Muslim self in the people he claimed to govern. The state integrated the former ADF rebels into its security apparatus and released it into the Muslim community to inform on the goings-on thereby turning the Tabligh against each other; it transformed a Muslim insurgence into an intra-Muslim civil war. The intrigue and in-fighting that gripped the Tabligh following the murder of the Muslim clerics was intensified by the circulation of information between the state and its informants.[99] As the following section shows, the outcome of the nature of the state's response to the ADF rebellion led to further splits within the Salafiyya as those granted amnesty felt protected by the state and used their temporary power positions to reorganize themselves to the detriment of others.

The 2014 split in the Tabligh

In 2014, a group of Sheikhs within the Salafiyya appointed Muhammad Yunus Kamoga to become their Amir. Their choice was dictated by the reconciliatory wave sweeping through the Muslim groups, and to his organizational abilities. Because he had received state amnesty, his new position would accord him a degree of protection. Internal Salafiyya politics however disrupted the reunion until Kamoga was 'dismissed' for 'dictatorship' and fanning 'hatred and division' among Muslims.[100] Kamoga resisted his 'dismissal' and an internal purge targeting all sheikhs opposed to him began. Yet the prelude to these spats had much to do with both internal management politics within the Salafiyya and the state's attempt to divide and rule Tabligh groups, while appointing state agents to

[97]   Ibid.
[98]   FGD with former ADF rebels, 19 July 2016.
[99]   Ibid.
[100] See also 'Muslim Tabliqs dismiss leader', *Daily Monitor,* 28 November 2014.

182 ISLAM IN UGANDA

become their custodians. The trouble began with the death of prominent Muslim clerics in 2012 that belonged to the rival group affiliated to Kibuli. Accusations and counter-accusations emerged within the group over complicity in murders of the clerics. When more clerics were murdered in 2013 and 2014, information reached various sheikhs that some leaders in the Salafiyya were colluding with the state to inform on other sheikhs within the group. As seen in the previous section, this was the very effect of the integration of the former ADF into the government security structure.

Further, Kamoga's mobilization skills had culminated in the conception of a fundraising drive to build a project – Ummah House. Before long, questions emerged regarding the signatories to the project's bank accounts and its details. Where was it to be built? Who would own it? Did it belong to only the Tabligh-cum-Salafiyya only or to all Muslims in Uganda? Who would manage it? Would all sheikhs from Kibuli and Old Kampala also have offices in it? As Kamoga's cohorts ran to media houses to improve public relations regarding 'Ummah House', a section of prominent sheikhs within the Salafiyya denounced the project and were abruptly stopped from conducting *darasa* sessions. The explanation was that they had gone to the media and spoken against 'Ummah House'.

But the problem was larger than Ummah House. Internal leadership politics regarding the management of different Muslim organs such as *zakat* (poor due), Hajj (pilgrimage) and *waqf* were considered 'lucrative' opportunities for many Tabligh youth in league with leadership to acquire some economic improvement and *ekitiibwa* (honour, better status), which brought internal competition among sheikhs to attract the Amir's approval. As Amir, Kamoga had stopped some sheikhs from preaching inside a *darasa* session, on various occasions. His group was also suspected of 'torturing' enemies, and rampant displays of 'dictatorship'.[101] State support for Kamoga was confirmed when General Salim Saleh (state official) attended one of the annual Tabligh *darasa* at Busega in which Kamoga requested that Saleh assist them with a ground to build Ummah House – together with Moses Kigongo, Salim Saleh had been identified as the state officials to provide custodianship over the Kamoga-led faction.

The Jjemba-led faction became convinced that Kamoga was the 'enemy' within, and at a 'farewell' *khutba* in Masjid Noor Ndawula, with emotion, revealed a tell-all about the wrongs within the Tabligh-Salafiyya, swore by the Quran and marked a formal split from Kamoga.[102] Unlike open con-

---

[101] 'Kirya's faction gives evidence for Kamoga's torture of Muslims', *Bukedde*, 1 January 2015.

[102] Umar Swidiq Ndawula, *khutba* at Masjid Noor, William Street, Kampala, August 2015.

frontation of the previous years, the new split undertook a discourse of recorded *darasa* and *khutba* whereby each faction critiqued the other. Yet the undercurrent within these recordings was the conversation of despair, disillusionment, hatred, betrayal and malicious lies directed against some sheikhs. In sum, the *busagwa* (poisonous discourse) of earlier years resurfaced, only that video and audio recordings carried it more effectively to its targeted audience. When Haruna Jjemba became the Amir of the 'new' Salafiyya faction, a wave of 'verbal terrorism' emerged from their counterparts. Trading insults and abuses reached the level where death threats surfaced. In one recording, the author threatens Ndawula and his group that unless they all faced death, Islam in Uganda would never progress.[103]

On 3 January 2016 at the Wandegeya Masjid in Kampala, the Jjemba-led Salafiyya faction convened a *darasa*, which they dubbed '*katubibagambe*' (let us reveal the secrets). The objective of this session was to explain to the Muslims the cause of the clerics' murders and the agent of death. I hope to return to this in the next chapter. But something emerged within the *darasa* about how a professing Muslim could become the enemy of Islam and Muslims. Sheikh Abdallah Wanji delivered a session that reported a Hadith of the Prophet (PBUH). He noted that

> the Prophet Muhammad (PBUH) said: 'After me, there will be two things: disagreements in understanding knowledge and factions. Composed of youthful people, with beards, shortened clothes, and shaven heads, their understanding will be thoughtless, their prayers would be frequent as is their fasting. Although reading the Hadiths of the Prophet would be their daily routine, their practice would be worse. They would be strong in reading Quran but it would not proceed beyond their throats to their hearts to inform practice. Their tongues would convince others to become Muslims but they would not practice what they preach. They would be the primary people to murder Muslims but the non-Muslims would look at them as their brethren since they would pronounce disbelief saying that so and so is Kafir and unworthy of Islam. If the infidels are safe from such a Muslim, then Islam is outside of such an individual. Whoever would be fortunate to rise up and fight such youth would have a great reward. The acts of such youth would take them outside Islam with the speed akin to that of an arrow leaving the bow. They would never return to Islam until the arrow returns to the bow. They are the worst of creatures and if you find them, kill them. For this is most honorable in the eyes of Allah.' The Sahabah

---

[103] Audio recording from one Sheikh, relayed in a *darasa* session, Lubiri ring road Masjid, 'Yahya Yaani', 20 December 2015. Sheikh Yahya Mwanje was the deputy leader of the Tabligh faction led by Sheik Yunus Kamoga.

asked: 'how shall we differentiate them?' The Prophet said, 'they would have shaved heads'.[104]

When Wanji delivered this Hadith, he was all the while interjecting with reminders that the Tabligh-Salafiyya had to watch out for members who looked like them (beards, shortened trousers, et cetera) but shaved their heads. The narration of this Hadith was important for the very reason that information circulating among the sheikhs was that their brethren were complicit in various ways in the murders of clerics. As this chapter has argued, the Tabligh was responsible for laying the language of radicalism on which the state rode as an alibi to liquidate them. When it successfully liquidated the ADF rebels and turned some of them into agents of state security, the NRM government turned the Tabligh 'problem' into an intra-Muslim civil war. Further violence ensued when the Tabligh allied themselves to the centres of Muslim power in Uganda (Kibuli and Old Kampala), which rattled the state. How the state undertook to contain Muslims culminated into the liquidation of former rebels and their supporters to extirpate signs of rebellion (both real and potential) from the NRM political gains in Buganda.

---

[104] Wanji Abdallah (2016), 'Who is Killing the Muslims?' Wandegeya, 3 January. This Hadith was reported as a combination of meanings from various narrators of the Prophetic tradition. Its full statement did not originate from the words of Ali Abi Talib (the third Caliph in Islam who also narrated some traditions of the Prophet). Author translation from Luganda.

CHAPTER 7

NRM Statecraft and Muslim Subjects

This chapter investigates the systematic murder of Muslim clerics beginning from 2012 to the end of 2016 as an entry point to understanding how the National Resistance Movement (NRM) regime re-articulated the Muslim conundrum. It argues that the murders fit within the attempt of the state to support Old Kampala-based Islam as a centre of Muslims' representation vis-à-vis Kibuli and other emerging centres of Muslim leadership. It shows that historical Muslim 'problems', such as social-political-economic marginalization, which the NRM inherited, influenced the political status and role of Muslims within the NRM regime while in turn cultivating a special role for state agents within the Muslim publics. Following from the previous deliberations, this chapter demonstrates the consequences of the attempt of various Muslim elites to articulate a particular interpretation of Islam that imagined political jihad as the antidote to Muslim historical social-political-economic marginalization, which invited state responses that turned Muslim violence into an internal civil war.

By situating the questions, 'who are the Muslims' and 'how do they express Islam?' it demonstrates how the NRM transformed the Muslim question from representation to belonging – understood as allegiance to NRM patronage of Muslims, This was born within the 1986 revolution, but intensified in the 1990s when the regime sought to thwart Muslim militancy (ADF) from its political gains in Buganda. Intra-Muslim schisms therefore also contributed to state intervention. The theoretical contribution of this chapter is to question the assumption that violent state action against forms of 'religious radicalism' from social groups arises from the state's desire to subdue political opposition, negating the internal agency and capacity for radical actions arising from particular forms of religious expression. Following Asad, my contribution fuses 'secular' and 'religious' explanations for violent action to demonstrate that the appeal to 'religious' expressions has consequences for 'secular' power.[1] Unable to marshal a

---

[1] Asad, Talal (2003), *Formations of the Secular: Christianity, Islam, Modernity,* Stanford University Press: Stanford, p. 11.

186 ISLAM IN UGANDA

spirited force to thwart its 'enemy', 'religious' agency *invites* the intervention of secular power to inscribe and continue instances of domination. As Foucault emphasized, violence here becomes its own victim.[2]

This chapter also speaks to some legacies of the colonial era that continued and intensified under NRM governance. First, the historical restriction of Muslims' political field had allowed the state to circumscribe expressions of Islam by pushing Muslim politics to private sites such as masjids. This had not 'withered' political Islam but it had relegated it to the private spaces where micro-politics had emerged. The NRM learned from colonial statecraft and proceeded to maintain the Muslim Supreme Council as an elite institution to represent and guard Islam for the Muslim masses. Unlike Amin, the NRM was a non-Muslim power that postured Muslim unity to achieve different political interests. As it tasked the Supreme Council to guard Islam, counter-elites challenged the state's choice.

Second, the attempt of multiple centres of Muslim power to challenge state-backed Muslim elites has colonial antecedents. When the Juma-Zukuuli theological schisms had emerged, the Mbogo/Kakungulu elite dominance had been challenged. Within this moment, alternative centres of Muslim power emerged when new Muslim elites (Abdallah Ssekimwanyi and Twaibu Magatto) emerged to attract Muslim masses and founded new groups. Under NRM governance, the emergence of Muslim counter-elites (Kibuli) to challenge the 'traditional' centres of Muslim representation (Old Kampala) gained importance in a context where political majorities were considered critical to the outcomes of national elections. The challenge for the state is that Muslim elite groups proliferated so much that majoritarian national electoral politics necessitated the forging of special alliances that would deliver Muslim majority votes to the incumbent. Muslim minorities were designated 'enemies' of the state.

Third, the history of Muslims' economic marginalization is situated within colonial land distribution and education policy. Unlike the Christian groups, the historical denial of adequate means of social-economic reproduction (land) put Muslims at the mercy of the colonial state. When Obote I founded NAAM, Muslims realized an opportunity to acquire economic emancipation, among other benefits. They could only progress as far as their importance to Obote's political project. Amin's revolution had returned some Muslims to the fore of economic prosperity when they

---

[2] Foucault, Michel (1977), 'The Subject and Power', *Critical Inquiry,* Vol. 8, No. 4, pp. 777–95 pp. 794–5.

inherited the businesses and properties of departing Asian communities, and the UMSC became the richest landowner in the country. Fearful of a Muslim resurgence, on the one hand, and desiring to liberalize the national economy with his open-door policy for returning Asians, Museveni undertook to control the UMSC by propping up a 'friendly' Mufti, which made him the patron of the Muslim leadership and its representation of the Muslim masses.

In various ways, the NRM era has witnessed the most consistent attempt of multiple Muslim leaderships to expand the field of Islamic interpretation beyond the ritualism identified with the colonial era. To contain what it perceives as a threat to its political gains, the NRM's response is to combine modes of governance. It has fused Obote's delicate balancing (supporting Mufti Ssemakula's NAAM while marginalizing Kakungulu's Kibuli-based Africa Muslim Community) and Amin's state patronage of Muslims, within the divide-and-rule tactics akin to the colonial era, which are directed at the multiple centres of Muslim leadership in Uganda. This recasting by the NRM of colonial-era tactics of governance over the Muslim groups I call the desire to recolonize society. What emerges in this chapter however is that some Muslims have broken allegiance with the centres of Muslim power and have proceeded to articulate a version of Islam that gels with the national agenda. Such individuals as professionals, business elites, politicians and others have achieved individual autonomy in expressing themselves in multiple ways. Born within the moment of frustration with Kibuli-Old Kampala leadership rivalry, this trend points to an attempt to individualize Muslim self-consciousness and shake off the 'group feeling' and its effect on individual choices.

The chapter is divided into three sections. The first provides a political context for the NRM regime and its articulation of the Muslim question. It argues that Museveni's 'broad base' was an attempt to integrate and govern diverse ethnic groups in the country, such integration including religio-political groups such as the Muslims. The Muslim groups, having tasted political power under Amin, were considered by the NRM to be a political threat to its revolution. Conceived under Obote II to respond to this 'threat', Muslim massacres[3] were unsustainable. The NRM therefore undertook to prop up a Muslim leadership favourable to it, one that would guard a particular version of Islam and accommodate Muslim masses within the new political structure.

---

3   Kiyimba, Abasi (1989), *Is the 1979 Muslim Blood Bath in Bushenyi History?* Kampala.

188 ISLAM IN UGANDA

The second section discusses the NRM's governance of Islam and Muslims. It demonstrates the *politics* of the state's attempts to prop up a particular Muslim leadership as the representative of Muslim masses. It argues that state support for the UMSC as the representative of Muslim masses met resistance from emerging centres of Muslim counter-elites such as Kibuli. The response of the Muslim elites to the state's control of the UMSC bred diverse debates that fragmented Muslim leadership.

The third section discusses the NRM's attempt to assert itself as the single patron of Muslims in Uganda. It contends that the assassination of Muslim clerics fit within the NRM's re-articulation of the Muslim question from being one of mere 'representation' to being both 'representation' and 'belonging'. From being a question of 'who are the Muslims' and 'who represents them' to national political power, the fragmentation of Muslim leadership within the context of majoritarian national electoral politics added a nuance of 'belonging' to re-articulate the Muslim question under later NRM statecraft. The response to Museveni's question: 'where are my Muslims?'[4] was understood to imply those who belonged to the NRM electorate, the objective being that the multiple centres of Muslim leadership would rally behind two centres: state agents who acted as trustees[5] of youthful Muslim groups (Tabliq) and thus linked them to NRM power and, the UMSC as the state-recognized representative of Muslim masses. Its effect was to designate 'moderate' and 'radical' Muslim elites. The former was identified as one who could also work for the NRM to deliver his faction to vote for NRM incumbency, and the latter was considered a political minority that had to be extirpated;

---

[4] Jamil Mukulu Recordings, 2012, reminiscing on how Museveni had on numerous occasions wondered: since 'there are Muslims for Iran, Libya, and Saudi Arabia, where are my Muslims?'

[5] The notion of trusteeship has colonial antecedents when British colonialism sought to found micro units of Muslim governance. Trustees were chosen from a Muslim committee related to a particular masjid. These functioned as the first link between the groups to state power; to which the Muslim subjects were accountable in case of emerging issues of governance. See Buganda Government: Matters Relating to Mohamedans, 1929–1945, doc. 44, p. 2. In 2012, the NRM placed its important personalities as the trustees of the Tabliq leaders. Moses Kigongo and Salim Saleh were the trustees of the majority Tabliq group (Kamoga faction). Inspector General of Police Kale Kayihura was initially the trustee of the minority faction (the Jjemba-faction), but was denounced upon Kirya's death in June 2015. These trustees functioned to 'introduce' integrating the Muslim Tabliq with the NRM structure. Interview with Tabliq leader, Makerere, 19 August 2016.

usefully justified when there was a history of militant rebellion against the state. This inscription of NRM power on the Muslim leadership manifests its desire to contain it within the national political structure under state patronage, with measurable success.

The NRM broad base as an experiment in political governance

Under what historical conditions did the NRM regime imagine the broad base as a system of rule that would solve the history of ethno-religious conflict in Uganda? How did this integration of diverse groups within the idea of a single party-state provide promises of stability in the country? What contradictions did the broad base as a unifying mode of governance engender, as seen in the delayed pacification of the northern parts of Uganda (see Chapter 6) and the Muslim phobia? This section provides a political context for the NRM regime and its articulation of the Muslim question. It argues that Museveni's 'broad base' was an attempt to integrate and govern diverse ethnic groups in the country, including such religio-political groups as Muslims. The NRM considered the Muslim groups, which had tasted political power under Amin, a threat to the revolution politically. Although Muslim massacres disguised as fighting 'Aminism' had been conceived to respond to this 'threat' under Obote II, they were unsustainable. The NRM therefore undertook to prop up a Muslim leadership favourable to it, one that would guard a particular version of Islam and accommodate Muslim masses within the new political structure.

When the NRM came to power in January 1986, it revolutionized the prevailing conception of democracy reflected in multi-party government. Its experience of Ugandan politics believed that elitism had subjugated society. Thus Museveni's new government went about purveying grass-roots popular participation in opposition to representative conceptions of democracy. The system it founded comprised Resistance Councils (RCs) at various levels (parish, county, district) leading to the National Resistance Council (NRC). This new structure allowed government accountability to the people and ultimately enabled the state to 'crack' the legacy of decentralized despotism.[6] But the RCs have to be seen in a tripartite perspective. As bureaucratic spaces, they implemented government policy and therefore became state organs. As democratic structures, they became popular organs to check the abuses of civil servants and other state functionaries. The RCs were, however, also perceived by some as 'sectarian' since they

[6]   Mamdani, 'Uganda in Transition', p. 1173.

were the organs of 'one single political group, the NRM'.[7] In pretending to construct a revolutionary structure of overall inclusion, the RCs thus ensured that the national image mirrored the ideas of NRM.

Alongside the RCs, citizenship was recalibrated to designate residence in a given location as the marker of belonging. The NRM modernizing project attempted to resolve the interlinked parochial projects such as Ganda federalism, which challenged the broader NRM Ugandan project by institutionalizing the latter's idea of the 'Movement' in which all Ugandans were free to 'belong'. The NRM – organized, as a coalition of small groups interested in power and privilege – was the external political wing of the National Resistance Army (NRA).[8] This externality very much explains the dictatorial turn within the NRM and the extirpation/ elimination of those opposed to it both from within and without. From its early days, the NRM was an exclusive group; the broad base merely camouflaged its interests. The appeal to social inclusion was the one-way ticket to political legitimacy.

Two years after coming into government, the NRM continued to incorporate groups considered friendly to its interests while excluding those perceived inimical to its agenda. General Moses Ali's Uganda National Rescue Front, for instance, became accepted within the NRM/A since he was 'content with a ministerial position' and could integrate his troops into the larger NRA. Other groups such as Uganda People's Democratic Army (UPDA) were also integrated within the NRM after a peace agreement in 1988.[9] The success of integration as a strategy of statecraft was predicated upon its strong emphasis on the comprehensive development of diverse groups. Disenfranchised constituencies rising up to demand rehabilitative politics while the regime pretended to integrate all social constituencies, but occluded comprehensive social-economic-political benefits, could spell disaster in Uganda.[10] Integration therefore was the NRM response to mitigating possible opposition from groups that desired power and privileges.

---

[7] Ibid., p. 1176.
[8] Ibid., p. 1160.
[9] Omach, Paul (2011), 'Understanding obstacles to Peace in Northern Uganda: Actors, their interests and Strategies', in Baregu, Mwesiga (Ed.) (2011), *Understanding Obstacles to Peace: Actors, Interests and Strategies in Africa's Great Lakes Region,* Fountain: Kampala, p. 283.
[10] For example, when the ADF and UNFM/A rebellions claimed that the state had historically treated them as third class citizens and the NRM government compounded this historical marginalization.

When the NRM regime came to power, it found a Muslim community divided by leadership crises. Beginning from the Obote II government, various Muslim leaders had chosen closeness to state power as the best way to maintain their hold on their offices. Museveni's government therefore inherited Muslim leadership factions.[11] He interpreted the history of Muslim conflict over masjids and other spaces as significant threats to the stability of the country, and he warned that government would not accept a 'breakdown of law and order in the name of religious conflicts'.[12] The NRM's interest in Muslim leadership is however identified with two important developments. First, the desire of Museveni to maintain the Supreme Council as the representative Muslim organization owing to the accruing social-economic benefits; second, the growth of the Muslim Tabliq as a phenomenon that threatened the Supreme Council. Regarding the first, the NRM declaration of an 'open-door' policy for the returning Asians informed its practice of identifying 'friendly' leaders in the Muslim Supreme Council that would relinquish Muslim control over the properties that they had inherited following Amin's decree, banishing the Asians. In the case *Rajab Kakooza v Saad Luwemba*, regarding the Muftiship of Uganda, the state allegedly influenced the Supreme Court to rule in favour of Sheikh Saad Luwemba who was considered easy to work with.[13] Rajab Kakooza was considered a 'difficult' Muslim leader because he was hesitant in returning Asian properties such as the Aga Khan building that housed the Supreme Council headquarters in Old Kampala. Kakooza was also supported by the Tabliq youth who looked to him as Mufti, as reflected in the Tabliq invasions of the Supreme Council in 1991. When the state chose Saad Luwemba as Mufti, Sheikh Rajab Kakooza proceeded on a diplomatic campaign in the Arab world to speak against Museveni's intervention in Muslim affairs.[14] This affected the regime's economic development since he had looked towards Arab finances to escape the conditions of Western aid and donations.

Museveni decided to arrange a World Muslim League (Rabitta)-brokered resolution of the internal Muslim conflicts by organizing a

[11] Kasumba, Yusuf (1995), 'The Development of Islam in Uganda 1962–1992 with Particular Reference to Religio-Political Factionalism', Masters Dissertation, Makerere University, Kampala', pp.207–8.

[12] Kaliisa, Anas Abdunoor (1994), 'Leadership Crisis Among Muslims of Uganda (1850–1993)', Masters Dissertation, Kampala: Makerere University, pp. 236–40.

[13] Ibid., p.238.

[14] Ibid., p.239.

192   ISLAM IN UGANDA

Muslim unity conference in Mbarara in May 1993. On the surface, he seemed to be interested in finding a solution, yet he declined to implement its resolutions and continued to front Saad Luwemba, a candidate that the delegates did not actually endorse.[15] It emerged later that Museveni stage-managed the Muslim unity conference to entice Arab economic support. As later events were to reveal, the government publicly indicated its dissociation from the outcomes of the unity conference when it invited two different leaders to represent the Muslims at the Independence celebrations in Kololo (Kampala) in the same year. Regardless of Muslim opinion, these events symbolized government determination to support Muslim leadership at Supreme Council. Its actions were however contradictory because they also accommodated the opposing Muslim power at Kibuli when the state officials would participate in Kibuli activities. This context of power rivalry was however difficult to sustain due to the desire of the Kibuli group to oust the leadership of the Supreme Council. In the ensuing altercation, various factors influenced the NRM choice of the Old Kampala Muslim leadership.

The NRM and 'its Muslims': Kibuli-Old Kampala Muslim power rivalry

How did the Kibuli-Old Kampala Muslim power/leadership rivalry come to assume national importance in the NRM era? And what implications did this rivalry engender for NRM politics and national Muslim leadership? In this section, I demonstrate that the NRM's desire to prop up Old Kampala as the 'legitimate' representative of Muslim masses met resistance from historical and emerging centres of Muslim counter-elites such as the new Salafiyya Tabliq spaces and Kibuli. Such opposition to state support of Muslim leaders considered 'unpopular' by Muslim elites bred a debate that further fragmented Muslim leadership, one that assumed national importance because the alliance of various Tabliq youth to both Kibuli and Old Kampala availed to each centre an 'army' of Muslim youth that could defend its claim to leadership by invading the Supreme Council. The implication is that a Kibuli alliance with the Tabliq could cause a Muslim revolution if a successful attack was undertaken, to the detriment of the state's support of the sitting Mufti. This fact explains the state's use of violence to prevent Kibuli-based Muslim marches to the Supreme Council.

---

[15]   Kanyeihamba, George W. (1997), *Reflections on the Muslim leadership question in Uganda*, Kampala.

The contemporary power rivalry between Kibuli and Old Kampala has historical antecedents, as discussed in earlier chapters, but here I concentrate on the recent history, especially the events after 2000. Since 1987, Muslim leadership was a contested affair that culminated in two leaders representing two factions. The election of Mufti Shaban Ramadhan Mubajje in 2000 had promised to end this 'double' leadership and return order to the Muslim community. On 13 December 2000, sharp divisions emerged among the Muslim leadership when members of the Kibuli Muslim faction retracted their support for the newly elected Mufti. About ten sheikhs denounced Mubajje's election.[16] Mufti Mubajje was the first non-Muganda to attain the position of Mufti.[17] Later on, there emerged statements that some of the sheikhs named had been misrepresented, but the reason for denouncing the Mufti whom they had elected in a peaceful three-day process of the General Assembly of the UMSC, was not clear at the time. It emerged later that Mubajje's 'ethnicity' had bred Ganda indifference.[18]

However, many delegates of the 2000 election have refuted the ethnic factor in denouncing the new Muslim leadership. According to them, the denouncement of Mubajje arose out of disgruntlement from some delegates who had fronted their own candidates. Once it was clear that their own candidates were losing, they became frustrated and looked for excuses to salvage their egos:

> the issue about Mubajje after his election was not about his tribe. It was Baganda who also elected him. You must know that there were some Baganda who voted against tribes-mates. Even within Baganda Muslims, there are those who consider themselves of a higher status than others. Those Baganda that were perceived weak by their leaders also decided to vote for Mubajje. They were tired of the decay and business-like running of the UMSC from fellow Baganda. They voted for change ... the ethnic factor is not the issue ... they were frustrated.[19]

---

[16] '10 Kibuli Sheikhs denounce Mubajje election', *New Vision*, 13 December 2000.

[17] Among the Ugandan students In the Islamic Universities in Saudi Arabia, the election of Mufti in 2000 saw a split between the Mubajje camp (non-Baganda) and the Kakooza camp. The Baganda of course saw themselves as the guardians of Islam in Uganda and said they were 'Quraish' (the noble tribe of Mecca from which is chosen the guardian of the Islamic Holy sites) juxtaposed to the non-Baganda.

[18] FGD, Iganga, 3 November 2016.

[19] FGD, Mbale, 1 December 2016.

Regardless, Mubajje's election to muftiship was seen as a revolution whereby some sheikhs in Buganda were to quietly retire from their years of leadership. The only way to resist the revolution was to denounce the elected leadership and identify a site of power that would safeguard a parallel Muslim administration. Kibuli was that site where some Baganda sheikhs and all those denouncing the new Mufti could find refuge; headed by a Buganda Prince Kassim Nakibinge who was seen as 'untouchable' by any other power including the state, also a trustee of many Muslim endowments and other properties he inherited from his father, Badru Kakungulu, and his grandfather Prince Nuhu Mbogo.

Careful scrutiny reveals that Mubajje's denouncement lay in the Islamic theological articulations of both the new Mufti and those that denounced his election. Mubajje had been the District Khadi of Mbale during the leadership of the late Sheikh Saad Luwemba. Many believed that Mubajje, a graduate of the Islamic University in Riyadh, Saudi Arabia, was a strict follower of the Salaf sect since his caucus-forming appealed to the youthful Tabliq: 'he used to grow his beard and shorten his clothes. Many Tabliq saw him as one of their own who could remove the rot at the Council'.[20] The fact that the Tabliq identified with him as opposed to the other leaders created enmity because the Bazeyi (old guard), as they are called, saw the triumph of the youth in Mubajje's election. The Tabliq were critical of particular practices of the Bazeyi (Chapter 6), which they considered *bida* (innovation in religion). The election of Mubajje ushered into the UMSC a member of the Tabliq sect against the wishes of the Bazeyi. According to others, Mubajje was opposed due to his links with the NRM government, where he served as an electoral mobilizer to campaign for Museveni's election as president in 1996. Mubajje's election as Mufti was perceived as a reward for his role in that successful election campaign. Although he identified with the Salaf, his NRM leanings attracted enmity from many Muslims who perceived Mubajje as an ally to the NRM regime, and considered him an 'enemy of Islam and Muslims' in Uganda.[21]

The bickering over Mubajje, including his denouncement, could not assume national importance because it originated from a few 'disgruntled' sheikhs. It was the court cases involving Mufti Mubajje and his alleged involvement in the fraudulent mismanagement of Muslim properties and endowments that drew the ire of the Muslim masses and bred an anti-NRM Muslim public that looked beyond Mubajje to his benefactor, the state.

[20]   FGD, Iganga, 3 November 2016.
[21]   Ibid.

In 2006, information emerged that Mufti Mubajje and members of his administration had been involved in the gross mismanagement of Muslim properties without the consent of other UMSC members, in which it is alleged that some properties had been sold off. This issue divided the UMSC into two camps and led to the expulsion of some members. During the investigation, voice recordings circulated whereby various sheikhs had dubbed the Mufti as 'dishonest', accusing him of the betrayal of Islam and Muslims. He was ridiculed in many *khutba*, and many sheikhs called for his resignation.[22] The Mufti declined to give verbal evidence to the Commission of inquiry constituted to investigate the matter, arguing that it had been turned into a 'court of law', beyond its mandate. As the members of the Commission declined to visit the Mufti's office, citing 'rules of procedure', they concluded their report without hearing from the key witness in the investigation.

The UMSC properties implicated in the alleged fraudulent sale were many but the focus came to those in prime locations. These included Plot 30 at William Street in Kampala, Plot 102, William Street, Kampala and Plots 12–16 in Port Bell Road, Luzira (near Kampala). Plot 30 William Street, Kampala, which houses Masjid Noor, had been leased to HAKS Express Ltd, a company owned by a prominent businessman, the then Chairman of the USMC. A copy of the Land Title registration shows that HAKS Express Ltd sold its interest in Plot 30 William Street to one city tycoon (Francis Drake Lubega) for a sum of Uganda Shillings 600 million, on 20 July 2005, ignoring the statutory declaration issued by concerned delegates of the UMSC General Assembly had issued a statutory declaration affirming their interest in these properties and challenging the transfer to a third party (Francis Drake Lubega), since HAKS Express Ltd was holding those properties in lease capacity as per a memorandum of understanding entered into with the UMSC; also regardless of the Caveat that the Chief Registrar of Titles in Kampala had placed on any possible disposal of the said properties. One of the affirmants of the statutory declaration issued on 4 July 2005 was Sheikh Ibrahim Hassan Kirya (assassinated 30 June 2015). Among other properties, the sale of Plot 30 William Street, housing Masjid Noor became a hot issue that would decide the future of Mubajje's muftiship. As he failed to appear before the Commission, Sheikhs Haruna Jjemba, Ibrahim Hassan Kirya and Abdul Hakim Ssekimpi, delegates to the UMSC General Assembly, took the matter to the secular Courts of Uganda.

---

[22] Many of the recordings were made in Luganda language. The language they use to depict Mubajje's 'wrongs' is so despicable that the English translations cannot reproduce the nuances.

In *Sheikh Ibrahim Hassan Kirya & 3 others v Sheikh Shaban Ramadhan Mubajje & 6 others*,[23] the High Court of Uganda declared that the accused had a case to answer. In the second stage of the hearing, the court's role was to declare whether they sold properties of the UMSC and if so, whether the Constitution of the UMSC granted them that right. Procedurally, the Mufti denied personal involvement in the sale of Muslim properties. Substantively however it came to light that his administration had actually sold the properties. It was ruled, however, that the UMSC Constitution granted him the power to dispose of Muslim properties. The contemporary split within the Muslim public in Uganda after years of seeming unity, began when the court deliberations revealed the Mufti as a poor leader. Subsequent to the court decision, the Assembly of Sheikhs and Muslim Scholars of Uganda was convened at Hotel Africana in Kampala on 22 January 2009 at which the delegates planned to withdraw their allegiance from Mubajje since several were of the view that his behaviour violated Islamic ethics.[24] Not all agreed with the assembled sheikhs. Many Muslims considered the assembly as a meeting of overzealous individuals hungry for power:

> we all felt that the Mufti had committed a big mistake by deceiving us about our properties. But taking him to court disgraced the community. We wanted to find out the truth of what actually happened at the Council. But the truth has hurt our community further. We are now a public joke.[25]

How and why did the Assembly of Sheikhs at Africana come to the conclusion that the problems affecting the Muslim community began with Mubajje's sale of properties and lying about it? The choice of words insinuated that all the challenges of the Muslim leadership began with and ended with those office holders, such that once dispensed with, new office holders would wash away both historical and contemporary challenges. According to the anxiety of the time, a hostile environment had declared the Mufti guilty before the inquiry was complete. Sheikhs were issuing competing fatwas as to the supposed guilt of the Mufti, and the applicants to the High Court of Uganda felt pressured to seek redress in 'neutral territory' already biased by the report of the Commission.

[23] HCT-00-LD-CS-0815-2006 (High Court of Uganda).
[24] Assembly of Sheiks and Muslim Scholars of Uganda, Hotel Africana, Kampala, 22 January 2009.
[25] FGDs, Mbarara (1 August 2016), Iganga (3 November 2016), Mbale (1 December 2016).

Yet, Mubajje's leadership tenure was not the first to lose Muslim properties. As many Muslims asked, why did the inquiry into the disappearance of Muslim endowments and properties begin with Mubajje? Why not with previous leaderships? Property was lost before but no-one could say a thing because it was thought that the owner could 'eat from his garden' without being accountable to anyone else? Was it their property to 'eat'? All these properties were in the hands of Baganda leaders, what is their responsibility over them?[26] Respondents decried the hypocritical proclamations of the sheikhs assembled at Africana since the disappearance of Muslim properties and endowments did not begin in 2000. It began much earlier when the trustees of various endowments had turned them into personal businesses.[27] Nevertheless, the resolutions of the Sheikhs assembled at Africana on 22 January 2009 must be situated in a context that surrounds the leadership climate preceding the election of Mubajje in 2000. The explanation at the time was that Mubajje came across as a unifying figure. As a fulcrum of unity, his caucus 'mobilized on the basis that he was coming to wash away the rot of past leaderships' in the Muslim community and usher in an era of accountability, transparency and honesty, restoring Muslim pride in their leadership and elevating the level of Muslims in all aspect of public life. The reason he garnered the support of groups such as the Tabliq and many non-Baganda was that his leadership promised a revolution in Muslim leadership in the country. His electoral promises had to be judged against the pragmatism of normal administration, especially the economic factor of maintaining the leadership structures, which made his leadership susceptible to the whims of wealthy chairman Hajji Hassan Basajjabalaba and his NRM constituency.

The Assembly of Sheikhs did not merely make suggestions for another committee to implement; it was the judge, jury and enforcing agency. It had tasked itself with choosing a new administration by the end of January 2009 without asking any legitimate authority of the UMSC. In a single sitting, it had resolved to undertake a non-violent 'coup'. If the denouncing of Mubajje in December 2000 had been misconceived, the outcome of the trial had given Mubajje's opponents a legitimate basis riding on Muslim public opinion that the coup was not only necessary but also desirable. The wave of Muslim public opinion forced Francis Drake Lubega to publish an offer to sell back Masjid Noor.[28] The hostile Tabliq environment regarding

[26] FGD, Nakalama (Iganga), 5 November 2016.
[27] Ibid.
[28] 'Offer to Sell Plot 30 William Street', 23 April 2008.

the Masjid probably pushed Lubega's hand, but national electoral and saviour politics was also high on the agenda since, in the following months, the Muslim community received word that President Museveni had promised to pay off Francis Drake Lubega and forthwith instructed the Governor of the Bank of Uganda to issue a promissory note for full compensation of his interest in the property, which was to be returned to the Muslims. On 12 February 2016, President Museveni visited UMSC at Old Kampala and handed over the land title for Plot 30 William Street during his campaign trail for the 2016 presidential elections. By returning the title of a property comprising a Tabliq stronghold, Museveni's act symbolized that Mubajje was in charge of whoever used or misused Masjid Noor and as a consequence, the Tabliq had to look beyond Mubajje to Museveni who had 'saved' their space from a city tycoon.

One of the resolutions at Africana had instructed the sitting members to announce a committee to elect an alternative administration to 'run the affairs of the Muslims of Uganda' until such a time when the Muslims would be capable of electing the Muslim leadership. How was this issue to be decided? Who was eligible for election in the tentative administration? Which rules, and under what procedure and mandate? These are questions that members asked themselves but brushed aside for expediency. On 28 January 2009, the Assembly of Sheikhs elected a new parallel administration and appointed Sheikh Zubair Kayongo as tentative leader, with a new title 'Supreme Mufti' to lead Muslims for a period of two years. Ironically, when the two years ended, the 'Supreme Mufti' is reported to have said that he would relinquish power after death, and indeed he held the position until his death. As delegations of Muslims supported him,[29] Mubajje derided the election of 'Supreme Mufti' and the possible ouster of himself.[30]

The NRM as Muslim patron

What made Mubajje feel secure in his position as Mufti? What kind of power did he possess in comparison to those who desired to oust him? What kind of power did the Kibuli faction, in turn, possess that emboldened their intentions to oust Mubajje? In this section, I demonstrate how the alliance of Muslim Tabliqs within the opposing centres of Muslim leadership in

[29] 'Eastern Clerics denounce rival mufti', *Daily Monitor*, 2 February 2009; Union of Eastern Muslim Scholars, meeting held at Iganga on 1 February 2009: its message emphasized Muslim unity.
[30] 'I am Still Mufti', *New Vision*, 2 December 2010.

Uganda set the stage for a politics of violent inclusion and exclusion. As Museveni challenged the Muslim leaderships to declare their belonging within the looming electoral process, the Kibuli-Tabliq alliance hesitated to respond to Museveni whom it considered the benefactor of its political nemesis, Mubajje. In this way, Kibuli had become a centre of Muslim opposition to NRM governance.

A gradual series of events combined to make Kibuli the centre of Muslim political opposition to the NRM regime. First, the Kibuli Muslim leadership accommodated the new Salafiyya Tabliq leadership when it split from the Kamoga-led Salafiyya. The sheikhs whose photographs were reproduced on posters and targeted for elimination – Haruna Jjemba, Najib Ssonko, Ibrahim Hassan Kirya, Mahmood Kibaate, Umar Swidiq Ndawula and Mustafa Bahiga – were those that formed the leadership of the new Salafiyya sect, who challenged the leadership of Muhammad Yunus Kamoga. Sheikh Ssekimpi was the deputy Mufti at Kibuli; Kirya was the spokesperson at Kibuli, while Kiggundu and Bahiga were all allied to the Kibuli faction. This leadership amassed a sizeable following of Muslim Tabliq youth that could be depended on to support an invasion of the Supreme Council.

Second, the election of a Supreme Mufti to challenge the state-supported Mubajje pointed to Kibuli as an alternative centre of Muslim leadership in alliance with Prince Kassim Nakibinge, a Ganda royal. All this worked against the context in which the President positioned himself as the only fountain of honour in the country. Electing a Supreme Mufti was one thing, but situating him at Kibuli was synonymous with pronouncing an eminent revolution in Muslim leadership without the approving 'stamp' of relevant state authority; thus Kibuli had been considered merely as a space of transition; Old Kampala was the target. Many attempts to move to Old Kampala and oust the incumbent Mufti Mubajje were thwarted by the Uganda Police, which used tear gas and bullets to disperse the crowds of Muslim youth who chanted 'Allahu Akbar' and 'out with Mubajje'. The Uganda Police was supposedly attempting to keep law and order but it was emboldened by the Consent Order of the High Court of Uganda[31] which had required that the status quo be maintained with regard to Mubajje's muftiship and that Supreme Mufti Kayongo was free to move anywhere as long as his intention was not to 'install Imams or District Khadis in Mosques' controlled by the UMSC. For the time being, the opposition was content with leading Muslims from Kibuli.

[31] MISC. APPL. No. 304 of 2009.

200 ISLAM IN UGANDA

Who would be the khadis to lead in its name if the court barred Kayongo's activities as Supreme Mufti? Various sheikhs defected to Kibuli. If the Supreme Mufti could not go to install the Khadis, they would come instead and pledge allegiance to him. The defection began with the District Khadi of Kampala, Sheikh Kasule Ndilangwa, who came with eight members of his leadership to bolster the Kibuli camp – he was later to become Supreme Mufti after Kayongo's passing. Kasule's group publicly pledged allegiance to Kayongo and prompted others to join them. In response, the UMSC accepted their defection in spiteful terms, labeling them antagonistic to the UMSC leadership and confirming the appointment of new office bearers to the various offices. Field visits have confirmed that, indeed, sheikhs defected. But the Supreme Mufti and his leadership could not have had a peaceful 'revolution' just because he was riding on the public mood surrounding Mubajje's mistakes. The defections were high in Buganda but minimal, if not absent, in other parts of the country.[32] The messages of support to Mubajje confirmed this. Also, since the UMSC did not actually have many masjids spread around the country, many belonging to private organizations and individuals, the offices of the district khadis were situated in other establishments.[33] The only way that Kayongo could govern outside Kampala was to establish parallel offices – a state of affairs continued for a while but eventually became unsustainable.

The opposition to Mubajje was never so widespread that the establishment of parallel offices would divide the Muslims to follow particular camps. As many respondents observed,

> If Kibuli wants to convince us that they are the rightful leader of Muslims in Uganda, let them show us their followers. When House of Zakat from Kibuli came to Busoga to distribute *zakat*, they were shunned in many places and instead performed the function on the outskirts of Iganga in a house of a fellow from Kampala. We got tired of this confusion. Islam is one, these divisions are meaningless.[34]

Faced with a Muslim public tired of what it perceived to be jostling for 'honours and wealth' using the Muslim flag, many considered the Kibuli-Old Kampala divisions a waste of time and resources. Many Muslims, especially outside the central region, saw (and continue to see) the division as a public display of need for recognition and the individual benefits that accrue to those displays, as opposed to a serious theological split

---

[32] FGD, Nakalama (Iganga), 5 November 2016.
[33] Ibid.
[34] FGD, Iganga, 3 November 2016.

that could mark off one as an enemy to Islam.[35] Others intimated that Kibuli must be given recognition for its titular leadership of Muslims in the country: 'what Nuhu Mbogo, Badru Kakungulu and their descendant Kassim Nakibinge have done for Islam in Uganda is invaluable. But they have to recognize that Muslims need educated leaders to empower the community'.[36] Without a theological explanation for the schism, the disunity is perceived as trifling. If only it were, because then the spilling of blood would be avoided.

The targeting of Kibuli-based Tabliq leaders arose within a specific moment of NRM electoral politics. It was revealed by an alliance between Sheikhs Kamoga, Kakeeto and Mubajje, dubbed 'Muslim unity meet', which was symbolic on two levels. On the one hand, it worked to attract all Muslims to 'come home' to the Supreme Council; the hordes of Muslim masses would confirm Old Kampala as the space of majority Muslim masses. On the other hand, this tactic of violent inclusion worked to demonstrate Kibuli as a less important space for Muslim organization. Museveni got his reply: the 'unity meet' at Old Kampala in February 2015, one year before the national elections in February 2016, showed that the majority 'Muslims' 'belonged' to him.

Many factions of the Tabliq had united under Mubajje's leadership up until the 2006 court case. When Sheikh Sulaiman Kakeeto was Amir, he had also managed to ensure Tabliq loyalty to UMSC and to avoid violent activities. The election of Muhammad Yunus Kamoga ensured that all possible opposition to Mubajje was dealt a blow when, in January 2015, Kamoga went with Sulaiman Kakeeto to pledge alliance to Mufti Mubajje at Old Kampala. By this time, the death of Muslim clerics had begun and although this trio had called a truce for their misdeeds against each other, many in the Kibuli faction had neither forgiven nor forgotten Mubajje's mistakes. The Kakeeto-Kamoga-Mubajje alliance therefore symbolized the attempt to unite all Muslim factions in Uganda under the leadership of Mufti Mubajje. On Friday 30 January 2015, during one of the largest gatherings of Muslims ever recorded at the National Masjid at Old Kampala, Mubajje sought forgiveness for his mistakes and called upon all Muslims in the country to unite under his leadership for the good of the Muslim community. Mubajje said:

> I request you to forgive me for what did not go well during the period of disunity in our community and I have also forgiven you … I am not an

[35] Ibid.
[36] Interview with prominent sheikh, Jinja, 6 November 2016.

angel that I don't sin. I am a mere servant before you. Welcome back home and this is the time for all of us to move as a solid group.[37]

Other speakers at the unity prayers noted that Old Kampala was the official seat of Muslims in Uganda as opposed to familial headquarters like Bukoto, Nnateete and Kibuli, which could be sold or inherited. Others in attendance noted that whoever had not turned up for the unity meeting was the 'enemy' of Islam and Muslim unity in Uganda. Many Muslim leaders opposed to Mubajje did not turn up. Some sheikhs allied to Kibuli turned up in individual capacity while others held corresponding *khutba* in other masjids in Masaka and Kampala, deriding not only the intention of the unity campaigns but also the character of the key players. Hassan Kirya, the then Kibuli spokesperson noted that big congregations were not real unity if the reasons of the disunity remained in the first place:

> Unity among Muslims does not mean bringing up a big congregation and everything stops at that. Islam preaches unity among its followers, but if Muslims develop division among themselves, we must critically look at the reasons why they separated, analyze those reasons and come up with solutions before we talk about reuniting ... We were all united under Sheikh Shaban Mubajje on his election but when he exposed dishonesty ... two years after he was elected, we had no alternative but to break away from his leadership.[38]

The *khutba* that circulated following the unity campaigns started a lively debate within the Muslim publics as to whether Mubajje's opposition should forgive him and unite with UMSC or whether he should listen and accommodate their grievances. Within the debate, many sheikhs, and Muslims generally, called for Hassan Kirya and colleagues to look beyond Mubajje and move towards unity; while others argued that Mubajje needed to move his 'forgive me' rhetoric to actual displays of remorse that called for serious investigations into his misdeeds. There were also many who debated the key question: 'we agree to unite with Mubajje, but on what? On his dishonesty, lies, deceit and corruption? Unity is not a value-free consequence, it has deliberations that some of us may not accept, so, unity at what cost? Words are not enough.'[39] According to this group, Mubajje's unity campaign attempted to unite Muslims by asking them to forget all the ills of the Muslim leaders who were alleged to have committed any

---

[37] 'Kibuli faction shuns Mubajje unity meet', *Daily Monitor*, 3 February 2015.

[38] Jumuah *khutba* at Wandegeya Masjid, Kampala, 30 January 2015.

[39] Sheikh Umar Swidiq Ndawula, 28 December 2014.

wrong against the community. Mubajje was also working with Sheikhs Kakeeto and Kamoga, from whom Kirya and colleagues had split. They wondered why Muslim unity was being chanted at the time of the forthcoming national elections in February of the following year (2016) and they called for caution in rushing to Old Kampala. As they debated the meaning of the unity campaigns, they were branded 'radical', 'unforgiving' and 'difficult' individuals. All attempts by various elderly sheikhs to 'talk sense' into those opposed to Mubajje's unity campaigns fell on deaf ears; at one time the reconciliation with Mubajje reached a forceful level such that one sheikh asked:

> Why are you forcing us to reunite with you? You do not need to hound us into joining you. All you need is to perform good works and we shall join you if and when we want. Do you have some other intentions that we do not know about? If so, tell us why you are hurriedly interested in our union with you.[40]

In the course of 2015, at a public function in Mukono, Sheikh Obeid Kamulegeya, who was then allied to Kibuli, received big 'envelopes' to mobilize the Muslim vote for President Museveni's election in 2016. Months after the election, in October 2016, he went to the media to announce his split from the Kibuli faction and that he had ceased all activities to do with Prince Nakibinge. He was critical of the UMSC and the state; he went to his offices at the World Muslim League (Rabitta) at Old Kampala but did not join the UMSC.[41] Yet, for all his abuses against Mubajje and the Museveni regime, Kamulegeya seemed untouchable. Why were particular others marked for elimination? What did majoritarian politics have to do with this phenomenon? And how did the Kamoga-Kakeeto-Mubajje alliance symbolize the death of minority Muslim leadership and thereby confirmed Mubajje as the favoured representative of the Muslim masses? My response to these questions is that the issue was beyond Mubajje; he was merely a player in a game decided outside the Supreme Council. The real winner of the unity meet was Museveni's political incumbency.

Beginning in 2012, in preparation for the February 2016 presidential elections, the NRM devised a plan to woo the Muslim electoral ticket. The Tabliq division was a serious concern to the NRM electoral strategy and

---

[40] Sheikh Umar Swidiq Ndawula, Wandegeya Masjid, 28 December 2014.
[41] Interviews in Busoga revealed how Sheikh Kamulegeya referred to himself as '*taata wa fitnah, ngisumulula nengizaayo*' (I can open and close up tribulations), FGD, Iganga, 3 November 2016.

ISLAM IN UGANDA

it had to be settled; these divisions divided the Muslim vote.[42] Although Mubajje's support was assured, electoral tactics required a sort of alliance between competing Tabliq factions to forge unity, however tentative.[43] Promises of finances for development projects greased the reconciliation of Muhammad Kamoga and Sulaiman Kakeeto who made an alliance to unite with the NRM-backed Mufti Mubajje at Old Kampala. In late January 2015, the UMSC announced that Kakeeto, Kamoga and Mubajje with all their respective followers had decided to unite for the sake of 'peace' within the Muslim community in a large gathering at Old Kampala (National Masjid). This togetherness reverberated countrywide in unity campaigns. When the Kibuli camp refused to attend, arguing that the real cause of disunity persisted,[44] its aversion to Mubajje's public 'repentance' was demonstrated. Such Kibuli attitude irked the Muslim public who were concerned about Kibuli's 'unforgiving' and 'radical' stance on Mubajje's mistakes.[45] Kibuli was thus designated as the 'enemy' of Muslim unity in Uganda. Actually, the various speakers at Old Kampala reminded the congregation that whoever had not appeared at the unity meet was the number one enemy of Islam and Muslim unity in Uganda.[46] Within this context, the Kibuli faction was this enemy.

On the other hand, few within the Muslim public critiqued the gesture of the unity campaigns. Many did not ask the fundamental question: to what was Mubajje uniting them? The political skill within which the unity campaign was undertaken belonged neither to Mubajje nor Kamoga and his partners. It was purely designed by NRM electoral strategists and given to their Muslim associates to implement. Promises of money proved the biggest carrot.[47] The tactic was to turn as many Muslims away from the opposition (Kibuli). In typical NRM political tactics, Kibuli and its sheikhs had become just another political opposition group to Museveni's

---

[42] Interview with NRM electoral strategist, Buganda region, Kampala, December 2016.

[43] Ibid.

[44] 'Kibuli faction shuns Mubajje unity meet', *Daily Monitor*, 3 February 2015.

[45] Muslims were wont to state: *'Abe Kibuli bazibu, balemera kunsonga, omusajja bamusonyiwe kasita yetonze'* (The Kibuli group is radical in its demands on the issue of Mubajje's misdeeds. Let them overlook his wrongs since he's sought forgiveness).

[46] The Luganda nuance *'abo bemutalabye wano bebalabe b'obusiraamu mu Uganda'* carried violent overtones.

[47] Interview with NRM electoral strategist, Buganda region, Kampala, December 2016.

government. The bigger challenge for the NRM was that many within this Kibuli alliance refused to accept state lures.[48] Mubajje and his associates could not reveal that the NRM had promised 'mobilization' funds for the Muslim groups scouring for votes in the forthcoming elections and that whoever opposed Museveni's campaign was the enemy. If not all at Kibuli were singled out and marked for death, what were the selection criteria; why were particular sheikhs to be eliminated and under what excuse?

The alibi for the elimination of Muslim clerics in Uganda has two sources. One is internal to the Muslim Tabliq community, and the other external to it. The internal source has much to do with the extremist turn of Tabliq *dawah* and how it turned against the social base (Muslim public) that it intended to fully Islamize while enabling the ADF idea of political jihad. As Chapter 6 revealed, this backlash created an intra-Muslim civil war, when the state defeated the ADF and turned its army into state agents, making the Tabliq Muslim community the most spied-on group in Uganda.[49] This internal politics of Muslim intrigue intensified by state espionage enabled a regime of peonage whereby the state 'owned' the former ADF that have now been reinserted to inform on fellow Muslims. To remain relevant and endear themselves to the dominating power, these informants have sometimes given false information based on lies and defamation as a tactic to fight political battles internal to the Salaf.[50] This scenario contributed significantly to the murder of various clerics.

The selection criteria regarding the choice of who, when and how to eliminate was decided at the high level of the NRM inner core.[51] Liquidation was considered because it would settle historical scores while serving contemporary benefits. Historically, these individuals had posed a serious (read military) threat to the NRM regime; vengeful politics informed this moment. Sheikhs Ssentamu, Ssekimpi, Kirya, Bahiga and Kiggundu were at various moments considered members/associates of the ADF and UFM/A. The amnesty agreement these individuals signed with the state had been conditioned on avowing all rebellious activities as a condition of their reintegration. As amnesty flushed them out of the bush, they had not 'repented' properly, as seen in their refusal to contribute to the success of the NRM party that had 'forgiven' their 'sins' and 'saved' them from annihilation. As one prominent official put it, '*abo Museveni yabaguumaaza*

---

[48] Interviews with Kibuli sheikhs revealed delegations of 'Elder' Sheikhs and NRM personalities sent to 'talk sense' into the Kibuli faction'. August, 2016.

[49] FGD with former ADF rebels, Kampala, 19 July 2016.

[50] Ibid.

[51] Interview with FM, December 2016.

206   ISLAM IN UGANDA

kubanga tasonyiwa buyeekera' (Museveni hoodwinked them because he does not forgive rebellion).[52]

The method of eliminating these designated 'enemies' of the NRM regime was a matter of collaboration between the state and its agents, especially within a particular Tabliq leadership supported by former ADF-cum state spies. Although Kamoga's election as Amir had accorded him a protective status, it could not protect him from state advances. Amnesty wrought a double dilemma. On the one hand if he declined the state advances he would be designated as a 'new enemy'. On the other hand, the Muslims would consider him a sellout if they learned of his alliance with the state. The state's advances won and Kamoga joined with notable NRM-leaning figures such as Sulaiman Kakeeto and Mufti Mubajje. The Muslim public described this new 'alliance' as surrender: *'ekintu ky'aba Tabliq kyayikamu amazzi'* (the Tabliq group has become diluted by state intervention).[53] This alliance divided roles; the assassin could only work on information provided by the internal spy, action on which could not however function within a vacuum; he had to operate in a context wherein the target had been excommunicated from the Tabliq community. The split of the Tabliq into new Salafiyya enabled this.

The systematic collaboration took various phases. The first act was to expel the target members from the group, a purge that saw the excommunication of over thirteen prominent clerics from the Kamoga camp. The expulsion notice (issued on 28 November 2014) reasoned that those individuals had founded their own group and challenged the leadership of Kamoga as Amir. The second act was to circulate a series of lists designating the names and describing the 'wrongs' of particular sheikhs. The first list had three names: Sheikhs Bahiga, Ssonko Najib and Hassan Kirya. Its heading reads: *'Bano Mubeewale'* (strictly avoid these individuals). Distributed at Masjid Noor in 2014, this list warned the Muslim public to stop any dealings they had with the mentioned individuals. The second list comprised six names and, unlike the first, it described the *dhulm* (wrongs) of the designated individuals alongside their names. Published in 2015, it added Sheikhs Umar Swidiq Ndawula, Mahmood Kibaate and Haruna Jjemba to the first published names. Its heading read thus: *'Bano ababbi ki kyebaagaza obusilamu?'* (What do these thieves want with Islam?) The descriptions of their wrongdoings ranged from funds misappropriation, property mismanagement, allegations of *shirk* (polytheism) and murder.

---

[52]   Interview, Kampala, 28 August 2016.
[53]   Interview with Sheikh AM, August, 2016.

The third list was circulated in 2016, after the murder of Mustapha Bahiga, to add Prince Kassim Nakibinge, the titular head of the Kibuli Muslim faction. The publication of the lists invoked the intervention of prominent Muslim personalities. In a meeting called at the residence of Hajji Moses Kigongo (Vice Chairman of the NRM) attended by some security agencies, the opposed Tabliq factions were reminded to resist from escalating their feuds. The circulation of the list could not however produce the desired effect on its own. The targeted individuals had to actually be derided and disgraced. The implication of the 'smear campaign' against prominent clerics in the opposition was that the publishing camp positioned itself as the guardian of 'pure' Islam and Muslim progress under NRM patronage. The opposing faction was thus threatened and the list was to instill fear into its clerics so as to check its political ambitions. As one member explained, there 'is a group of Muslims who believe it their duty to guard Islam and Muslims, and that without them neither can prosper. Such Muslims are spreading persistent rumours for the elimination of clerics they consider obstacles to Muslims' prosperity in Uganda.'[54]

What was it about these particular individuals that made them targets? The six Sheikhs on the hit list were the core leaders who had in November 2014 dismissed Kamoga as Amir on grounds of 'dictatorship' and 'incompetence'.[55] The silenced reasons were allegations that Kamoga's camp had accepted state advances against the wishes of his electoral body. These six individuals also formed the core of the administrators of the *zakat* (poor due) and Hajj (pilgrimage) offices of the Tabliq. Crucially, they were the trustees of Masjid Noor and thus signatory to bank accounts on which the rent from the businesses at the Masjid was posted. They were thus seen as having both power and economic means. Prince Kassim Nakibinge was (is) also a signatory to the Tropical Bank accounts of Masjid Noor. When the six sheikhs declared Haruna Jjemba as the new Amir, Kamoga allegedly refused to vacate his position and used his mobilization skills to convince the largest Tabliq faction not to accept the split. As Haruna Jjemba left with his supporters, Kamoga could not allow them to leave with the instruments of office. Sheikh Ssonko Najib, the victim of an assassination attempt, argues that the assumption that Masjid Noor 'minted' money because its premises housed lock-up shops was false: 'many of us including Omulangira (Prince Kassim Nakibinge) are targeted because of the trusteeship at Masjid Noor ... that there are

---

[54] Sheikh Sharif Ssennoga, Wandegeya, 3 January 2016.
[55] 'Muslim Tabliqs dismiss leader' *Daily Monitor*, 28 November 2014.

strong businesses renting from these premises gives the impression that the administrator is minting millions. Then we are seen as the corrupt enemies of Islam and Muslims.'[56]

But how many know what actually goes on? – asks Sheikh Ndawula. The 'truth is the Masjid management committee decided to allocate the rental proceeds from the rent of the plot premises and decided to put fixed deposit payments regarding utilities and a monthly five million shillings to develop Muslim schools in the country.'[57] Kamoga denied targeting the six sheikhs personally and instead told his camp that the six were banking masjid proceeds on personal bank accounts in Tropical Bank.[58] Within this conflict for masjid space and its rental proceeds, the concern was not that the present managers and trustees were 'corrupt' but that they were in opposition and possessed access to a lucrative Muslim property within the city. Jjemba's camp was unwilling to relinquish Masjid Noor due to the history of alleged financial mismanagement identified with the opposing leadership. The alternative was to have new trustees. Only death would force the change but, before this, other tactics were considered.

On 28 November 2014 an expulsion notice was issued for some sheikhs following a series of humiliating and demeaning acts directed at sheikhs critical of Kamoga's leadership. Some of these acts included threats of bodily harm. In one incident, one sheikh rented strong muscled goons from the Kampala abattoir to 'discipline' Umar Ndawula. The decision to escalate proceedings followed a series of meetings in the Kamoga camp, born of the desperation for results since the prevailing tactics were inef-fective. One sheikh's house, dubbed the 'white house' became the space for deliberating on alternatives to deal with the opposition. One meeting, on 28 July 2014, allegedly resolved to eliminate Bahiga, Kirya, Kibaate, Jjemba, Ndawula, Ssonko and Nakibinge.[59] A series of death threats sent via phone texts and voice recordings began.

In several recordings that circulated among the Muslim publics, the authors were threatening death to the opposition as the enemies of Muslim progress in Uganda. In one message, Sheikh Ssonko Najib received a pic-ture of the *Qabr* (grave), warning him that his demise was imminent.[60]

---

[56] Sheikh Ssonko Najib, 3 January 2016.
[57] Sheikh Umar Swidiq Ndawula, Jumuah *khutba* at Masjid Noor, August 2014.
[58] Sheikh Muhammad Yunus Kamoga, Masjid Noor, William Street, Kampala, 30 December 2014.
[59] Interview with Sheikh SS, January 2016.
[60] Sheikh Ssonko Najib, 3 January 2016.

Several messages reminded Kirya that he would eat bullets for dinner.[61] These activities were allegedly orchestrated by teams within the Kamoga camp headed by 'experts' in abusing, physical confrontation and acid attacks. To avoid possible retaliation, the deputy Amir of the Kamoga camp, on Sunday 3 August 2014, ordered for Masjid Noor to have 'weapons of war' such as 'stones, pangas, ropes, and etcetera' to fend off 'enemies' who want 'us to lose Masjid Noor'. He warned the Muslims not to beat up individuals in the Masjid but to tie them up and throw them to the street.[62] A wave of paranoia swept into the Masjid over new faces unknown to the usual attendees. It was worse if one had a chubby physical makeup. On 22 August 2014, one Yahya Ssegujja (a national boxing athlete) was mistaken to belong to the 'enemy', was 'arrested' and received aggravated harm on the orders of the deputy Amir, and afterwards handed over to the police as the 'murderer' of Sheikh Abdul Karim Ssentamu.[63] Regardless of the fact that the police investigation discovered the culprits, none was held accountable for the aggravated bodily harm. The Ssegujja incident sparked off a heated debate within the opposing Tabliq camps; it manifested Kamoga's determination to extirpate opposition at all costs.

The Jjemba camp was resolved that no reconciliation was possible. It would seem that the exit to found another operating space depended on how many followers the Jjemba camp could command. Regardless of his mobilization skills, Kamoga could not confidently know how many followers he could command after the split. The tactic was to deny the Jjemba camp operating space. The new faction decided to call a *darasa* at Wandegeya Masjid to inform the Muslim public about the 'betrayals' in the Kamoga camp. Sheikh Mustapha Bahiga was the coordinator of the *darasa* slated for Sunday 28 December 2014; planned to make the formal split from the Kamoga-led Tabliq. Fearful that the breakaway faction would lead to a mass exodus of Tabliq members from the old to the new, Kamoga allegedly threateningly warned Sheikh Muhammad Kizza (custodian of the Wandegeya Masjid) in a phone-call to deny the new group space to organize the *darasa*.[64] Kizza informed Kamoga that preaching to Muslims was more important than the personality and leadership feuds

---

[61] When the targeted sheikhs reported the matter to the Uganda police authorities, their phones and other gadgets were confiscated as police 'evidence'. The individuals wrote statements to the police but no concrete investigations and arrests were done until 2015.

[62] Interview with Sheikh KM, August 2016.

[63] Sheikh Jibril Matovu, Wandegeya Masjid, 3 January 2016.

[64] Ibid.

obtaining within the Tabliq leadership. Kamoga retorted that a 'tsunami' loomed if the *darasa* proceeded as planned.[65] On 28 December 2014, the *darasa* actually took place, attended by a large section of Muslims (Tabliq and non-Tabliq) who sympathized with the breakaway sheikhs. The convener, Sheikh Mustapha Bahiga, said in the *darasa* that he witnessed unusual attendees of the *darasa* (about five men) standing within the precinct of the Wandegeya Masjid. These allegedly followed and murdered him at Bwebajja on Entebbe road the same evening.[66]

Further, the threatening recordings targeting the Jjemba faction were availed to the police and the office of the Inspector General of Police (IGP), Kale Kayihura. The state was aware of which sheikhs threatened the Jjemba camp with death at various places. The nature of NRM electoral politicking was that various individuals within the NRM had been chosen and tasked with reaching out to various political constituencies. The IGP Kale Kayihura was much spoken about within the Muslim side because the NRM electoral strategists had tasked him to deliver the Muslim electorate to vote for Museveni in February 2016.[67] The IGP choice for the Muslim constituency was not innocent; it was calculated to consider a measure of violence for a community of which some of its members desired no alliance with the state.[68] Politically, the IGP calculated that he could only work with the camp that had the larger numbers. The alliance of Kakeeto-Kamoga-Mubajje eased his choice since they commanded the majority. What to do with the opposition now allied with Nakibinge at Kibuli? These had to be debased as 'unworthy' of Muslim leadership and the campaign described above was to incite the Muslim public against this opposition. If they were opposed to Museveni's election, it was prudent to identify those with a 'history of rebellion' and liquidate them.[69] Blood would be the price of opposition to Museveni's presidency,[70] which also revealed the enduring cost of the ADF rebellion.

The easiest excuse for the IGP was that the ADF (already designated a terrorist group) was eliminating those with information about its operations. Beginning with the 2012 murder of Sheikh Ssentamu, the IGP had appeared at the mourning ceremony to declare the ADF as the assassins

---

[65]   Ibid.

[66]   Sheikh Jibril Matovu, Wandegeya Masjid, 3 January 2016.

[67]   Interview with FM, December 2016.

[68]   Ibid.

[69]   FGD with Joint Anti-Terrorist Taskforce (JATT) contractors, Kampala November 2016.

[70]   Deputy Supreme Mufti Sheikh Mahmood Kibaate, 3 January 2016.

even before any investigations could be done. This explains why state inquiries into the clerics' murders produced no reports. The ADF functioned as a language of distraction for state indifference towards dead clerics belonging to a 'small' faction of the Tabliq. Even when the state arrested Jamil Mukulu (the ADF leader) in May 2015, the murders continued. When Sheikh Ssonko Najib escaped an assassination attempt, he considered seeking political asylum in China where he had gone for a business trip only for the IGP to call him up and plead his return to Uganda with promises that his would-be assassin had been apprehended; in fact, Ssonko was yet to meet his would-be assassin.[71] The IGP responded to the continued murders and death threats by issuing police bodyguards to all the targeted sheikhs. To the targeted individuals, the bodyguards were meaningless since they could be called away if one was due for elimination, as happened with the murder of Hassan Kirya, or they could also be sacrificed altogether and be considered as 'killed in action',[72] as happened with the murder of Muhammad Kiggundu in November 2016. Issuing the police guards was thus not so much to protect threatened clerics but to act as tools of surveillance towards the clerics, to know their movements and daily activities[73] – in a manner akin to George Wilson's 'honourable surveillance' of Prince Nuhu Mbogo.

The Kamoga-IGP alliance reached a level where it could no longer be defended within the Muslim public due to the overwhelming recordings of statements implicating Kamoga's knowledge of the assassinations. In 2015, the state prosecutor arrested Kamoga and thirteen others, remanding them to Luzira prison. The initial charge sheet alleged that Kamoga and his co-accused were complicit in the murder of Muslim clerics. When the murders continued even after his incarceration, Kamoga's lawyers argued that their client had no capacity to orchestrate murders inside the walls of a prison cell. The state changed its charge sheet to read that Kamoga and others were imprisoned on the orders of the Jjemba camp and if this latter group could accept some offices for status and honour in Kamoga's camp then the detainees would be released.[74] It is for these changes in the charge sheet that some Sheikhs labeled *Uganda v Kawooya & 13 Others* as *katemba* (drama) to confuse the public.[75] The change in state charges had the same implication as before: it drew and directed the anger of the

---

[71] Sheikh Najib Ssonko, media briefing at Wandegeya Masjid, 3 January 2016.
[72] Sheikh Umar Swidiq Ndawula, Wandegeya Masjid 3 January 2016.
[73] Ibid.
[74] Ibid.
[75] Ibid.

majority Tabliq Muslim public towards the minority Jjemba camp for having no concrete evidence to imprison leaders in the former camp for the cleric's murders except desiring *ebitiibwa* (status and honours).

The IGP purveyed such 'conflicting information': on one hand

> he told us that he imprisoned Kamoga for ridiculing others. Other times, he came and said the case was about the title of Amir. We cannot be party to this confusion. The reason Kamoga and co-accused were imprisoned is because we suspect them as collaborators in the clerics' murders. In many meetings, witnesses provided information on how Kamoga and his cohorts discussed the murder of clerics in 'white house'. IGP has all the information. If he thinks that the issue is now about ridicule and dignity, let him release all the accused.[76]

But the matter of Kamoga's incarceration revealed the tactics of the state, which portrays its fusion of law and naked violence as policing tactics of statecraft that deploy cyclical violence to continue domination.

Concluding observations

First, the integration of Muslims within the NRM political structure was not an innocent tactic of statecraft. The history of Muslim conflict over masjids and other sites of Muslim power had enabled a perception under the NRM that Islam and Muslims were a threat to its political interests. To ensure that the state maintained its powerful relations vis-à-vis the Muslim leadership, the state displayed its dominance by propping up Supreme Council leadership alongside existing and emerging centres of Muslim power. The resistance of these groups to the state's choice of Muslim leaders, as reflected by Mubajje and his 'misdeeds', bred an intra-Muslim debate that further fragmented the Muslim community. As new counter-elites emerged to challenge the elite representation, violence became a referential means of the state's desire to direct Muslim leadership to its electoral politics.

Second, the NRM electoral strategy reflects the core of Museveni's concern with political jihad, realized by the ADF, and the deceptive character of his politics. As the NRM used Muslims in 1993 to stage-manage a Muslim unity conference so as to improve their image in the Arab world and acquire economic benefits, it also used Muslims to finally settle the scores regarding the enduring cost of the ADF rebellion. In the defeat of

[76] Ibid.

the ADF, the NRM had captured, retrained and turned the foot soldier into a state spy. Having given the leaders amnesty, he also chose a few and turned them against their colleagues. Having turned a Muslim rebellion into an intra-Muslim civil war, the murder of Muslim clerics reflected the NRM state's desire to totally eliminate the symptoms of military opposition in Buganda.

Third, the efforts of the NRM government to influence Muslims' national political consciousness reflect its desire to enforce its understanding or vision of the role of Islam within a non-Muslim state. I call this a desire to enforce political morality: to integrate Muslims within the national political platform regardless of their diverse articulations of Islam has been core to the NRM struggle to ensure security, stability and continuity for itself within Uganda. As the above tactics of statecraft have clarified, the history of the NRM government anchored in its idea of the broad base tried to enforce a uniform understanding of national duty and obligation, which would end tribalism and parochial politics. Even when multi-party politics were introduced, the undercurrent was that emerging political constituencies would still support the 'Movement' system as a matter of appreciation for the 'fundamental change' the NRM claimed to usher in. Although residence in a particular location was presented as the best way to overcome tribal, ethnic and religious identity, this did not happen as thought. In reality, multiple forms of identity especially religion, continued to influence people's political consciousness. Although the NRM government could appeal to the heads of religious denominations such as the Catholic and Protestant clergy to advise their flock to support NRM electoral politics, this could not be said when it came to some Muslim groups – simply because Islam has no known 'ministry' whose order may be followed by *everyone* without contest. The expectation of the NRM regime has been that many Christians would follow the political advice of their leaders in 'public' issues like elections. Islamic jurisprudence accepts unity and diversity but also internal differentiation. Religious rulings given by a mufti could be challenged by other sheikhs convinced that theirs is the best interpretation of the primary sources. In this way, the national political consciousness of a Muslim individual could be conditioned by many factors that inform their understanding of a Muslim's political role within a non-Muslim state, regardless of how much a mufti may convince them otherwise. I explore more on political morality in the concluding chapter.

CHAPTER 8

Conclusion

I began this book with the claim that the broader historical Muslim question, which concerns the role of Islam as ideology and Muslims' quest for autonomy in their relationship with shifting configurations of power over time, explain the violence witnessed within the Muslim community in contemporary Uganda. To unpack that claim, I have argued and showed that successive regimes of political power in Uganda's long history have witnessed violence either committed against Muslims or arising from within the Muslim community. These episodes of violence were the symptoms of larger issues that concerned Muslims' internal relations with each other and their whole relationship, in turn, with the larger political regimes under which they subsisted. The preceding chapters have shown that patterns of political governance of Islam and Muslims constructed in one historical epoch were either discontinued or refined and continued in another era using different agents under new strategies and tactics of governmentality. The prevailing issues concerning Muslims' relationship with political power and how that power envisioned its relationship with Islam, constituted the Muslim question under a particular regime. Every regime of power therefore framed its Muslim question.

I have also argued that Uganda has witnessed two moments in its history whereby Muslims acquired and lost political power. The first was under Kabaka Muteesa I (1854–84) when he chose Islam as a vehicle to achieve two major goals. On the one hand, proclaiming Islam as state religion would allow him to centralize power and reorganize Buganda, thus overcoming other powerful checks that balanced his power as Kabaka. This was the internal goal that Islam played for Muteesa I. On the other hand, it also fulfilled an external goal for the Kabaka. Islam would position Buganda as a Muslim state and thus thwart the attempts of the Khedive of Misr (Egypt) to colonize Buganda. Also, using Islam, Muteesa I sought to befriend the business minds of the Zanzibar coastal Arab traders who would bring wares of foreign trade, especially guns and ammunition that strengthened Buganda's military to defeat domestic and foreign enemies.

The cost of Muteesa I's attempt to Islamize Buganda was quite high for both Muslims and non-Muslims. Native Ganda who refused to Islamize met a wave of violence orchestrated by the Ganda state, thus tarnishing the image of Islam among Baganda. On the other hand, the desire of Muslim pages to establish individual autonomy after receiving instruction in different interpretations of Islam from Egyptian Muslim visitors challenged Muteesa I's control over the discursive coherence of Islam in Buganda. The execution of Muslim pages in 1876 revealed the dangers that accrue from unmoderated exertion in religious consciousness.

As with Muteesa I, Islam also played a similar role during the regime of Idi Amin (1971–79), the second time in Uganda's history where Muslims held and lost political power. Idi Amin became president on the backdrop of a military coup. Owing to various internal and foreign circumstances, he ended up embracing the local and global Muslim communities. Amin was determined to right the wrongs of historical Muslim marginalization in Uganda and since he saw the nation as 'black', native Muslims were *supposed* to benefit from his nationalization of corporations following the Asian expulsion. The international backlash following the Asians' exit, however, affected Uganda's foreign image. Required to identify with his Muslim identity to garner local support and legitimize his regime, Amin looked to the global Muslim community to assist with development aid. Like Muteesa I in nineteenth-century Buganda, Idi Amin used his Islamic identity to advance the interests of state power and authority. Yet, his patronage over the leadership of the Supreme Council, which he founded, revealed that even he as a Muslim was concerned about Muslims' autonomy, and the affairs of the UMSC were closely run from a desk inside State House. Both Muteesa I and Idi Amin presented themselves as patrons of Islam and Muslims. There are some theoretical implications that accrue from such a posture whereby political power seeks to direct the trajectory of religious belief and practice as a matter of public life. The attempt by political authority to intrude into spaces that relate to an individual's soul is one of the most consistent tropes that can be teased from all the periods studied in this book. The acts of intrusion also imply particular intentions of statecraft. Let me highlight this in other periods and I hope to return to it in the sections below.

Towards the end of the nineteenth century, religion (especially Islam and Christianity) became a form of identity that determined access to social-economic-political goods in Buganda. With the entry of British colonial officers like Lugard and others, Christianity gained the upper hand and successive leaders like Apollo Kaggwa influenced political outcomes regardless of Lugard's secular pretensions. Using its concerns over Islam and Muslims, no doubt gained from other colonial experiences, British colonial statecraft constructed levels of Muslim governance that begun in various phases. To securitize the state, Muslims were allocated inferior territories between Christian groups as a way to buffer and containerize them. To subdue them, elite representatives like Prince Nuhu Mbogo were chosen to link the Muslim masses to colonial political power. With representation, Muslim politics was driven from the public to the private arena. Once the colonial state stabilized, matters of Muslim concern were dealt with at the level of native customary courts, which played tactics that humbled and humiliated Islam and Muslims. These acts of colonial governance of Islam and Muslims were intended to establish a secure environment for the Protectorate Government by curtailing the potential of Muslim autonomy to preach free ideas for social emancipation.

During the era of independence, Muslims' political oblivion meant that they could not provide a meaningful programme to participate in debates for national independence. The few Muslims who participated like Abu Mayanja did so as individuals. Faced with the recalcitrance about Buganda's exceptionalism, Milton Obote realized the opportunity to also use Baganda Muslims as a way to establish a base for governing over Uganda and Buganda. By founding NAAM as a Muslim organization, Obote twitched the Muslim question and tied it alongside the nationality question. By founding NAAM as a way to mobilize Muslims to support his government, he failed to transcend the influence of ethnic identity because this time he was using non-royal Ganda to support his political designs. Unlike the Mengo establishment, the Ganda Muslims who led NAAM could be easily dispensed with. Again, Islam and Muslims were vehicles for rearticulating Obote's idea of a unified Ugandan nationality. Desperate to escape political oblivion, some Muslims joined NAAM and worked with Obote's government in a symbiotic relationship that displayed an asymmetry of power. By founding NAAM and accommodating some Muslims in the national political platform, Obote positioned the state as the patron of Muslims in Uganda. Muslims who claimed they belonged to Kakungulu's camp were considered the enemy of NAAM, which sparked off waves of violence in various spaces. The same tactic was used by the NRM government as it maintained the UMSC as an institution linked to the state as its patron. Here, Yoweri Museveni failed to dismantle some of the legacy of the Idi Amin era however much he derided him in public speeches. The above instances whereby political power seeks to intrude into religious spaces as a way to direct the actions and behaviours of individuals reveal that power rarely intrudes for the its own sake. Rather, power conceives of specific intentions when it chooses to intervene in society. The process by which such intentions are conceived by powerful actors has theoretical implications on political morality, either from below or above.

Thinking about political morality

Political morality arises as a central issue in all the periods that have formed the core of this study. By political morality I mean the range of actions and behaviours surrounding particular political practices that seek to engage in the national public domain. It includes the sort of actions that are perceived as acceptable by each political constituency according to the existing social-economic-political circumstances. I relate it to the very constitution of power and how its configuration changes within time, on the one hand, and how it also festers within society to effect governance and its desired (or undesired) outcomes. Some practices of power have been embedded within the very nature of its constitution. For instance, the decisions by Muteesa I to execute non-Muslims who declined his Islamization were inherent components of the nature of Ganda power, which considered that the Kabaka's words were unassailable. In this way, these decisions displayed an amoral politics inherent in Ganda statecraft of that time. Also the brave responses from Mudduawulira (Muteesa I's page) on why he refused to pray behind Muteesa and eat meat slaughtered in the palace because the Kabaka had refused circumcision, displayed a moral breakdown in social order and discipline on the one hand, and limited exertion in Islamic knowledge on the other. Political morality seems to operate on a sliding scale whereby the full weight of the actions of powerful actors seems to cause a measured response from its subjects. Political morality also demands political actors working in asymmetrical power relations to be realistic and recognize the changing configurations of power within a political community and therefore marshal discipline to analyse their situation and attenuate the danger that can flow from their possible actions or inactions.

Political morality demands weaker political actors to be smart and recognize the context in which they seek to act. Consider for instance the nature of colonial governance of Islam and Muslims in Uganda. As officers in the early phase of the colonial government were convinced of the Muslim 'threat', and some like Harry Johnston declared how they were fine to accommodate Muslims but not their 'nonsense', this showed that the colonial project presented an amoral political project towards its Muslim subjects and that is why influential Protestant leaders like Apollo Kaggwa could tell Lugard what to do with Muslims. Such an amoral politics could not advance Islam and Muslims. It fell to the genius of Prince Nuhu Mbogo the Muslim representative to recognize that the future of

Islam and Muslims in Uganda depended on humbling themselves to power, to accept a humiliating status in the short run while hoping to overcome subjugation in the long run. Mbogo was humbled when he accepted to leave Butambala and live close to the colonial officers at Nakasero where his movement was 'honourably' surveilled; he refused to join the soldiers in the Sudanese Mutiny even when they appealed to his religious sensibilities as a fellow Muslim; he even vacated his house in Nakasero and went to Kibuli to allow colonial officials take up his former residence. By maintaining discipline and loyalty to the holders of power, Mbogo was able to win for himself and the Muslim community an opportunity to advance Islam. When the amoral politics of the colonial state drove Islam from the public sphere into the private domain, it enabled Muslim political consciousness to emerge in the sacred sites such as masjids, Maulid festivals, burial ceremonies, marriages et cetera, which enabled Muslims to increase their fields of operation; as a result Islam prospered in the long run. Although some would argue that the context of the colonial system when Muslims were a numerical minority has since changed and that over time Muslims' demography increased, the principle still stands that political actors must recognize their situation and the effects that could accrue from their actions or inactions.

Theoretical and practical implications

This book has been based on three areas of scholarly inquiry: first, the governance of Islam and Muslims; second, the construction of the nation-state project; and third, the diverse and contradictory articulations of Islam. Each would seem to be different, but they have a common trope linking them all. All debates concern the political management of a human person considered amenable to various forms of subjectivity. As has been seen throughout the book, debates on how particular forms of power sought to govern Islam and Muslims aim at the fact that the primary sources in the discursive tradition of Islam (Quran and Sunnah) claim a metaphysical origin, which is in itself a claim to higher sovereignty (*hakimiyyah*) – simply the belief that sovereignty belongs to Allah. With this in mind, the intellectual revolutions that ushered in the political revolution in Westphalia in 1648 (Chapter 1) sought to displace theocracy and replace it with 'popular sovereignty'. But the merchants of ideas – as Philpott calls them – who convinced others to accept new social traits and allow religion to be separated from politics, thereby ensconcing state sovereignty over society and territory, had political and economic agendas to secure and maintain. This separation gave birth to the idea of the secular, understood as the best way to divest religious feeling from the public domain and relegate it to the private realms of individual consciousness. Religious identity continued to influence statecraft, however.

By delineating the boundaries of politics and religious life, the holders of state power created an alibi by which they could intrude into the private domain and thus intervene in social spaces as a way to assert themselves and claim to enforce the common good as they define it. This delineation is what has turned political principles into tools and tactics of statecraft. In the very ideologies that seek to construct a nationalistic outlook are embedded a claim to majoritarian niceties that operate to create a shadow of undesirable minorities considered anathema to the very functioning of public life. Whereas Muteesa I conceived the non-Muslim as his political minority, the colonial project constructed the Muslim community as its political minority. The difference is that the latter outlived the colonial state to the contemporary moment.

The practical implications of political constructs are that they fail to imagine the broad range of actions that are available to the subjects in exercising religious freedom. One of the outcomes of the Islamic reform movement (especially after 1980) in Uganda was the attempt by the state to enforce a vision of Islamic practice using its institution, the UMSC (yes, the Supreme Council is a state institution) that attempted to circumscribe Islam into disparate parts. Many reformers were wont to receive information that advised them to consider the *deen* (religion) as separate from *dawla* (state). These appeals sought to advance the rituals of social cohesion such as daily prayer and at the same time impede the revolutionary potential of violent jihad. In searching for discursive coherence in Islamic practice, the NRM government ended up establishing divide-and-control tactics in the Muslim community. Like its broad-based experiment of the late 1980s whereby Resistance Councils were conceived to manage society, the state's desire to entrench, control and direct the affairs of diverse Muslim publics, especially in urban areas, created a way in which to recolonize the diverse Muslim community to secure and consolidate its gains in central Uganda.

Bibliography

Primary sources

Agreements and treaties

Agreement between Captain F.D. Lugard and Nuhu Mbogo, Mwera, 1892.

Agreement between Chiefs of the Roman Catholics and Protestant Parties, Bulingugwe, 3 February 1890.

Agreement between the Chiefs of the Protestant and Roman Catholic Parties, 22 April 1893.

Agreement between the Uganda Government and the UNFM/A, of Nairobi Peace Talks May 2000.

Provisional Agreement between King Mwanga and Sir G. Portal, 29 May 1893.

Public Health Ordinance, Mohammedan Cemetery, Kampala, Legal Notice No. 242, 10 October 1953.

The Buganda Agreement, 1900.

Treaty between Henry Edward Colville, Her Britannic Majesty's Acting Commissioner for Uganda, and Mwanga, King of Uganda, 27 August 1894.

Treaty between the Imperial British East Africa Company and Mwanga, 30 March 1892.

Treaty between the King of Buganda and the Imperial British East Africa Company, 26 December 1890.

Archive correspondence

Letters from A.M. Mackay, 17 November 1878, *CMS Intelligencer,* Vol. I. (1877).

Letters from C.T. Wilson, *CMS. Intelligencer,* Vol. I (1877).

Letter from Zaid Bin Juma bin Saalem to Hashir bin Mselem (nd), received in Zanzibar on 13 February 1890, Zanzibar Archives.

Letter from Mwanga to the Queen, 17 June 1892.

Portal to Rosebery, included in Portal's Report on Uganda, 14 April 1894, Colonial Blue Book, Vol. I, Africana Section, Makerere University.

Provincial Commissioner (Buganda) to Prince Badru Kakungulu, 22 January 1930, Uganda Archive, Wandegeya, Kampala.

Provincial Commissioner Eastern Province to Chief Secretary, 25 July 1931, Uganda Archives, Wandegeya, Kampala.

Provincial Commissioner Western Province to Chief Secretary, 29 July 1931, Uganda Archives, Wandegeya, Kampala.

Provincial Commissioner Kampala to Chief Secretary, 14 March 1932, Uganda Archives, Wandegeya, Kampala.

Secretary, Ahmadiya Association, Kampala to Chief Secretary, 22 February 1932, Uganda Archives, Wandegeya, Kampala.

Secretary to Government of India, Coded telegram dispatched 22 March 1932.

Legal case

Sheikh Ibrahim Hassan Kirya & 3 others v Sheikh Shaban Ramadhan Mubajje & 6 others, HCT-00-LD-CS-0815-2006

Sermons and media briefings

Sheikh Jamil Mukulu Embeera y'obusalafi', 'The state of Salafism', Kampala, 1994.

Sheikh Jibril Matovu, Wandegeya Masjid, 3 January 2016.

Sheikh Mahad Mbaziira, Masjid Noor, William Street, Kampala, 30 December 2014.

Sheikh Mahmood Kibaate, 3rd January 2016.

Sheikh Muhammad Yunus Kamoga, Masjid Noor, William Street, Kampala, 30 December 2014.

Sheikh Murtadha Bukenya, Masjid Noor, William Street, Kampala, 30 December 2014.

Sheikh Najib Ssonko, media briefing, Wandegeya Masjid, 3 January 2016.

Sheikh Sharif Ssennoga, Wandegeya Masjid, 3 January 2016.

Sheikh Ssonko Najib, Wandegeya Masjid, 3 January 2016.

Sheikh Umar Swidiq Ndawula, Jumuah Khutba Masjid Noor, 15 August 2015.

Sheikh Umar Swidiq Ndawula, Wandegeya Masjid, 28 December 2014.

Sheikh Umar Swidiq Ndawula, Wandegeya Masjid, 3 January 2016.

Sheikh Wanji Abdallah 'Who is Killing the Muslims?', Wandegeya Masjid, 3 January 2016.

Sheikh Yasin Kakomo, Wandegeya Masjid 3 January 2016.

Interviews

Interview with AK, Makerere University, 24 July 2017.

Interview with Chief Khadi, Masaka, 13 August 2017.

Interview with Hajji HS, Mbale, 1 December 2016.

Focus group discussions

Elder sheikhs, Iganga, 3 November 2016.
Five former ADF rebels, Makindye (Kampala), 11 July 2016.
Former ADF rebel, Kampala, 13 July 2016.
Former ADF rebels, Makindye Masjid, 19 July 2016.
Former ADF rebels, Wandegeya Masjid, 14 July 2016.
Former Mukulu-Tabliq members, Kampala, 19 July 2016.
Umar Swidiq Ndawula, *khutba* at Masjid Noor, William Street, Kampala,15
    August 2015.
Kidichi, Zanzibar, 19 January 2016.
Kisenyi, 6 July 2016,
Kisenyi, 10 July 2016.
Mbale, 1 December 2016.
Mbarara, 1 August 2016.
Mbarara, 3 August 2016.
Nakalama (Busoga), 5 November 2016.
Nakasero, 2 July 2016.
Nungwe, Zanzibar, 18 December 2016.
Wandegeya, 4 July 2016.
Wandegeya, 8 July 2016.

Secondary sources

Books

Al-Ghazali, Zainab (2006), *Return of the Pharaoh: Memoir in Nasir's Prison,*
    Leicester: The Islamic Foundation.
Althusser, Louis (1971), *Lenin and Philosophy and Other Essays,* London:
    Monthly Review Press.
Allman, Jean, Geiger, Susan and Musisi, Nakanyike (2002), *Women in African
    Colonial Histories*, Bloomington: Indiana University Press.
Anderson, Benedict (1983), *Imagined Communities: Reflections on the Origins
    and Spread of Nationalism*, London: Verso.
Asad, Talal (2003), *Formations of the Secular: Christianity, Islam, Modernity,*
    Stanford: Stanford University Press.
Ashe, Robert P. (1889), *Two Kings of Uganda: Life by the Shores of Victoria
    Nyanza,* London: Sampson Low (reprint 1971 Frank Cass).
Asif, Manan Ahmed (2016), *A Book of Conquest: The Chachnama and the
    Muslim Origins in South Asia*, London: Harvard University Press.

Barth, F. (1969), *Ethnic Groups and Boundaries,* London: Oxford University Press.

Belloc, Hilaire (1938), *The Great Heresies,* London: Create Space Independent Publishing.

Benjamin, Ray C. (1991), *Myth, Ritual, and Kingship in Buganda*, Oxford: Oxford University Press.

Bhargava, Rajeev (1998), 'What is Secularism For?' in Bhargava, Rajeev (Ed) (1998), *Secularism and Its Critics*, New Delhi: Oxford University Press.

Bishara, Fahad Ahmad (2017), *A Sea of Debt: Law and Economic Life in the Western Indian Ocean,* 1780–1950, Cambridge: Cambridge University Press.

Bose, Sugata (2006), *A Hundred Horizons: The Indian Ocean in the Age of Global Empire.* Massachusetts: Harvard University Press.

Cabral, Amilcar (1970), *Return to the Source: Selected Speeches of Amilcar Cabral*. New York: Monthly Review Press.

Chabal, Patrick (1994), *Power in Africa: An Essay in Political Interpretation.* New York: St. Martin's Press.

Chadwick, Owen (1975), *The Secularization of the European Mind in the Nineteenth Century,* Cambridge: Cambridge University Press.

Charles, Ed. (2002), *Modernist Islam 1840–1940: A Sourcebook,* Oxford: Oxford University Press.

Chatterjee, Partha (1986), *Nationalist Thought and the Colonial World.* London: Zed Books.

Clancy-Smith, Julia (2011), 'Ruptures? Governance in Husaynid-Colonial Tunisia, c. 1870–1914', in Maussen, Marcel, Bader, V. & Moors, A. (Eds) (2011), *Colonial and Post-Colonial Governance of Islam: Continuities and Ruptures*, Amsterdam: Amsterdam University Press.

Cohen, A. (1960), *British Policy in Changing Africa,* London: Routledge & Kegan Paul.

Comaroff, Jean & John (1992), *Ethnography and the Historical Imagination.* Boulder: Westview Press.

Davis, Horace B. (1978), *Towards a Marxist Theory of Nationalism*, New York: Monthly Review Press.

Ddamulira, Abdunoor & Ssebayigga, Burhan (nd), *Textbook of Islam: Biography of the Prophet, Orthodox Caliphate, and History of Islam in Uganda,* Kampala.

Derrick, Jonathan (2008), *Africa's 'Agitators': Militant Anti-Colonialism in Africa and the West, 1918–1939,* London: Hurst & Company.

Devji, Faisal (2011), 'The Idea of a Muslim Community: British India, 1857–1906', in Maussen, Marcel, Bader, V. & Moors, A. (Eds), *Colonial and Post-Colonial Governance of Islam: Continuities and Ruptures*, Amsterdam: Amsterdam University Press, pp. 118–21.

El-Affendi, Abdelwahab (1991), *Turabi's Revolution: Islam and Power in Sudan,* London: Grey Seal.

Escobar, Pepe (2006), *Globalistan: How the Globalized World is Dissolving into Liquid War*, Ann Arbor: Nimble Books.

——(2009), *Obama Does Globalinistan*, Ann Arbor: Nimble Books.

——(2014), *Empire of Chaos*, The Roving Eye Collection Vol. I., Ann Arbor: Nimble Books.

Falola, Toyin (2005), 'Mission and Colonial Documents', in Phillips, John E. (Ed.), *Writing African History*, Rochester: University of Rochester Press.

Feldman, Allen (1991), *Formations of Violence: The Narrative of the Body and Political Terror in Northern Ireland*, Chicago: University of Chicago Press.

Foucault, Michel (1972), *The Archaeology of Knowledge,* translated by A.M. Sheridan Smith, London: Tavistock Publications.

——(1978), *Security, Territory, Population*, Lectures at the Collège de France, 1977–78, Ed. Michel Senellart, trans. Graham Burchell, Palgrave Macmillan: Houndmills and New York.

——(1977), *Language, Counter-Memory, Practice: selected essays and interviews,* translated from French by Donald F. Bouchard and Sherry Simon, Ithaca: Cornell University Press.

——(1990), *The History of Sexuality: An Introduction Vol.1*, translated by Robert Hurley, New York: Vintage Books.

Geertz, Clifford (1968), *Islam Observed: Religious Development in Morocco and Indonesia,* Chicago: Chicago University Press.

Gellner, Ernest (1981), *Muslim Society,* Cambridge: Cambridge University Press.

Gingo G.W. (nd), *Pulaani Y'Obote Gyeyakola Okusanyalaza Uganda*, Nakivubo, Kampala.

Gray, John Milner (1950), *Chronicles of Uganda*, London:Frank Cass.

Green, Nile (2011), *Bombay Islam: The Religious Economy of the West Indian Ocean, 1840–1915*, New York: Cambridge University Press.

Gregory, Robert C. (1993), *South Asians in East Africa: An Economic and Social History, 1890–1980*, Boulder: Westview Press.

Hamilton, Carolyn, Harris, V.S., Taylor, J., Pickover, M., Reid, G. & Saleh, R. (Eds) (2002), *Refiguring the Archive,* Dordrecht: Kluwer.

Hanson, Holly (2002), 'Queen Mothers and Good Government in Buganda: The Loss of Women's Power in Nineteenth-Century East Africa', in Allman, Jean, Geiger, Susan and Musisi, Nakanyike (Eds) (2002), *Women in African Colonial Histories*, Bloomington: Indiana University Press.

——(2003), *Landed Obligation: The Practice of Power in Buganda*, Portsmouth: Heinemann.

226 BIBLIOGRAPHY

Harrison, Christopher (1988), *France and Islam in West Africa, 1860–1960,* Cambridge: Cambridge University Press.

Hobsbawm, Eric (2008), *On Empire: America, War, and Global Supremacy,* New York: Pantheon Books.

Horowitz, D.R. (1985), *Ethnic Groups in Conflict,* Berkeley: University of California Press.

Hussin, Iza R. (2014), *The Politics of Islamic Law: Local Elites, Colonial Authority and the Making of the Muslim State,* Chicago: University of Chicago Press.

Ibingira G.S.K. (1973), *The Forging of an African Nation: The Political and Constitutional Evolution of Uganda from Colonial Rule to Independence, 1894–1962,* New York: Viking Press.

Iliffe, John (2007), *Africans: The History of A Continent,* New York: Cambridge University Press.

Ingham, Kenneth (1962), *A History of East Africa,* London: Longmans.

——(1994), *Obote: A Political Biography,* London: Routledge.

Jacques, Le Goff (2015), *Must We Divide History Into Periods?* Translated by M.B. DeBevoise, New York: Columbia University Press.

Kabaka Muteesa II (1967), *Desecration of my Kingdom,* London: Constable.

Kabuga, C.E.S. (1972), *History of the Kingdom of Buganda: Birth of the Late King Kintu and the First Kintu,* trans. from Luganda into English by James Wamala.

Kabwegyere, Tarsis B. (1995), *The Politics of State Formation and Destruction in Uganda,* Kampala: Fountain.

Kaggwa, Sir Apollo (1971), *The Kings of Buganda,* trans. Ssemakula Kiwanuka, Nairobi: East African Publishing House.

Kakungulu, Badru & Kasozi, A.B.K. (1977), *Abasimba Obuyisiraamu Mu Uganda,* Kampala: Equator Books.

Kaliisa, Anas Abdunoor (1994), 'Leadership Crisis Among Muslims of Uganda (1850–1993)', Masters Dissertation, Kampala: Makerere University.

Kanyeihamba, George W. (1997), *Reflections on the Muslim Leadership Question in Uganda,* Kampala: Fountain.

Karugire, S.R. (1980), *A Political History of Uganda,* Nairobi: Heinemann.

Kasozi, A.B.K. (1996), *The Life of Prince Badru Kakungulu Wasajja and the Development of a Forward-Looking Muslim Community in Uganda, 1907–1991,* Kampala: Progressive Books.

——(2013), *Bitter Bread of Exile: The Financial Troubles of Sir Edward Muteesa II during his last exile,* Kampala: Progressive Publishing House.

Kasule, Umar Mukasa (1992), *The Impact of Islam on the Death, Funeral and Marriage Customs of the Baganda,* Kampala: Makerere University.

Kasumba, Yusuf (1995), *The Development of Islam in Uganda 1962–1992 with Particular Reference to Religio-Political Factionalism*, Masters Dissertation, Kampala: Makerere University.

Katungulu, M.M. (1968), *Islam in Buganda*, translated into English by Mr. Busulwa, Kampala.

Katungulu, Haruna Jemba A. (2012), 'Religion and the Search for Peace and Reconciliation in Buganda', PhD Dissertation, Kampala: Makerere University.

Kiwanuka, Ssemakula (1972), *The History of Buganda, from the Foundation of the Kingdom to 1900*, New York: Africana Publishing Corporation.

Kiyimba, Abasi (1989), *Is the 1979 Muslim Blood Bath in Bushenyi History?* Kampala.

——(2001), *Gender Stereotypes in the Folktales and Proverbs of the Baganda*, PhD Thesis, Dar es Salaam.

——(2012), 'The Domestic Relations Bill and Inter-Religious Conflict in Uganda: A Muslim Reading of Personal Law and Religious Pluralism in a Postcolonial Society', in Smith, James H. and Hackett, Rosalind I.J. (Eds) (2012), *Displacing the State: Religion and Conflict in Neoliberal Africa*, Notre Dame: University of Notre Dame, pp. 240–80.

Kkulumba, Ali (nd), '*Ebyafaayo by Obuyisiraamu mu Uganda*'.

Kodesh, Neil (2010 [2004]), *Beyond the Royal Gaze: Clanship and Public Healing in Buganda*. London: University of Virginia Press.

Kurzman, Charles Ed. (2002), *Modernist Islam 1840–1940: A Sourcebook*. Oxford: Oxford University Press.

Lauzière Henri (2016), *The Making of Salafism: Islamic Reform in the Twentieth Century*, New York: Columbia University Press.

Low, D.A. (1962), *Political Parties in Uganda 1949–1962*, London: University of London.

——(1971), *Buganda in Modern History*, London: Weidenfeld & Nicolson.

——(2009), *Fabrication of Empire: The British and the Uganda Kingdoms, 1890–1902*, Cambridge: Cambridge University Press.

Lugard, F.J.D. (2005 [1926]), *The Dual Mandate in British Tropical Africa*, London: Routledge.

——(1968), *The Rise of Our East African Empire: Early Efforts in Nyasaland and Uganda*, London: Frank Cass & Co.

Mahmood, Saba (2005), *Politics of Piety: The Islamic Revival and the Feminist Subject*, Princeton: Princeton University Press.

——(2016), *Religious Difference in a Secular Age: A Minority Report*, Princeton: Princeton University Press.

Mahoney, James & Thelen, Kathleen (Eds) (2010), *Explaining Institutional Change: Ambiguity, Agency, and Power*, Cambridge: Cambridge University Press.

Mamdani, Mahmood (1976), *Politics and Class Formation in Uganda,* London: Heinemann.

——(1996), *Citizen and Subject: Contemporary Africa and the Legacy of Late Colonialism,* Princeton: Princeton University Press.

——(2008), S*aviors and Survivors: Darfur, Politics and the War on Terror,* Dakar: CODESRIA.

——(2012), *Define and Rule: Native as Political Subject,* Cambridge: Harvard University Press.

Mantena, Karuna (2010), *Alibis of Empire: Henry Maine and the Ends of Liberal Imperialism,* Princeton: Princeton University Press.

Maussen, Marcel, Bader, V. & Moors, A. (Eds) (2011), *Colonial and Post-Colonial Governance of Islam: Continuities and Ruptures.* Amsterdam: Amsterdam University Press.

Marloes, Janson (2005), 'Roaming about for God's Sake: The Upsurge of Tabligh Jamat in the Gambia', *Journal of Religion in Africa,* Vol. 35, No. 4, pp. 450–81.

Mehta, Uday Singh (1999), *Liberalism and Empire: A Study in Nineteenth-Century British Liberal Thought,* Chicago: University of Chicago Press.

Miti, J.K. (nd) *Ebyafaayo bya Buganda*, Kampala.

Mudimbe, V.-Y. (1988), *The Invention of Africa: Gnosis, Philosophy, and the Order of Knowledge*, Bloomington: Indiana University Press.

Mudoola, Dan M. (1992), *Interest Groups and Institution Building Processes in Uganda: 1962–1971,* Kampala: Makerere Institute of Social Research.

Muhammad, 'Abduh (1881), 'Ikhtilaf al-qawanin bi-ikhtilaf ahwal al-umam' (Laws Should Change in Accordance with the Conditions of Nations)', in Muhammad 'Imara (Ed.), *Al-A 'Mal al-kamila* (The Complete Works), Lebanon: Mu'assasat al-'Arabiyya li al Dirasat wa al-Nashr, 1972, pp. 309–15.

Muhammad, Ibn Abdul Wahhab (1998), *Kitab-at-Tawheed Explained,* Riyadh: IIPH.

——(1938), *Simuda Nyuma*, London: S.P.C.K.

——(1998 [1904]), *Uganda's Katikkiro in England*, Manchester: Manchester University Press.

Mumtaz, Ahmad (1995), 'Tabligh Jamat', in Esposito, John L. (Ed.), *The Oxford Encyclopedia of the Modern Islamic World*, 4 New York: Oxford University Press, pp. 165–9.

Mutibwa, Phares (1992), *Uganda Since Independence: A Story of Unfulfilled Hopes,* Kampala: Fountain.

NanoWisdoms Archive of Imamat Speeches, Interviews and Writings, 'Wandegeya Mosque Opening Ceremony' by the Agha Khan, Thursday 17 September 1959, pp. 1ff, available from www.nanowisdoms.org/nwblog/4593 (last accessed 17 February 2022).

Ngendo-Tshimba, D. (2020), *Transgressing Buyira: An Historical Inquiry into Violence Astride a Congo-Uganda border*, PhD Thesis: Makerere University.

Nietzsche, Friedrich (1998), *On the Genealogy of Morals*, translated by Douglas Smith, Oxford: Oxford University Press.

Nsimbi, M.B. (1989a), *Amannya Amaganda N'Ennono Zaago* (Ganda Names and their Origins) Kampala: Longman.

Nsimbi M.B. (1989b), *Siwa Muto Lugero* (I do Not Tell Proverbs to a Young One), Harlow: Longman.

Oliver, Roland (1952), *The Missionary Factor in East Africa*, London: Longman.

Pape, Robert A. & Feldman James K. (2010), *Cutting the Fuse: The Explosion of Global Suicide Terrorism and How to Stop It,* Chicago: University of Chicago Press.

Perham, Margery (1960), *Lugard: The Years of Authority 1898–1945,* London: Collins.

Phillips, John Edward (Ed.), *Writing African History*, Rochester: University of Rochester Press.

Qaradawi, Yusuf (1987), *Islamic Awakening: Between Rejection and Extremism,* Herndon: American Trust.

Pulford, Cedric (1999), *Eating Uganda: From Christianity to Conquest*, Banbury: Ituri.

Qutb, Sayyid (2006), *Ma'alim fi'l-tareeq* (Milestones), Birmingham: Maktabah.

——(2015 [nd]), *Fi Dhilal Al-Quran* (In the Shade of the Quran) Vol. 1, Markfield: The Islamic Foundation.

Reid, Richard J. (2002), *Political Power in Pre-Colonial Buganda: Economy, Society & Warfare in the Nineteenth Century*, Kampala: Fountain.

Robinson, David (2004), *Muslim Societies in African History*, Cambridge: Cambridge: University Press.

Roscoe, John (1911), *The Baganda: An Account of Their Native Customs and Beliefs*, New York: Barnes & Noble.

Roy, Olivier (2007), *Secularism Confronts Islam,* translated by George Holoch, New York: Columbia University Press.

Said, Edward W. (1978), *Orientalism,* New York: Pantheon Books.

Sathyarmurthy, T. V. (1986), *The Political Development of Uganda: 1900–1986,* Aldershot: Gower.

Schoenbrun, David Lee (1998), *A Green Place, A Good Place: Agrarian Change, Gender, and Social Identity in the Great Lakes Region to the 15th Century,* Kampala: Fountain.

Schwartz, Michael (2008), *War Without End: The Iraq War in Context.* New York: Haymarket.

Serjeant, R.B. & Griffiths, V.L. (1958), *Report by the Fact-Finding Mission to Study Muslim Education in East Africa,* Nairobi: East Africa High Commission.

Shahab, Ahmed (2016), *What is Islam? The Importance of Being Islamic,* Princeton: Princeton University Press.

Ssekimwanyi, Abdallah (nd) (*Ebyafaayo Ebitonotono ku Ddiini Y'ekiyisiraamu Okuyingira mu Buganda*).

Stock, Eugene (1899), *The History of the Church Missionary Society: its Environment, Its Men and Its Work,* London: CMS.

Stoler, Anna Laura (2002), 'Colonial Archives and the Arts of Governance: On the Content in the Form', in Hamilton, C., Harris, V.S., Taylor, J., Pickover, M., Reid, G. & Saleh, R. (Eds) (2002), *Refiguring the Archive,* London: Kluwe, pp. 83–5.

Tabawebbula, Kivubiro (1998), *Ebintu By'abaganda Eby'ekinnansi N'ennono Zaabyo, Mu Mirembe Gya Chwa N'egya Muwenda Mutebi (Baganda Material Culture Since 1900, An Indigenous Interpretation),* PhD Thesis, Flinders.

Taylor, Charles (1998), 'Modes of Secularism', in Bhargava, Rajeev (Ed.) (1998), *Secularism and Its Critics,* New Delhi: Oxford University Press.

Theobald, A.B. (1951 [1899]), *The Mahdiyya: A History of the Anglo-Egyptian Sudan: 1881–1899,* London: Longmans, Green & Co.

Tucker, Alfred R. (1908), *Eighteen Years in Uganda and East Africa,* London: E. Arnold.

Young, Crawford (1994), *The African Colonial State in Comparative Perspective.* London: Yale University Press.

Zimbe, Musoke B. (1939), *Buganda ne Kabaka,* Kampala

Zizek, Slavoj (2005), *Iraq: The Borrowed Kettle,* New York: Verso.

Journal articles

Asad, Talal (2009), 'The Idea of An Anthropology of Islam', *Qui Parle,* Vol. 17, No.2, pp. 1–30.

——(2001), 'Thinking About Secularism and Law in Egypt', *ISIM Occasional Papers.*

Bezabeh, Samson (2014), 'Review of Terje A. Østebø, *Localising Salafism: Religious Change among Oromo Muslims in Bale, Ethiopia*', *Contemporary Islam,* Vol. 8, No. 2, pp. 181–3.

Bourdieu, Pierre (1991), 'Genesis and Structure of the Religious Field', *Comparative Social Research: A Research Annual,* Vol. 13, pp. 1–44.

Brantlinger, Patrick (1985), 'Victorians and Africans: The Genealogy of the Myth of the Dark Continent', *Critical Inquiry*, Vol. 12, No.1, pp. 166–203.

Church Missionary Society (1841–1921), *The Church Missionary Gleaner*, London: CMS.

Daniell, E.S. (1913) 'Our Great Opportunities in Uganda', *The Church Missionary Gleaner*.

Deacon, Gregory, Gona, G., Mwakimako, H. & Willis, J. (2017), 'Preaching Politics: Islam and Christianity on the Kenya Coast', *Journal of Contemporary African Studies,* Vol. 35, No. 2, pp. 148–67.

Düsterhöft, Isabel K. & Gerlach, Antonia I. (2013), 'The Successes and Failures of the Interventions of the European Union, the African Union and Neighbouring Powers in Somalia', *Sicherheit und Frieden,* Vol. 31, No. 1, pp. 18–23.

Erlich, Haggai (2015), 'Review of Terje A. Østebø, *Localising Salafism: Religious Change among Oromo Muslims in Bale, Ethiopia*, Brill: Leiden', *Northeast African Studies,* Vol. 15, No. 1, pp. 199–202.

Gee, T.W. (1957), 'A Century of Muhammadan Influence in Buganda 1852–1951', *The Uganda Journal,* Vol. 22, No. 2, pp. 139–50.

Gould, L.N. & Garrett, J.L. (1977), 'Amin's Uganda: Troubled Land of Religious Persecution', *Journal of Church and State,* Vol. 19, No. 3, pp. 429–36.

Kasozi, A.B.K. (1985), 'The Uganda Muslim Supreme Council: An Experiment in Muslim Administrative Centralization and Institutionalization (1972–82)', *Institute of Muslim Minority Affairs Journal,* Vol. 6, No. 1, pp. 34–52.

Kasumba, Yusuf (2015), 'Attempts at a Rejuvenation of Muslim Identity in Uganda: The Era of Idi Amin (1971–1979)', *Danubius*, No. XXXIII, pp. 379–408.

Kiyimba, Abasi (1990), 'The Muslim Community in Uganda through One Hundred and Forty Years: The Trials and Tribulations of a Muslim Minority', *Journal of African Religion and Philosophy,* Vol. 1, No.2, pp. 84–120

——(2012), 'A Detailed Account of the Massacre of Muslims in Western Uganda', *The Campus Journal,* 31 July.

Kodesh, Neil (2008), 'Networks of Knowledge: Clanship and Collective Well-being in Buganda', *The Journal of African History,* Vol. 49, No. 2, pp. 197–216.

Larkin, Brian (2016), 'Entangled Religions: Response to J.D.Y. Peel', *The Journal of the International African Institute,* Vol. 86, No. 4, pp. 633–9;

Mamdani, Mahmood (1988), 'Uganda in Transition: Two years of the NRA/NRM', *Third World Quarterly,* Vol. 10, No.3, pp. 1155–1181

Mazrui Ali A. (1977), 'Religious Strangers in Uganda: From Emin Pasha to Amin Dada', *African Affairs,* Vol. 76, No. 302, pp. 21–38.

——(1980), 'Between Development and Decay: Anarchy, Tyranny and Progress under Idi Amin', *Third World Quarterly,* Vol. 2, No. 1, pp. 44–58.

Menkhaus, Ken (2009), 'They Created a Desert and Called It Peace (Building)', *Review of African Political Economy*, Vol. 36, No. 120, pp. 223–33.

Meyer, Birgit (2016), 'Towards a Joint Framework for the Study of Christians and Muslims in Africa: Response to J.D.Y. Peel', *The Journal of the International African Institute,* Vol. 86, No. 4, pp. 628–32.

Musoke, D.R. (1917), *Ebifa Mu Buganda*, No. 120. Buddo.

Obadare, Ebenezer (2016), 'Response to "Similarity and Difference, Context and Tradition, in Contemporary Religious Movements in West Africa" by J.D.Y. Peel', *The Journal of the International African Institute*, Vol. 86, No. 4, pp. 640–45.

Oded, Arye (2006), 'Israeli-Uganda Relations in the Time of Idi Amin', *Jewish Political Studies Review* 18:3–4, pp. 65–79.

Peel, J.D.Y. (2016), 'Similarity and Difference, Context and Tradition, in Contemporary Religious Movements in West Africa', *The Journal of the International African Institute*, Vol. 86, No. 4, pp. 620–27.

Reid, Richard (1997), 'The Reign of Kabaka Nakibinge: Myth or Watershed?' *History in Africa* Vol. 24, pp. 287–97.

Robinson, David (1999), 'France as a Muslim Power in West Africa', *Africa Today,* Vol. 46, Nos 3–4, pp. 105–27.

Schoenbrun, David Lee (1996), 'Gendered Histories between the Great Lakes: Varieties and Limits', *International Journal of African Historical Studies,* Vol. 29, No. 3 (1996), pp. 461–92.

Soares, Benjamin (2016), 'Reflections on Muslim-Christian Encounters in West Africa', *The Journal of the International African Institute,* Vol. 86, No. 4, pp. 673–7.

Soares, Benjamin & Osella, Filippo (2009), 'Islam, Politics, Anthropology', *Journal of the Royal Anthropological Institute,* Vol. 15, No. s1, pp. S1–S23.

Solzbacher, Regina (1969), 'Continuity Through Change in the Social History of Kibuli', *Uganda Journal,* Vol. 33, No. 1, pp. 163–74.

Summers, Carol (2009), 'Catholic Action and Ugandan Radicalism: Political Activism in Buganda, 1930–1950', *Journal of Religion in Africa,* Vol. 39, Fasc. 1, pp. 60–90.

Twaddle, Michael (1969), 'The Bakungu Chiefs of Buganda under British Colonial Rule: 1900–1930', *Journal of African History,* Vol. 10, No. 2, pp. 309–22.

Weismann, Itzchak (2009), 'Genealogies of Fundamentalism: Salafi Discourse in Nineteenth-Century Baghdad', *British Journal of Middle Eastern Studies,* Vol. 36, No. 2, pp. 267–80.

Newspapers

10 Kibuli Sheikhs denounce Mubajje election', *New Vision*, 13 December 2000.

'Deadlock in London over Buganda's Sovereignty', *Uganda Argus*, 22 September 1960.

'Dr. Obote hits at opposition to Penal Bill', *Uganda Argus*, 27 January 1966.

'Eastern Clerics denounce rival mufti', *Daily Monitor*, 2 February 2009.

'Fire Arms Stolen from Kisubi Armoury', *Uganda Herald*, 26 January 1954.

'I am Still Mufti', *New Vision*, 2 December 2010.

'Katikiro's motion on Penal Bill', *Uganda Argus,* 20 January 1966

'Kibuli faction shuns Mubajje unity meet', *Daily Monitor*, 3 February 2015.

'Killings: Police, Muslim leaders clash', Mukisa, F., *Daily Monitor,* 7 January 2015.

'Kirya's faction gives evidence for Kamoga's torture of Muslims', *Bukedde*, 1 January 2015.

'List of Muslim Clerics killed in two years in Kenya', *The Star*, 11 June 2014.

'Lukiiko votes in favour of secession', *Uganda Argus*, 24 September 1960.

'Museveni blames Sheikhs' killing on ADF', *Daily Monitor*, 1 July 2016.

'Muslim clerics who have been killed', *Daily Monitor*, 26 November 2016.

'Muslim Tabliqs dismiss leader', *Daily Monitor*, 28 November 2014.

'Muslims Elect Uganda Leader', *Uganda Argus*, 3 April 1967.

'New Law may restrict K.Y. movements', *Uganda Argus*, 10 January 1966.

'Police link Killing of Muslim leaders to ADF rebel group', *Daily Monitor*, 31 December 2014.

'This is Our Only Home', Joshi, Ravi, *Uganda Argus*, 18 February 1959.

'Trouble in Africa', *The Spectator*, 31 January 1964.

Uganda Argus, 1 October 1968

Uganda Organization Newspaper, Vol. 108, No. 97, 12th July 1973

Reports and government publications

Amin, President Idi Dada, 'Message to the Nation by his Excellence General Idi Amin Dada, On British Citizens of Asian Origin and Citizens of India, Pakistan and Bangladesh living in Uganda', during the weekend of 12 and 13 August 1972, pp. 1–7. *Uganda Gazette,* Government Printer, Entebbe.

Amin, 'President Idi Dada, Midnight Address to the Nation', 17 December 1972. *Uganda Gazette,* Government Printer, Entebbe.

Gomotoka, J.M.T. (1940), 'Makula, kye Kitabo kye Bika Ekilangira Ky'oloyo lwe Buganda', on microfilm at Makerere University, Kampala.

Johnston, Harry (1901), 'Report by His Majesty's Special Commissioner on the Protectorate of Uganda', *Parliamentary Papers: Africa*, No. 7, pp. 4–5.

Kayunga, Simba Sallie (1993), 'Islamic Fundamentalism in Uganda: A Case Study of the Tabligh Youth Movement', Centre for Basic Research, Kampala, Working Paper No. 37.

Sadler, Hayes J. (1904), 'General Report on the Uganda Protectorate', No. 12.

Stuart, Ramsay (1898), 'The Mutiny in Uganda, 1897–98: A Précis of Events', 9 March.

Internet

'Inside Kenya's Death Squads', *Al Jazeera Investigations*, 8 December 2014, www.youtube.com/watch?v=lUjOdjdH8Uk (accessed 19 May 2016).

Index

Abadahemuka 123
Abakaafiri 49
Abakongozzi 36
Abakyala 42
Adam 46
Ahmadiyya 91–5
Ahmadiyya Movement 92–3
Ahmed, Shahab 14
Al-Afghani, Jamal al-Din 154
Al-fajr 58, 161
Al Jazeera 29
Ali, Moses 140, 146, 190
Allah 33, 44, 46, 48, 53, 55, 59–60,
  93–4, 153–6, 161, 170, 179, 183, 218
Allied Democratic Forces (ADF) 2,
  6, 25, 28–30, 151–3, 162, 166, 168, 173,
  177–8, 180–2, 184–5, 205, 210–13
Algeria 70–1
Althusser, Louis 96
Amasabo 34, 38
Amin, Idi 5–6, 13, 15–16, 21, 131–48,
  150–1, 157, 170, 186, 189, 215–16
Anglican 11, 64–6, 109, 127
Anglo-Mohammedan Law (India) 7,
  69
Ankole xiv, 125, 129, 147, 160
Anthropology 13, 23
Arabs 5, 46–9, 51, 55–8, 72–3, 76, 132
Arua 103, 178
Asad, Talal 187
Asians xv, 5, 115, 118, 132, 135–8, 150,
  187, 191, 215
  Community 90, 118, 144, 157, 162
  Expulsion 5, 132, 134–5, 137–9, 141,
  215
Assembly of Sheikhs 196–8

Baana ba Kintu 34
Baganda xix, 13, 20, 32–5, 47, 51, 53,
  56–7, 59, 85, 106, 111, 114–16, 118–19,
  122, 125, 127–8, 131, 177, 193–4, 197,
  215–16
Bagisu 115
Bahiga, Mustapha 26, 29, 199, 205–10
Bahima 115
Bakembuga 42
Bakopi 39, 79
Bakungu 39, 60, 120
Balangira 38
Balinda, Abasi 125
Balunywa, Ali 125
Bambejja 39, 42
Banyarwanda 115–18
Bataka xix, 35, 37–9, 44, 46, 88, 115,
  120, 122
Bazeyi 155–8, 161–3, 166, 169, 172, 194
Bemba 37
Bey, Selim 80
Bible 55
Bifurcated state 4, 68
Biggwa 35, 38
Biggya 35
Bika-Nnansangwa 37
Bilal Islamic Institute 155
Bilal, Janna 81–2
Bito dynasty 38
Black Africanist 137, 116
Bodaboda taxi 27
Bombo 103
Boras 91
Britain xiii, 29, 73, 120–1, 124, 138,
  145
British administration 81

236 INDEX

British colonial statecraft 11, 216
Broad base 41, 187, 189–90, 213
Buddo xiv, 99, 100
  Kings College 127
Buddu 75–7, 81, 84–5, 98, 110
Buganda
  Agreement (1894) 68, 121
  Agreement (1900) xiv, 75, 120
  Agreement (1955) 121
Bugembe 105, 128
Bugerere 129
Bukenya, Murtada 29, 159
Bulemeezi 42, 60, 76
Bulingugwe (Treaty) 74
Bunyoro kingdom xiii, 38
Busiro 37
Busoga 76, 106, 116, 125, 128–9, 148,
  171–2, 177, 200
Busujju 79
Butaka 35, 37, 39, 88, 114
Butambala 79, 88, 90, 102–3, 107, 218
Butonda 34
Buvuma 55
Bwanda 98

Caravan trade 31, 43–5
Catholic xiii, xv, 64, 75, 87, 99, 123–5,
  127, 213
  Roman Mission xiii, 64, 74
Chief Khadi 145–6, 149–50
Choli 49, 51
Christ, Jesus 55–6, 61–2
Christian Power 80, 107, 140, 172
Christianity 3, 10–11, 21–2, 32, 45, 48,
  54–7, 60–1, 63–6, 75, 78, 215
Church Missionary Gleaner 22
Church Missionary Society xiii, 22,
  64, 97
Circumcision xiii, 57–8, 60–1, 217
Civil law 67, 70, 90–2
Colonial
  Governance 4–5, 7–9, 66–8, 70–1
    86, 90, 100, 107, 109, 112, 114, 130,
    216–17
  Library 21–2

Statecraft 9, 11, 21–2, 69, 86, 96, 98,
  112, 186, 216
Colville, Edward Henry 74
Commonwealth Heads of Government
  meeting (1971) 134
Communique (Tripoli) 141
Constitutional Committee (1959–1960)
  115

Darasa xix, 17, 25, 28, 37, 103, 159–61,
  164, 172, 175, 179–80, 182–3, 209–10
Dar Fur (Sultanate of) 45, 139
Dark Continent 23
Dawah xix, 6, 152–3, 155–9, 161–3,
  165, 168–9, 205
Ddunda 34
Democratic Party xv, 124–5
Designated Mosque Sites 68, 105
Discursive
  Coherence 19, 152, 215, 219
  Field 20
  Formations 31, 44
  Practices 17
  Tradition 13–14, 18, 218

East Africa 22, 69, 90
East African Federation 120
Education policy 96–9, 186
Egypt xix, 9, 31, 44–5, 52, 69, 72, 142,
  168, 214
Eid 129, 146
Elizabeth, Queen of England 124
Ekitiibwa 36, 182
Empisa 36
Elite polygyny 42
Enju 35
Entebbe 81, 94, 157, 163, 210
Ethna Ashari Jammat 92–3
Ethnic identity 11, 147, 216
Eve 46

Faisal, king of Saudi Arabia 141
Ffumbe 37
Fitrah 20
Foucault, Michel 186
France xiii, 71, 73

INDEX

Gaddafi, Muammar 141
Ganda
  Chiefs 65
  Federalism 190
  Nationalism 5, 131
  Royal power 113, 130
  Traditions 40, 53
Gayaza xiv, 98, 123
Geertz, Clifford 13
Gellner, Ernest 13
Genealogy 15–16, 20
Gordon, Charles, General 62–4

Hadeeth 37
Haggai, Erlich 168
Hakawat, Sheikh 155–6
Harrison, Christopher 70
Hussin, Izza 144

Ijtihad 14–15, 156
Imperial British East Africa Company
  (IBEAC) xiv, 73
India xx, 7–9, 69–70, 91, 93–5, 138,
  153
Indian Ocean 90
Indirect rule 8–9, 22, 86, 104, 111, 114
Inspector General of Police 2, 28, 210
Intra-Muslim
  Debates 54, 152
  Disputes 90, 95, 103
  Politics 68, 162
  Violence 5, 131, 151
Iran 162
Iraq 25, 142
Iron smelting 38
Islamic
  Calendar 50
  Development Bank 143
  Flag 49, 52, 173, 200
  Governance 180
  Ideology 5, 132
  Knowledge 25, 98–9, 100, 102–3,
    156, 158
  Reform 6, 150–3, 155, 157–8, 169, 219
  Reform Movement 6, 150–1, 153,
    157, 219

  State 44, 52, 54, 65, 151
  University in Uganda 141–3, 194
Islamization 3, 20, 31–2, 44, 48, 51,
  53–5, 63, 65, 155, 217
Ismail, Khedive of Egypt 44, 215,
  63–4
Israel 29, 61, 138, 141

Jaluo 115
Jami 'at Dawah Salafiyya 165
JEEMA 165
Jinja 92, 105–6, 128
Jjemba, Haruna Katungulu 27, 182–3,
  195, 199, 206–12
Juma-Zukuuli 68, 88, 100, 102, 105,
  154, 186
Jumuah 49, 102–4, 173
Johnston, Harry 78, 80–1, 217

Kaate, Joshua 122
Kaawokadda 115
Kabaka xix, 33–4
  Chwa 50
  Chwa Nabakka 40
  Jjunju 41
  Kagulu 40
  Kalema, Nuhu xiii, 73
  Kimera 38–9
  Mutebi 38
  Muteesa I xiii, 3–4, 15, 38, 41, 43–4,
    63, 139, 214–15, 217, 219
  Muteesa II xiv, xv, 120, 145
  Mwanga xiii, xiv, 72–4, 76, 85
  Nnakibinge 40
  Ssemakookiro 41
  Ssuuna II 41, 44, 46
Kabaka Yekka (KY) party xv, xix,
  120–1, 125
Kabarega, Omukama of Bunyoro xiv,
  52
Kabejja 42
Kabula 79
Kaddulubaale 42
Kaggwa, Apollo xiv, 21, 41–2, 47, 49,
  88–9, 102, 109, 215, 217
Kailan, Sheikh 155

238 INDEX

Kakeeto, Sulaiman, Sheikh   159, 163–5, 174, 176, 201, 203–4, 206, 210
Kakolobooto   50
Kakooza, Rajab, Sheikh   162, 173, 191
Kakungulu, Badru, Prince   88, 98–107, 109–10, 112, 126–30, 133, 145–7, 167, 186, 194, 201
Kalanzi, Abdallah, Sheikh   159, 163
Kale, John   123
Kaliisa, Anas, Sheikh   130
Kamoga, Muhammad Yunus, Sheikh   29, 158–9, 162–3, 166, 169, 174, 181–2, 199, 201, 203–4, 206–12
Kamulegeya, Abdul Obeid, Sheikh   126–7, 130, 133, 140, 145, 149–50, 203
Kasangwaawo   115
Kasozi, A.B.K.   120, 127–8, 147, 167
Kasolya   35
Kasule, Ndilangwa, Sheikh   200
Kasumba, Yusuf   139–40, 147
Katikkiro   xiv, 48, 64, 77, 88–9, 102, 109, 124
Katonda   20, 33–4, 47, 53
Katwe People's Council   123
Kauta   48
Kayongo, Zubair, Sheikh   27, 198–200
Kayihura, Kale, General   28, 210
Kenya   2, 29, 90, 123, 163, 169, 174
Khojas   91–2
Khutba   xix, 17, 25, 28, 37, 103, 158–60, 172–3, 179, 182–3, 195, 202
Kibaate, Mahmood, Sheikh   27, 199, 206, 208
Kibirige, Muhammad   165
Kibuli   1–2, 26–7, 29, 87, 89, 99, 102, 127, 133, 145, 147, 152, 164, 167, 182, 184–8, 192–4, 199–205, 207, 210, 218
Kiggundu, Muhammad, Sheikh, Major   27, 159, 166, 176, 178, 199, 205, 211
Kiggundu, Sulaiman   149
Kigongo, Moses   182, 207
Kinaawa-Kabojja   49
Kintu   xix, 33–4
Kirya, Hassan Ibrahim, Sheikh   26, 159, 164, 195–6, 199, 202–3, 205–6, 208–9, 211

Kisingiri, Zakariya   76
Kisubi Mission College   123
Kiswahili   61
Kiwanuka, Joseph   120
Kiyimba, Abasi   78, 124
Kizikiti   49
Kololo   93
   Cemetery   93, 95
   Independence Grounds   192
Kusamila   48
Kyabazinga   116
Kyaddondo   37, 98
Kyaggwe   42, 48, 76, 98

Lauzière, Henri   154
Liberation War (1979)   xvi, 15, 147, 165
Libya   141–2, 151
Lubaga   149
Lubaale   34–5, 38, 51–3, 65, 114
Lubiri   xv, xix, 38, 54, 58, 122, 175, 178
Lubuga   43
Lubwama, Ntege   125
Lugaba   34
Luganda   xix, 32, 102, 120
Lugard, Fredrick   72–84, 90, 109, 215, 217
Lugave   37
Lukiiko   xix, 120–1
Lukwago, Isa K.K.   129–30, 149
Lutwa, Okello Tito   xvi, 150
Luwemba, Saad, Mufti   162–3, 165, 173–4, 176, 191–2, 194
Lwaazi, Idris Sheikh   159, 164

Macmillan, Harold   124
Madrasa   96, 99
Magatto, Twaibu   xiv, 102, 107, 186
Mahdi rebellion (Egyptian-Sudan)   72
Mahmood, Saba   12
Malaya   9, 69
Male, Kassim, Hajji   124–5
Maliki   54, 58–9
Mamdani, Mahmood   45, 67–8
Marxist theory   96

Masaka 105, 129, 142, 147, 162, 171, 176, 202
Masjid
  Makerere University 164
  Nakasero 156–9, 163–4, 173
  Noor, William Street 26, 29, 162, 173, 182, 195, 197–8, 206–9
  Old Kampala 174
  Wandegeya 183, 209–10
Masilo 35
Mau Mau Rebellion 123
Matovu, Abdul Razzaq, Sheikh xv, 145–6, 155
Matovu, Sulaiman Yusuf, Sheikh 146
Maulid 68, 108–9, 149, 159, 218
Mawokota 37
Maxim gun 82
Mayanja, Abu 125, 128, 142, 149, 216
Mayuge district 26–7
Mazrui, Ali 137
Mbale 26, 90, 142, 162, 194
Mbogo, Nuhu Kyabasinga, Prince 76, 82, 87, 88, 98, 102, 105, 108, 194, 201, 211, 216, 217
Mbugo 50
Mecca 51, 72, 126, 141–2
Mengo establishment 111, 120, 125, 216
Military coup 132
  1971 xv, 134
  1985 xvi, 150
  Military weaponry 31
Mill Hill mission xiv, 87, 97
Missionaries 21–2, 54, 56, 65, 91, 99
Miti, James Kabazzi 47, 58–9
Mombasa 90, 169
Monotheism 47–8, 52–3, 62, 65, 179
Mubajje, Ramadhan, Mufti 193–206, 210, 212
Mudduawulira 59–60, 66, 217
Mudimbe, Valentin-Yves 21
Mufta, Darlington 61
Mufti See Chief Khadi 145–6, 149–50
Muganda wawu 115
Muganzirwazza 41
Mugwanya, Leonard 118
Mugwanya, Matayo 124

Muhammad, Abduh 154, 166
Muhammad, bin Abdul Wahhab 156
Muhammad, Munir al-Dimashqi 154
Multifurcated society 4, 68, 86, 110, 130
Mulumba, Kassim, Sheikh 149
Mukasa, Ham 21, 42, 47, 54, 57–9, 62, 73
Mukama 34
Mukulu, Jamil 25, 28, 159, 162–4, 169–72, 174–81, 211
Mukwenda 42
Munyonyo-Salaama 49
Musambwa 34
Museveni, Yoweri Kaguta xvi, xvii, 24, 28, 162–4, 170, 178, 187, 191–2, 198–9, 201, 203, 205–6, 210, 216
Musisi, Nakanyike 40, 42
Muslim
  Autonomy 7, 9, 37, 68, 101, 103, 112, 133, 168, 216
  Communities 3–4, 15, 67, 215
  Diversity 13
  Elites 4, 9, 45, 48, 67–8, 70, 80, 86, 101, 109, 112–13, 125, 131, 147–50, 185–6, 188, 192
  Factions 5, 108, 132, 139, 143, 148, 153, 201
  Factionalism 133, 143
  Identity 5, 27, 49, 69–70, 88, 122, 126, 152, 167–8, 170, 215
  Marginalization 6, 132, 134, 165, 215
  Minority 4, 6, 12, 15, 113, 151
  Murders 15, 62
  Pages 54–5, 57, 60–2, 65, 215
  Publics 9, 167, 185, 202, 208, 219
  Question 2, 15, 18, 23, 44, 66–9, 80, 86–7, 89, 96, 98, 112, 125, 139, 149, 186–9, 214, 216
  Subjects 3, 72, 79, 185, 217
  Supreme Council xv, 6, 130, 133, 144, 169, 173–4, 176, 186, 191–2, 199, 201, 203, 212, 215, 219,
Mutibwa, Phares 119
Mutuba 35, 50
Muwanga, Paulo 123, 149

Muwaya, Adbul Kadir, Dr.   26–7
Muzimu   35
Mwera (Agreement)   74, 76–8, 80, 85

Nadiope, William   116
Nakasero Hill   88–9
Nakawa   49
Nakivubo   89
Namasagali   98
Namirembe Conference (1955)   121
Naqd   6, 152
Nasiha   6, 152
National Association for the
   Advancement of Muslims (NAAM)
   125–6, 133
National elections   6, 167, 174, 186,
   201, 203
National Resistance Movement (NRM)
   xvi, 6, 13, 151, 185
   Statecraft   6, 185, 188
National Resistance Army (NRA)
   190
Nationality question   5, 111–15, 118–20,
   125, 132, 137, 216
Native
   Administration   89, 101, 106
   Chiefs   xiv
   Government   104
   Ordinances   xiv
Ndawula, Umar Swiddiq   27, 199,
   206
Nekyon, Adoko   126–7
Nigeria   29, 69–70
Njaza   37
Nkumba   51, 53
Nkutu, Shaban   125, 127–8, 145
Nnabulagala-Kasubi   49
Nnakalanga (Battle)   55–6, 58, 61
Nnakibinge, Kassim, Prince   27, 194,
   199, 201, 203, 207–8, 210
Nnakku, Queen of Buganda   40
Nnannono, Queen of Buganda   40
Nnono   35
Nsambya Hill   87
Nsiriba   35, 155
Nyonyi   37

Nŋanda   32
Nŋonge   37

Obote, Milton Apollo   xv, xvi, 5, 13,
   15–16, 21, 111–13, 117, 120–2, 125–6,
   128–31, 133–4, 139, 144–5, 147–50, 152,
   157, 186–7, 189, 191, 216
Obukulu   35
Obuntu bulamu   36
Obuyonjo   37
Obwangor, Cuthbert   118
Obweetowaze   37
Okugatta   36
Okulanya   57, 115, 117
Okwaabya olumbe   35
Olwendo   36
Omusenze   114–15
Omusika   35–6
Omutabuuza   48
Omutaka   35, 114
Omuwanika   48
Old Kampala   1–2, 26, 75, 145, 152,
   167, 173–4, 176–7, 182, 184–7, 191–3,
   198–204
Organisation of Islamic Cooperation
   (OIC)   141, 143–4
Orthodoxy   14
Østebø, Terje   155, 168

Pakistan   142, 151, 159
Pasha, Emin, Sir   80, 82
Patel, C.K.   118
Pentateuch   61–2
Political
   Governance   106, 189, 214
   Identity   32, 66
   Institutions   32
   Minority   3–4, 10–12, 112, 130, 188,
      219
   Morality   213, 217
   Neutrality   12
   Strategy   32
Portal, Gerald, Sir   xiv, 72, 77
Polygamy   53, 101
Polytheism   47, 155, 179–80, 206
Prescriptive power   14

Pre-colonial Buganda   3, 15, 31–3, 139
Pre-Islamic Buganda   32
Primary sources   14, 37, 213, 218
Private domain   7, 11, 49, 101, 107, 112, 218–19
Prophet Muhammad (PBUH)   xix, 14, 93, 108, 153–4, 163, 168, 183
Protectorate Government   117, 216
Protestantism   11
Protestant Ganda (chiefs)   73–4
Public sphere   12, 218

Qadi courts   71
Qaradawi, Yusuf   158
Qasamallah Unity Accord   149
Quran   14, 18, 20, 37, 46, 48, 58–9, 61, 86, 99, 144, 170, 182–3, 218
Queen Mother   40–2

Ramadhan   51, 56
Reid, Richard   35, 38
Religious Field   19, 54, 57, 65–6
Religious System   31–2, 66, 43–4, 47, 51, 53, 60, 65–6
Resistance council   xvi, 189
Rida, Rashid   154, 158
Robison, David   72
Ruzinda, Ausi, Hajji   123
Rwakaikara, Ausi   125

Sadler, Hayes   72, 85
Salaf Salih   xix, 2, 14
Salafism   xix, xx, 2, 6, 14, 25, 154–5, 157, 168
Salafiyya   151, 153, 165–6, 181–4, 192, 199, 206
Salat   48–9, 51–2, 57–9, 61, 100, 102–3, 106, 155–6, 159–61, 167
Saleh, Saleh, General   182
Saudi Arabia   141–2, 151, 169, 194
Saum   51, 100, 155
Secular   5, 11–13, 17–18, 96–100, 127–8, 149, 172, 185–6, 195, 215, 218
   Power   5, 185–6
   State   11–12, 13
   Transformation   11

Secularism   11–12, 14
Sendikwanawa   116–18
Senegal   70–1, 78, 96
Sepoy Mutiny (India)   7–8
Settler Muslims   67, 90, 93–4
Shaafi   54, 91
Sharia   68, 90–2, 95, 101, 144, 158, 168, 170–1, 178–9
Shia   26–7, 173
Singo   42, 74, 76, 78
Social power   11–12, 131, 150
Somalia   xvii, 25
Somo la kwanza   61
Speke, John Hanning   xiii, 55, 61
Spiritiual Kabaka   34, 37
Ssaabakaaki   48, 52
Ssaabawaali   48
Ssaza   xx, 39, 102–3
Ssebalu, Musa   103
Ssebo   42, 59, 63
Ssekabaka   50
Ssekiboobo   42
Ssekimpi, Abdul Hakim   27, 164–5, 195, 199, 205
Ssekimwaanyi, Abdallah   88, 102–3, 105–7, 186
Ssemakula, Swaibu, Sheikh   128–30, 187
Sseŋŋendo, Paul   123
Ssentamu, Abdul Karim   26, 28, 159, 164, 169, 174, 176, 179, 205, 209–10
Ssiga   35
Ssonko, Najib   27, 199, 206–8, 211
Stanley, Henry Morton   55–6, 61
Sudan   54, 69–70, 72, 142, 152, 158
Sudanese Mutiny   80, 218
Sunnah   14, 170, 179, 218
Sunni   25, 27, 46, 90–4, 105, 146
Sunni Muslim Community   92–3
Supreme Mufti   27, 198–200

Tabligh   152–88, 194, 197–8, 201, 203, 205–7, 209–11
Tabliq   xx, 25, 29, 153, 157, 191–2, 198–9, 201, 204–6, 210, 212
Tanzania   27–9, 147

Tawhid   155, 166, 179
Toro   84
Treason   54, 59
Tucker, Alfred   22
Tunisia   70, 89
Turkiya   54
Turks   58–60, 65

Uganda Army   80, 134, 141
Uganda Muslim Community (UMC)
  126, 133
Uganda National Congress   120
Uganda People's Congress (UPC)   121,
  124, 125–7, 145, 147–9
Uganda Polytechnic Kyambogo   142
Uganda Protectorate   75
UPC-KY Alliance   121, 125–7
United States   29, 138

Verona Fathers   87
Victoria (Lake)   73, 75–6

Wafula, Abdu Rashid, Sheikh   26–7
Wakibi   48
Wakiso   155
Wasswa, Yona   49
War on Terror   25, 29
Wegulo, Badru   125
West Africa   70
Westphalia   11, 218
Western civilization   99
Wild Committee   118
Wilson, George   83–4
World Muslim League   127, 149, 191,
  203

Zanzibar   31, 43, 44, 46, 54, 55, 76,
  83–5, 91, 214
Zionist   29–30
Zzimbe, Musoke Batulumayo   21, 47,
  54–6, 64, 73
Zziwa, Muhammad Kizito   158–9

Previously published titles in the series

Violent Conversion: Brazilian Pentecostalism and Urban Women in Mozambique, Linda Van de Kamp (2016)

Beyond Religious Tolerance: Muslim, Christian & Traditionalist Encounters in an African Town, edited by Insa Nolte, Olukoya Ogen and Rebecca Jones (2017)

Faith, Power and Family: Christianity and Social Change in French Cameroon, Charlotte Walker-Said (2018)

Contesting Catholics: Benedicto Kiwanuka and the Birth of Postcolonial Uganda, Jonathon L. Earle and J. J. Carney (2021)

Islamic Scholarship in Africa: New Directions and Global Contexts, edited by Ousmane Oumar Kane (2021)

From Rebels to Rulers: Writing Legitimacy in the Early Sokoto State, Paul Naylor (2021)

Sacred Queer Stories: Ugandan LGBTQ+ Refugee Lives and the Bible, Adriaan Van Klinken and Johanna Stiebert, with Sebyala Brian and Fredrick Hudson (2021)

Labour & Christianity in the Mission: African Workers in Tanganyika and Zanzibar, 1864–1926, Michelle Liebst (2021)

The Genocide against the Tutsi, and the Rwandan Churches: Between Grief and Denial, Philippe Denis (2022)

Competing Catholicisms: The Jesuits, the Vatican & the Making of Postcolonial French Africa, Jean Luc Enyegue, SJ (2022)